PAINT, PAPER
& GOING PLACES

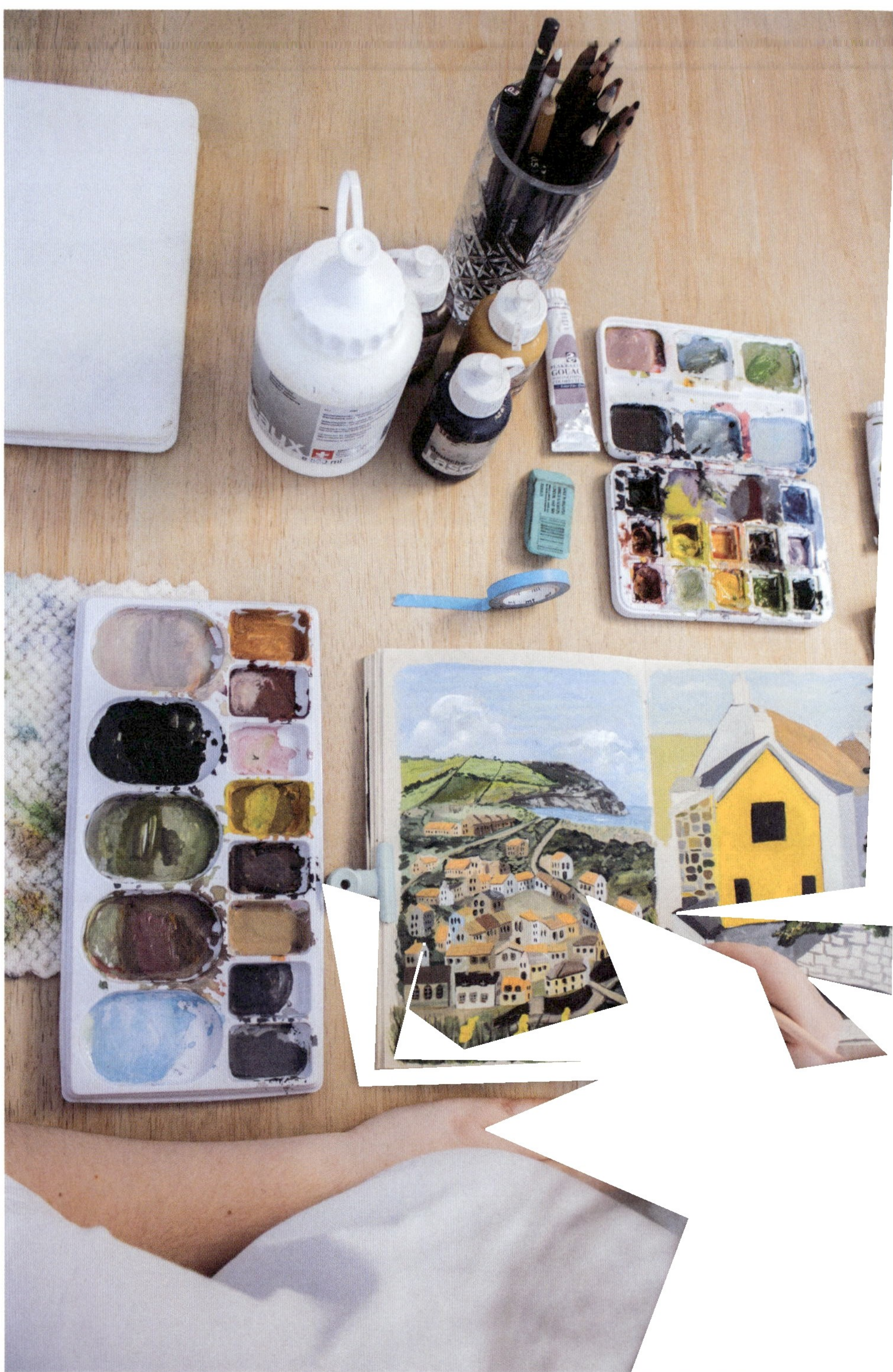

PAINT, PAPER & GOING PLACES

A GUIDE TO CREATIVE TRAVEL JOURNALING

Merel Djamila
Hoekstra

CONTENTS

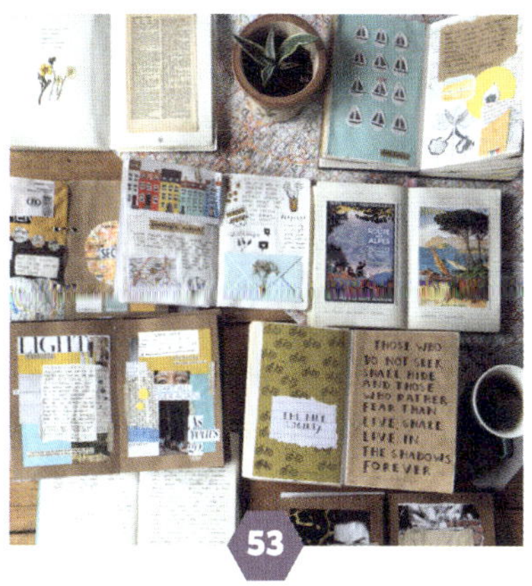

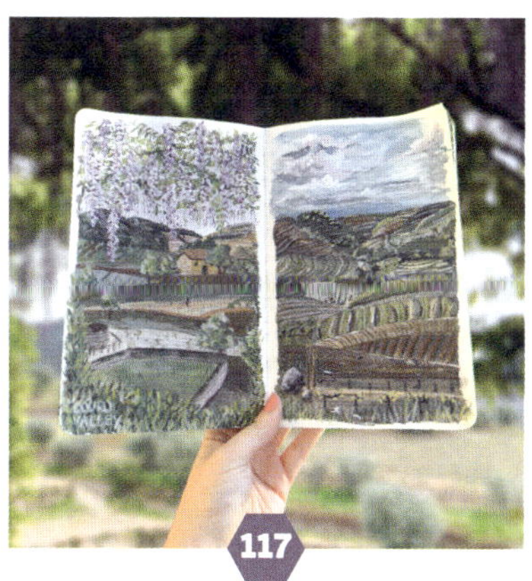

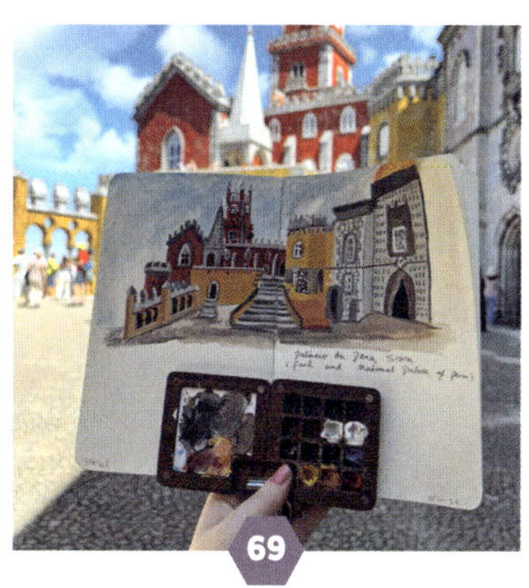

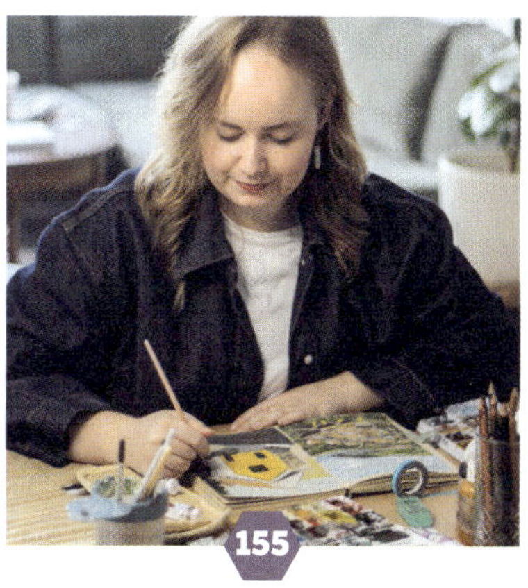

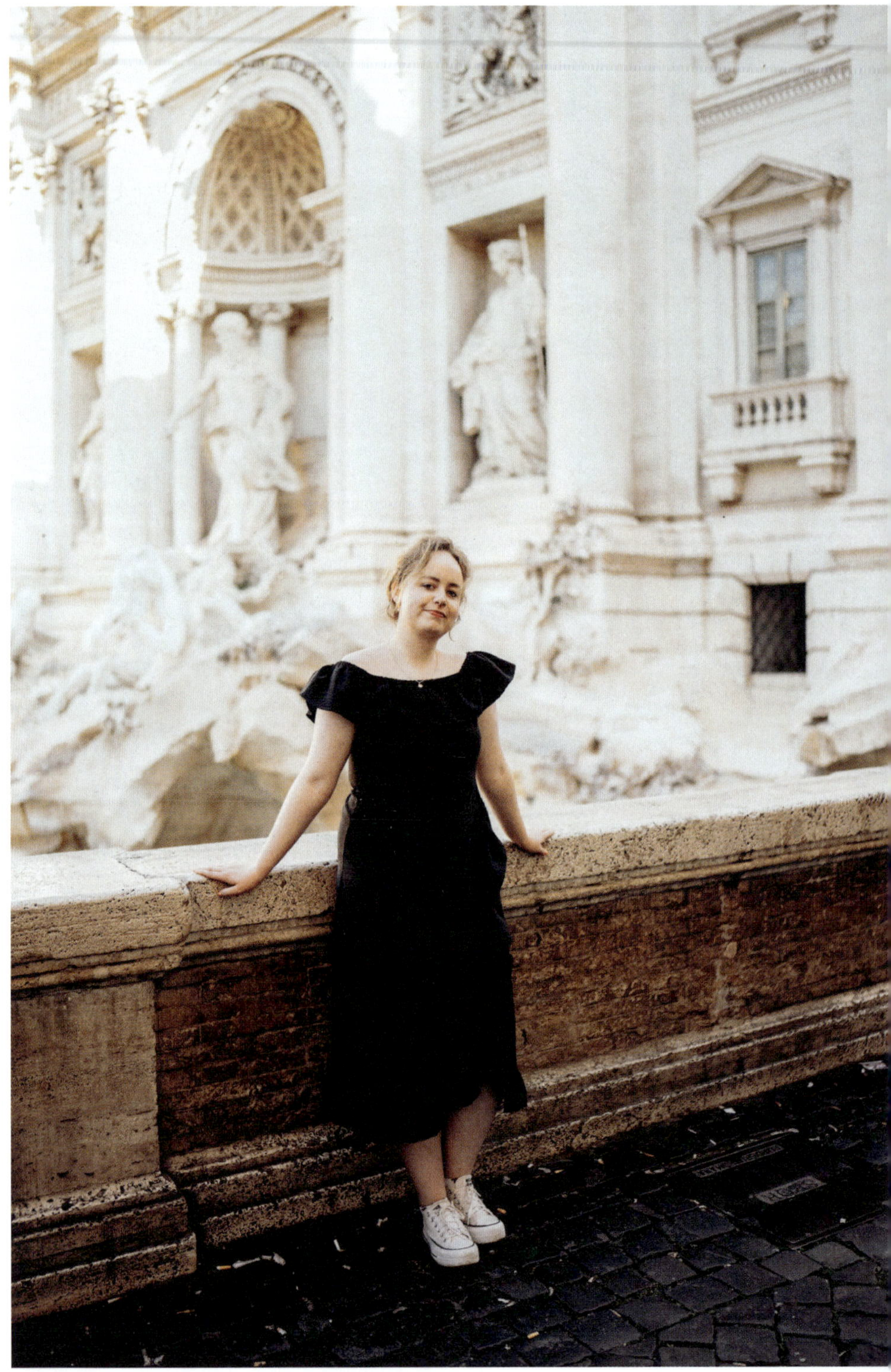

Dear reader,

Perhaps you've already created a travel journal before, or maybe you have attempted to at some point. Capturing stories in texts, images, or sketches is of all times, and it has always been an outlet for me as well.

Since 2017, I've been sharing my creative journals online. My portfolio has grown into a collection of keepsakes, from glossy photos paired with pressed flowers to gouache paintings of landscapes and buildings.

This book is for anyone who wishes to document their travel stories in their own unique way. For travellers who like to create as they go, but also for those who only find time to journal after their return. It doesn't matter whether you use pen, paper, glue, or paint. I prefer gouache paint, and most tutorials are based on it, but in your travel journal, what matters most is that you enjoy the process as well as the result. Journaling is about experimenting, stepping away from your phone, and fully embracing the present moment. The key is finding a technique and routine that feels right for you and makes you happy.

On my social media (*@mereljournals*), I hope to continue inspiring you with my illustrated travel diaries. Please, feel free to share your creations with me. For now, I wish you lots of fun observing and capturing your travels on paper. I hope you get to explore and bring your paints and papers while going places.

Love,
Merel

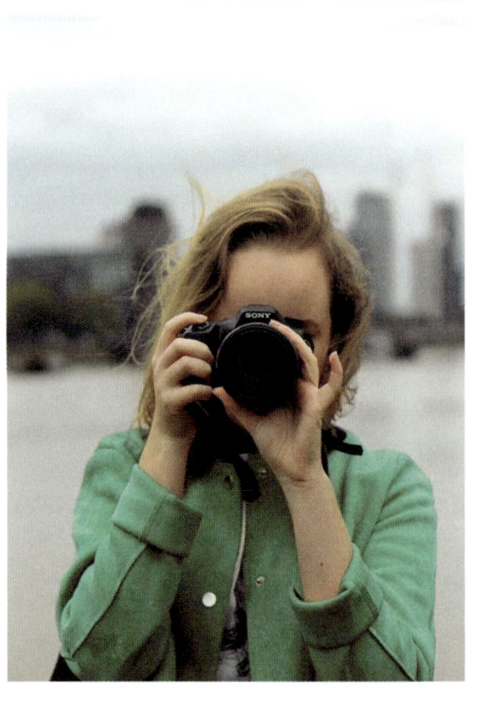

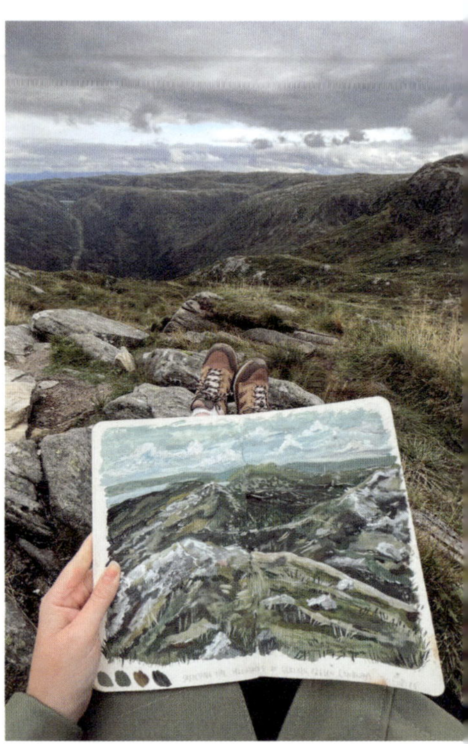

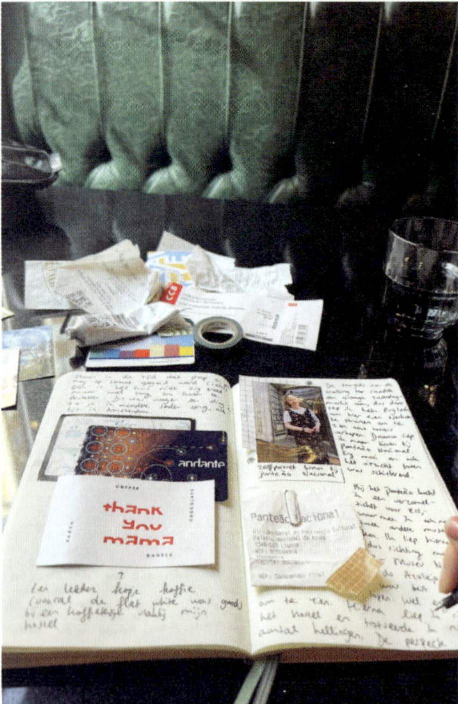

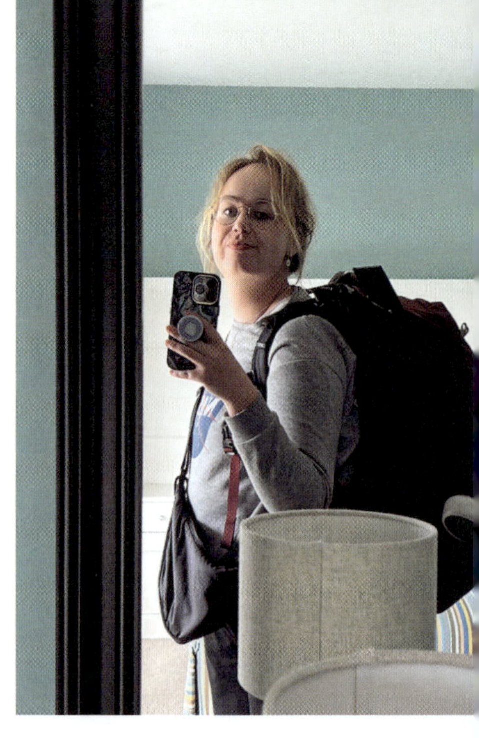

Travelling solo

Travelling at my own pace, doing whatever I felt like, and meeting new people were just a few of the reasons I had always longed to embark on a longer solo trip. So, in April 2023, I left my job, packed my bags, said goodbye to friends and family, and travelled to my first destination: Portugal. From there, my journey took me through Spain, Italy, Slovenia, Croatia, and Montenegro.

Of course, I was nervous. Being alone didn't scare me; I enjoy spending time by myself. In my home country, the Netherlands, I regularly venture out solo, whether it's visiting museums, wandering through town, or enjoying lunch on my own. But doing the same things in unfamiliar countries where I didn't speak the language felt like stepping into a whole new level of discomfort.

As it turned out, my worries were unfounded. Whenever I needed a break from travelling or didn't feel like venturing out, I found solace in my travel journal. I wrote about my experiences and printed photos with my portable mini printer, sticking them onto the pages. I saved receipts, train tickets, and museum passes. With my paints and sketchbook, I felt just like Van Gogh, spending hours in cafés or on location, capturing the most beautiful scenes on paper. These moments alone gave me time to truly unwind. Portraying the places I visited in this way gave my journey a deeper sense of purpose.

No matter how beautiful all these destinations are, after a while, they begin to blur together. That's why I found it so rewarding to observe more closely, using pens, brushes, and paper. This practice not only helps you appreciate the places more, but also preserves the memories in a unique way. It doesn't matter if you're working with a pen, a paintbrush, or glue; what matters is that you're preserving memories that might otherwise get lost among the thousands of photos on your phone, as I believe these memories deserve more space.

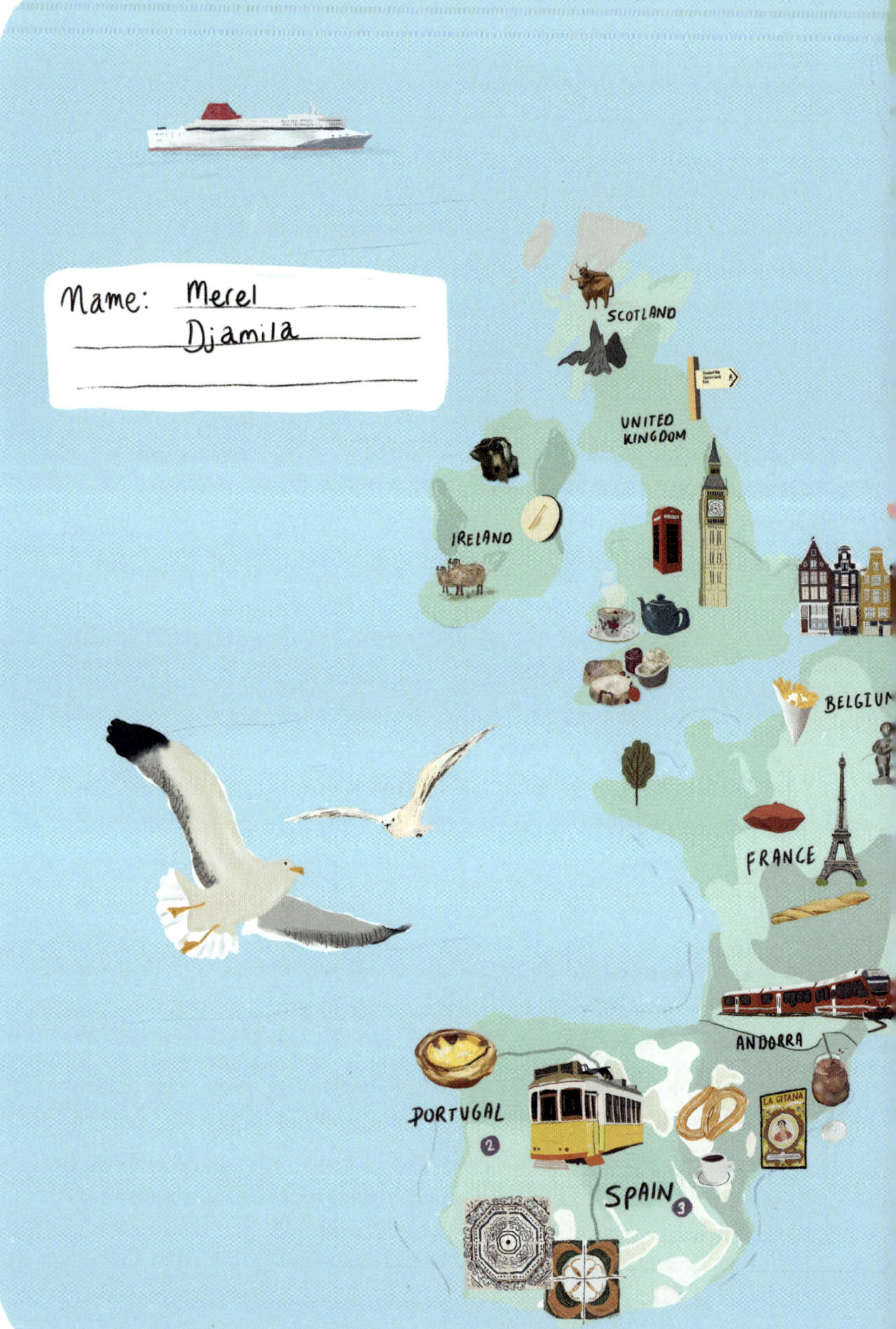

Name: Merel
Djamila
SCOTLAND
UNITED
KINGDOM
IRELAND
BELGIUM
FRANCE
ANDORRA
PORTUGAL
SPAIN
LA GITANA

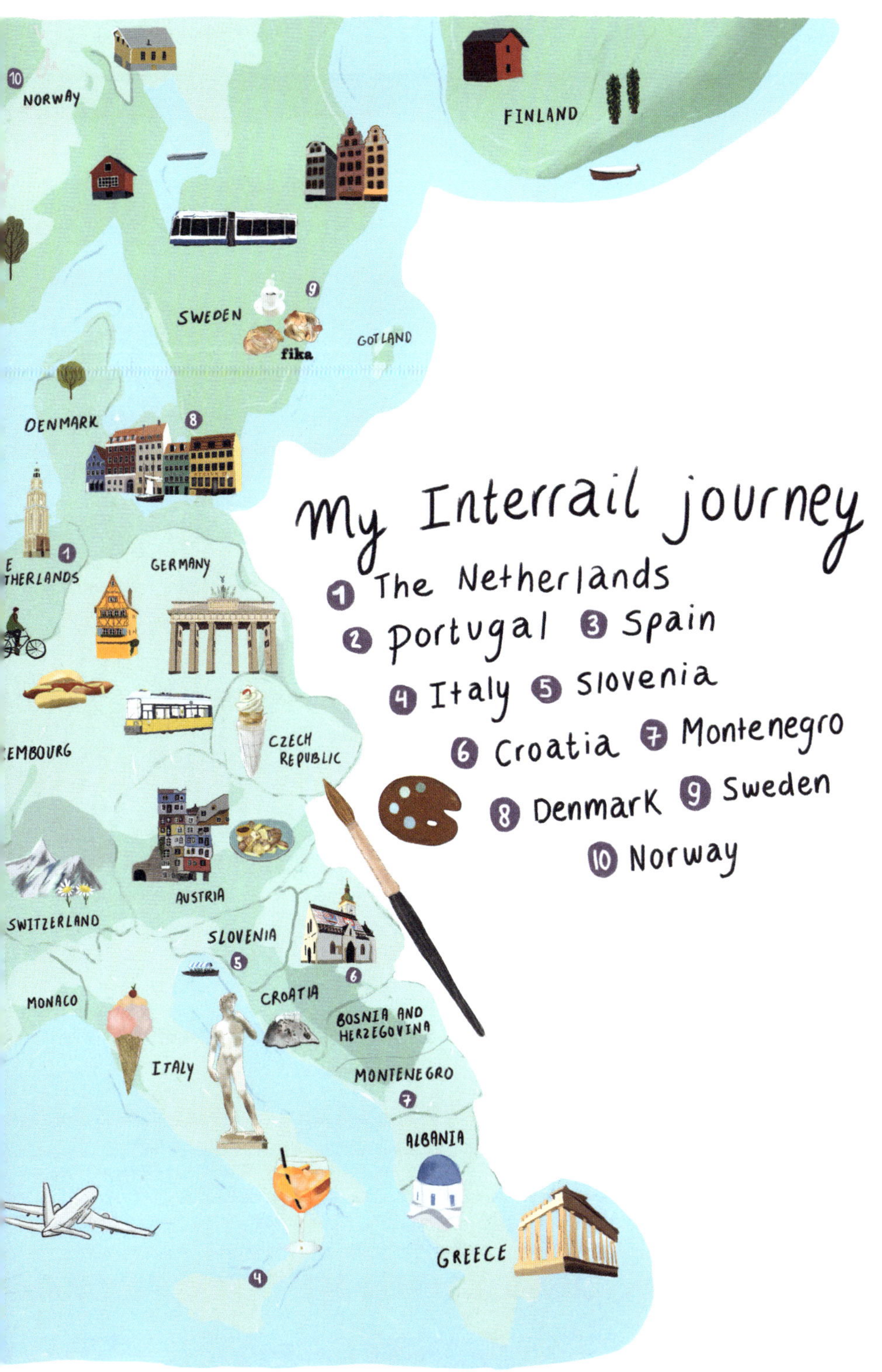

NORWAY
FINLAND
SWEDEN
fika
GOTLAND
DENMARK
NETHERLANDS
GERMANY
LUXEMBOURG
CZECH REPUBLIC
AUSTRIA
SWITZERLAND
SLOVENIA
MONACO
CROATIA
BOSNIA AND HERZEGOVINA
ITALY
MONTENEGRO
ALBANIA
GREECE
My Interrail journey
1 The Netherlands
2 Portugal   3 Spain
4 Italy   5 Slovenia
6 Croatia   7 Montenegro
8 Denmark   9 Sweden
10 Norway

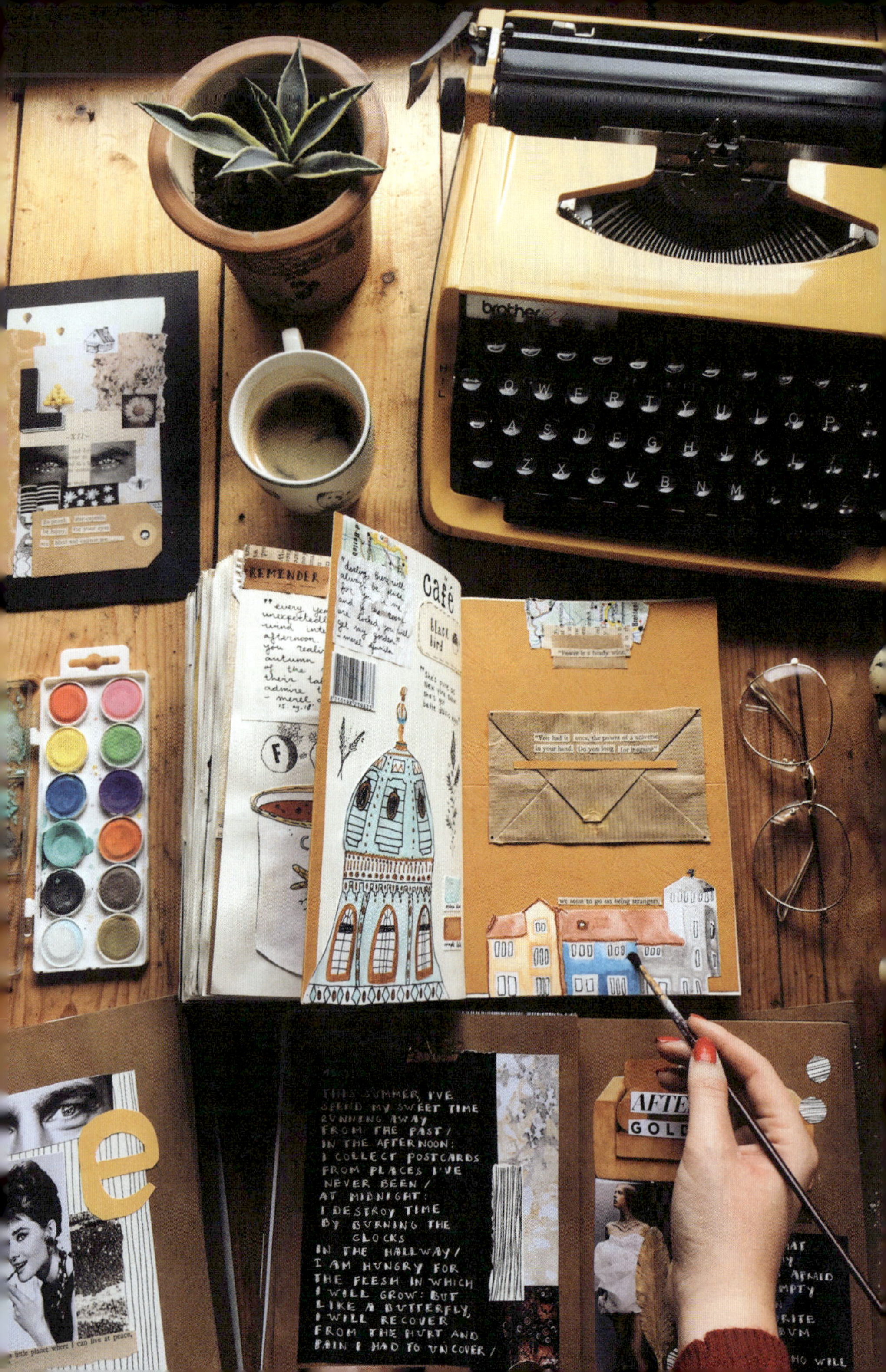

REMEMBER
café
black bird
THIS SUMMER, I'VE
SPENT MY SWEET TIME
RUNNING AWAY
FROM THE PAST /
IN THE AFTERNOON:
I COLLECT POSTCARDS
FROM PLACES I'VE
NEVER BEEN /
AT MIDNIGHT:
I DESTROY TIME
BY BURNING THE
CLOCKS
IN THE HALLWAY /
I AM HUNGRY FOR
THE FLESH IN WHICH
I WILL GROW; BUT
LIKE A BUTTERFLY,
I WILL RECOVER
FROM THE HURT AND
PAIN I HAD TO UNCOVER /
AFTER
GOLD

WHY START A TRAVEL JOURNAL?

Keeping a travel journal – whether during or after your trip – offers a great way to reflect on your experiences, the people you meet, and the moments you cherish, while shaping and preserving memories in a meaningful way. Can you think of a greater gift than dusting off one of your journals after several years, flipping through its pages, and reliving your memories?

Reflecting through ink

As a child, I always kept diaries because I felt the need to reflect on my day. When nothing special happened, I sometimes made up my own stories with fictional characters. I was never very consistent, though, and would sometimes forget to write for days.

But during holidays, I would collect receipts and tickets. If I didn't manage to stick them into my notebook that same evening, I made sure to do it the following day. At the time, I didn't realise I was actually journaling, but as it turns out, I had been doing it all along. My twin sister and I were both fascinated by capturing moments through photography. In 2011, she started her first blog to share her photos, while I remained dedicated to keeping a paper journal and reflecting on my life through ink.

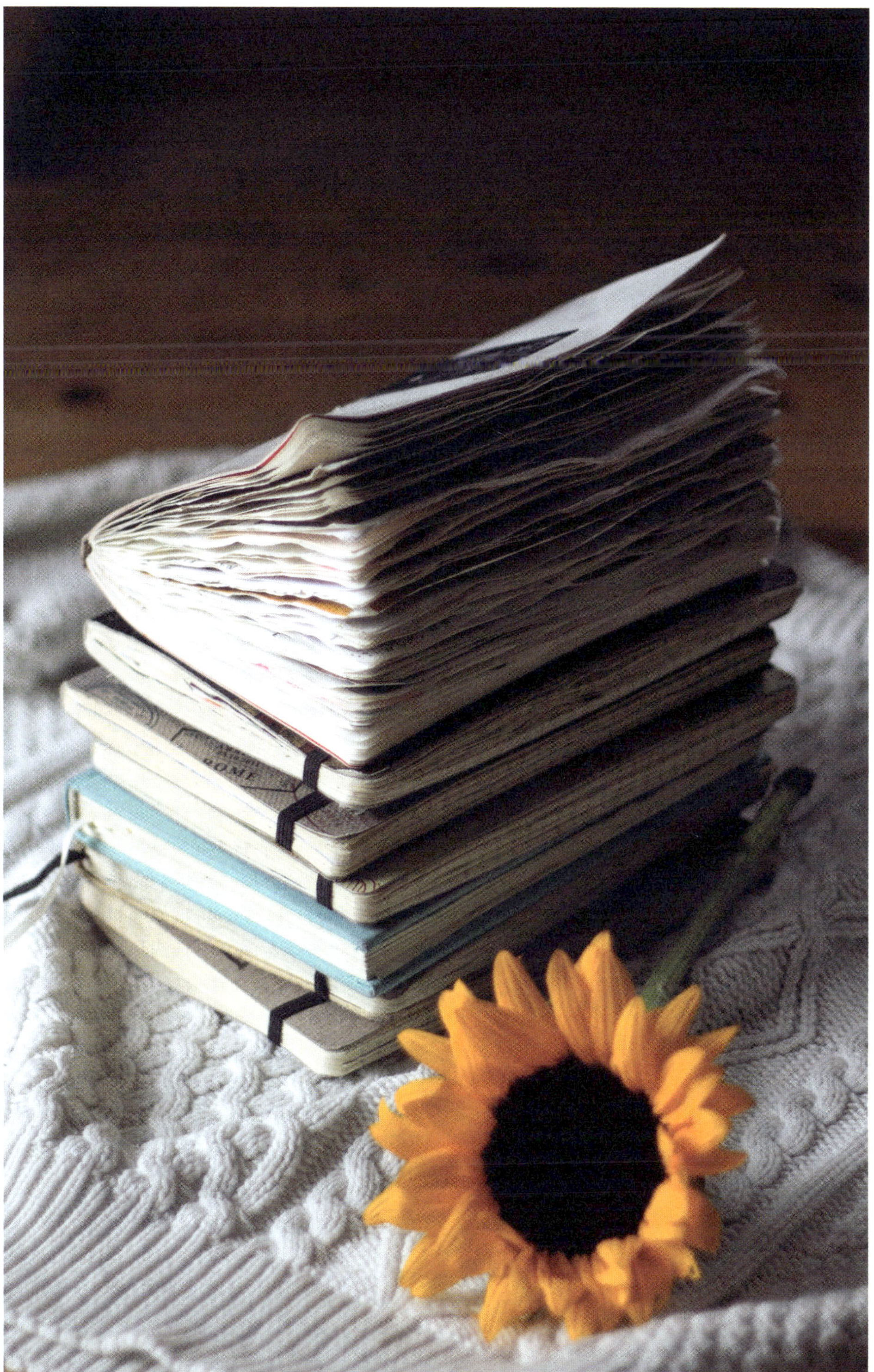

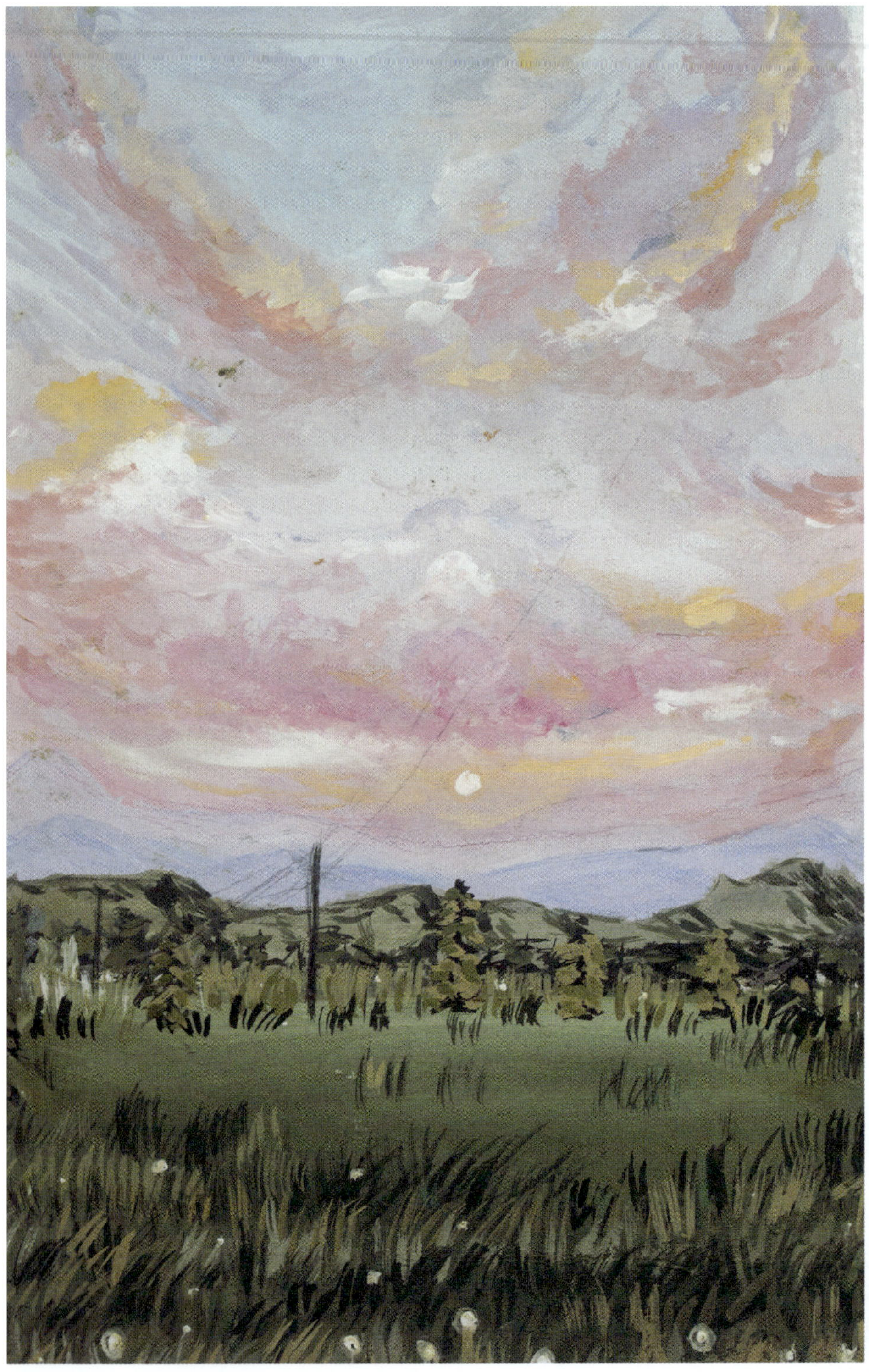

The power of paper

When you consider that you are constantly receiving and processing new stimuli, it is not surprising that you might feel overstimulated from time to time. On social media, you may scroll through entertaining videos for hours, in town you are confronted with countless advertisements, and at school or at work you might be constantly interrupted by classmates or colleagues.

As a place becomes more familiar, chances are you're filtering out most stimuli and only notice sounds, smells, and sights that are out of the ordinary. However, when you're in a new, unfamiliar setting – such as when travelling – you're far more aware of everything around you. As a result, you may become overstimulated.

Journaling can help you focus on the moment and take a break from the background noise, but its benefits go beyond that. For one, keeping a journal provides space for self-reflection. Writing about your thoughts allows you to explore your emotions and mindset, fostering a deeper understanding of yourself. Reflecting on challenges, fears, or difficult experiences can offer relief and contribute to mental well-being and clarity. Additionally, writing down your aspirations and goals can help you stay organised and motivated during hectic periods. Ultimately, journaling teaches you to appreciate the small things and cultivate a positive mindset.

Disconnect to reconnect

Embracing paper over screens

Have you always been the kind of traveller who likes to see as much as possible in a short amount of time? Or do you prefer beach holidays to escape from your busy life? Either way, a travel journal is an excellent tool for documenting your adventures. A traditional paper journal encourages you to focus and stay present in the moment. Chances are, you already spend enough time staring at screens in your everyday routine anyway.

As holidays are supposed to be relaxing, it is an excellent time to put away your phone and truly take in your surroundings. Recording them in a travel journal helps you become a better observer, because you must take in some details to draw or paint something. Journaling also slows you down: it simply takes more time to draw or paint then it does to snap a photo, and you'll end up with a physical memento of your trip that you can still flip through years later.

Travel journals are much more personal than printed photo books, as they are uniquely you. As you build your collection of travel journals, you will also shape your history and development as an artist, improving your drawing and painting skills with each one along the way.

Do you want to start a travel journal, but don't have a holiday planned?
Go out and explore your own neighbourhood. Take a sketchbook, pencil or pen, pick a building or location, and just begin!

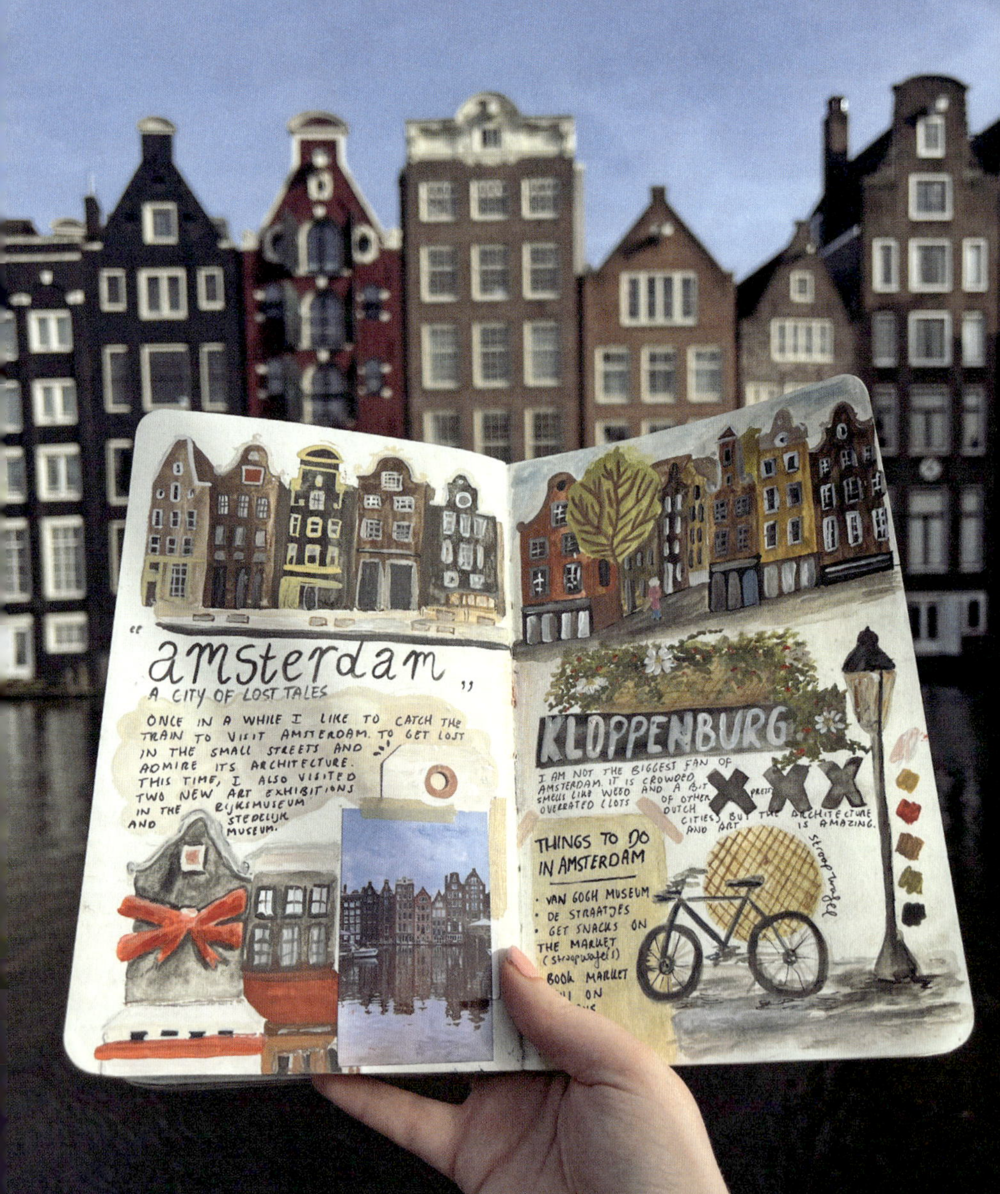

" amsterdam "
A CITY OF LOST TALES
ONCE IN A WHILE I LIKE TO CATCH THE TRAIN TO VISIT AMSTERDAM. TO GET LOST IN THE SMALL STREETS AND ADMIRE ITS ARCHITECTURE. THIS TIME, I ALSO VISITED TWO NEW ART EXHIBITIONS IN THE RIJKSMUSEUM AND STEDELIJK MUSEUM.
KLOPPENBURG
I AM NOT THE BIGGEST FAN OF AMSTERDAM. IT IS CROWDED, SMELLS LIKE WEED AND A BIT OVERRATED (LOTS OF OTHER DUTCH CITIES) BUT THE ARCHITECTURE AND ART IS AMAZING.
XXX
THINGS TO DO IN AMSTERDAM
• VAN GOGH MUSEUM
• DE STRAATJES
• GET SNACKS ON THE MARKET (stroopwafels)
BOOK MARKET ON
stroopwafel

CHAPTER 2

THE ART OF OBSERVING

In this day and age, it's not uncommon to feel rushed –
even while relaxing. Think about how little time you
spend standing in front of a painting at a museum,
or how quickly you work through the list of the most
important sights and landmarks during a city trip.
What would happen if you took more time? Allow me
to explain the magic of observing.

observe

/əbˈzəːv/

notice or perceive (something) and register it as being significant

Learn to linger

You may have heard of "slow living" before. In a world where we constantly rush from one appointment to the next, with little time to recover, it's no surprise that burnouts are becoming increasingly common. We often forget to hit the brakes and take time to process the constant stream of stimuli, signalling a need for change. One way to achieve this is by slowing down.

During a trip, you can slow down by loosening your schedule. Instead of trying to see everything, focus on the details: the decorations on buildings, a balustrade, or the view from a tall church tower. This kind of observation allows you to fully absorb the atmosphere of a place – its sights, sounds, and smells. It also gives you time to reflect on what you're seeing, deepening your understanding and appreciation. Observing isn't about seeing more, but about being selective, noticing details, and remembering them.

And, as you've probably guessed, a travel journal is the perfect tool for slowing down and observing. You can use it to note down your observations, thoughts, and the interesting details that catch your eye.

The basics of observation

Observing is about looking at the world with more attention and focus. Start with a low-threshold activity that you can do at your leisure, or on your terms. For example, sit on a bench and count the people passing by, the ducks in the pond, or the green cars in the street.

As a result, you will pay more attention to details rather than to the overall scene. You will begin to appreciate things you never noticed before. This helps you to develop a better understanding of both people and the world around you.

For example, by analysing a painting in a museum, you will think more about the painter's techniques, or about the story being depicted. Thoughts and emotions can be observed and written down accordingly. For instance, if you felt disappointed today, it's through the art of observation that you can identify what triggered that feeling and understand why.

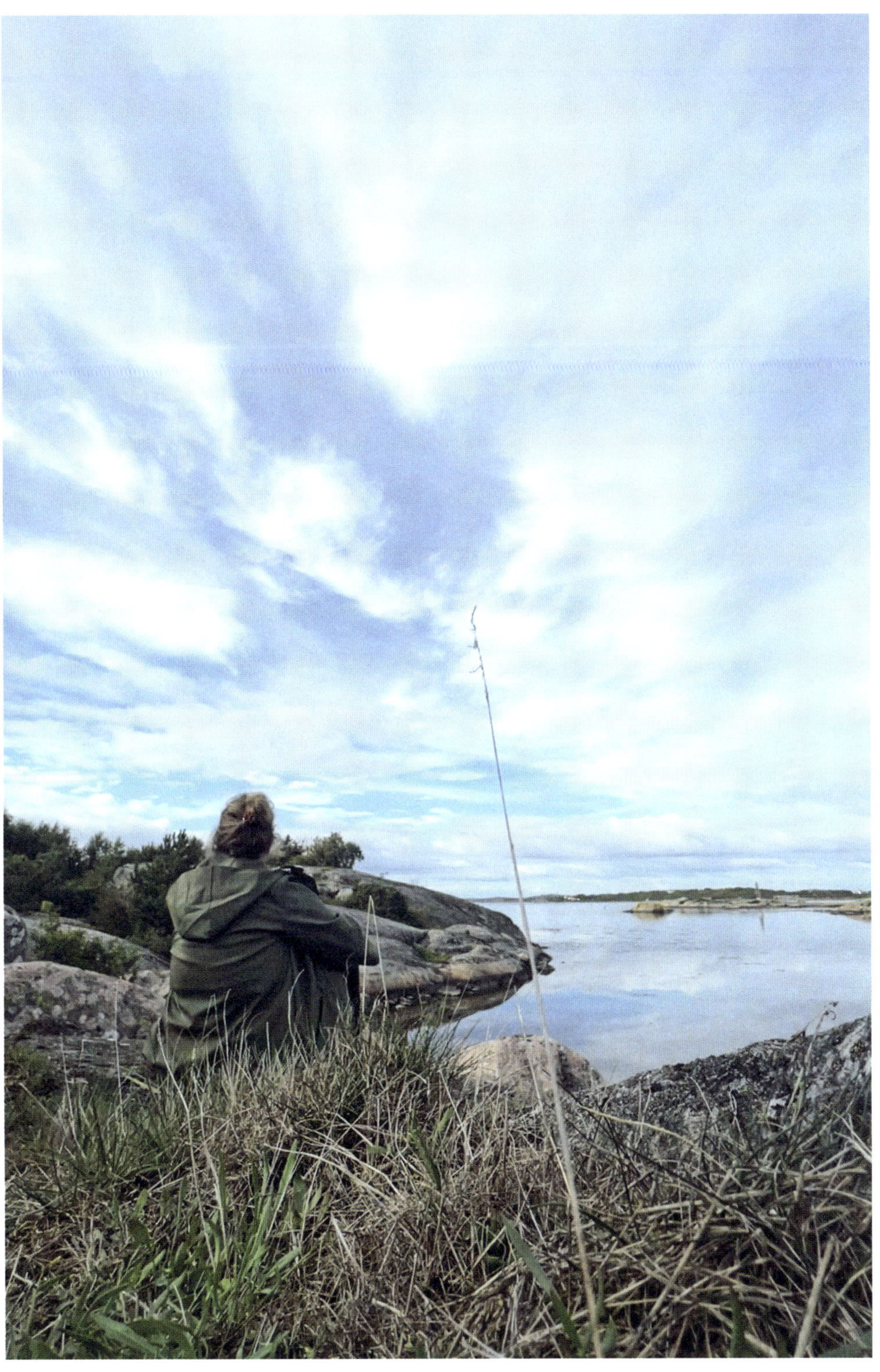

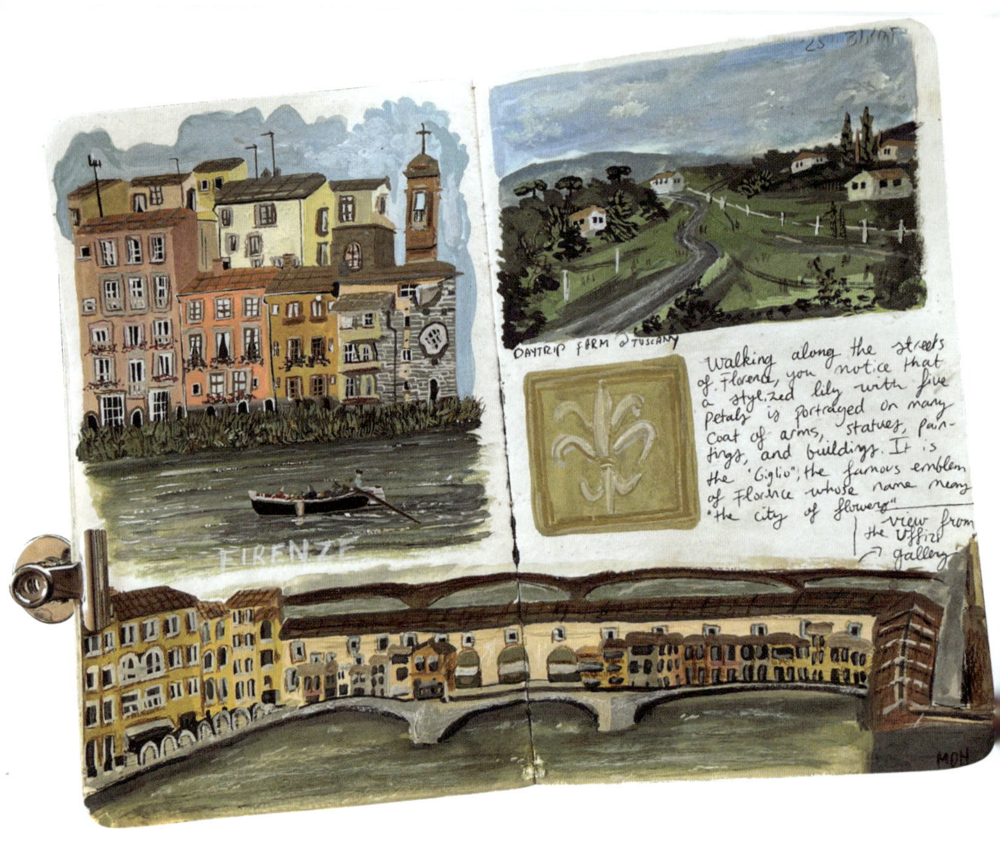

Recognising patterns

An example of what happens when you take your time to be aware of your surroundings is this journal spread that includes the Florentine *Giglio*. Walking through the streets of Florence, I often came across the *giglio*, a French lily with five petals. It is depicted on many coats of arms, statues, paintings, and buildings. It is the emblem of Florence, which means 'the city of flowers'. Once you have noticed it, you will encounter the symbol hundreds of times as you stroll through Florence. So, you see, when you observe closely, you'll start to recognise patterns and notice more.

Training your observational skills

Build habits

Schedule half an hour each week for hands-on activities, such as writing, drawing, or gardening. This enhances focus on details, like soil texture or word choices, while helping you slow down and absorb your surroundings, from gardens blooming to evolving sketches.

Find your rhythm

Experiment to find out what works well for you. If that means taking out your journal once every six months to work in it, that is absolutely fine.

Wander with intention

Do your research before visiting a place and make a list of sights (such as museums, churches, or shops) you don't want to miss to help avoid feeling overwhelmed.

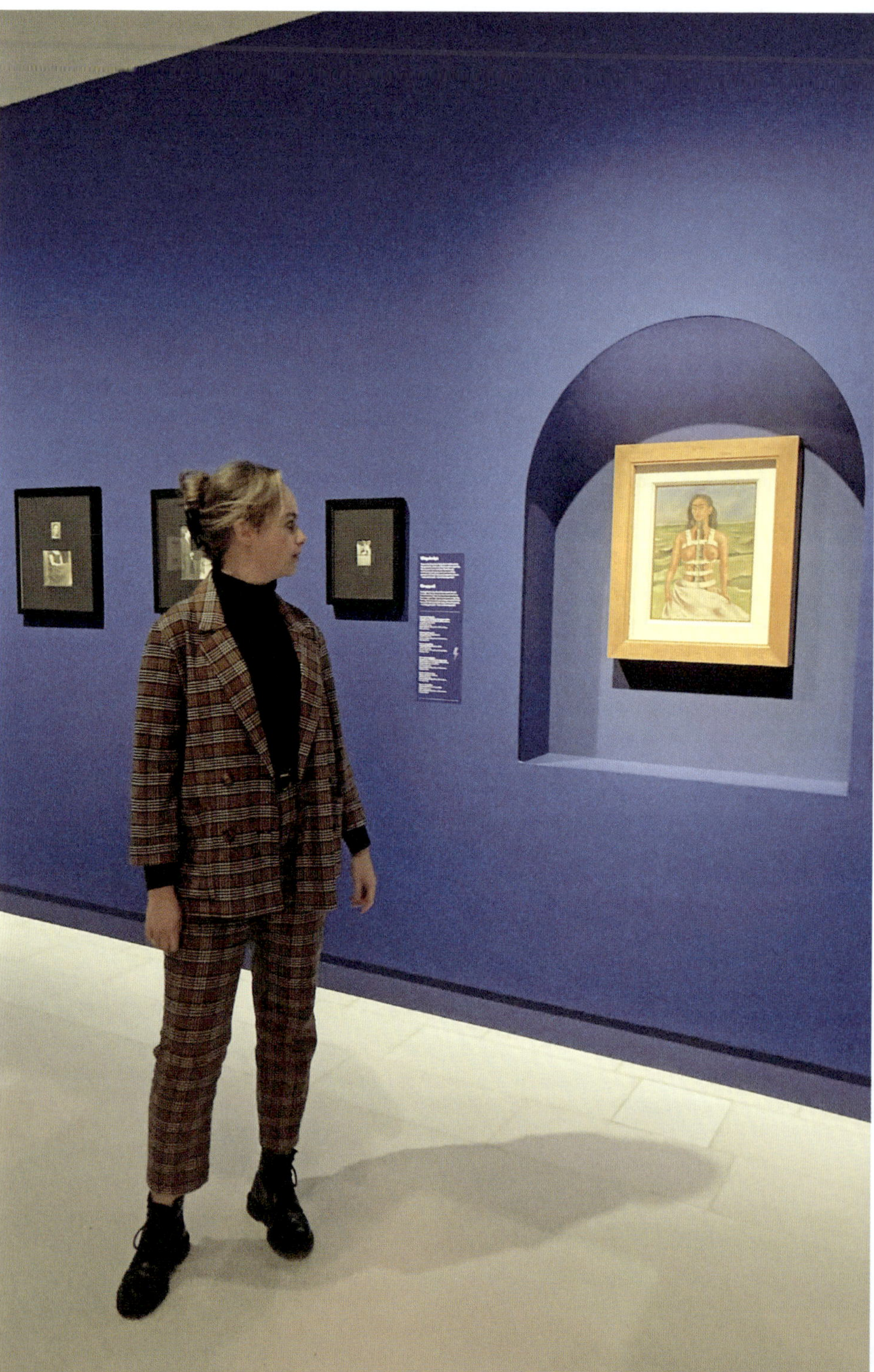

Engaging with your surroundings

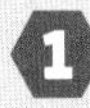

Through new eyes

Rediscover your own environment by walking through it. Pick a route and make a list of everything you encounter that you haven't noticed before.

Look up

Especially in a city, don't forget to look up. You'll often find the most beautiful details of buildings high above.

Dive deep into art

During a museum visit, take a longer look at a work of art that appeals to you. Before reading the information about the painting, focus on a few details. Is there a lot happening in the painting that draws your attention? Choose one or two elements to concentrate on. Imagine the conversations you might overhear if you were among the people in the painting. Or consider the time of day – is it morning or perhaps evening?

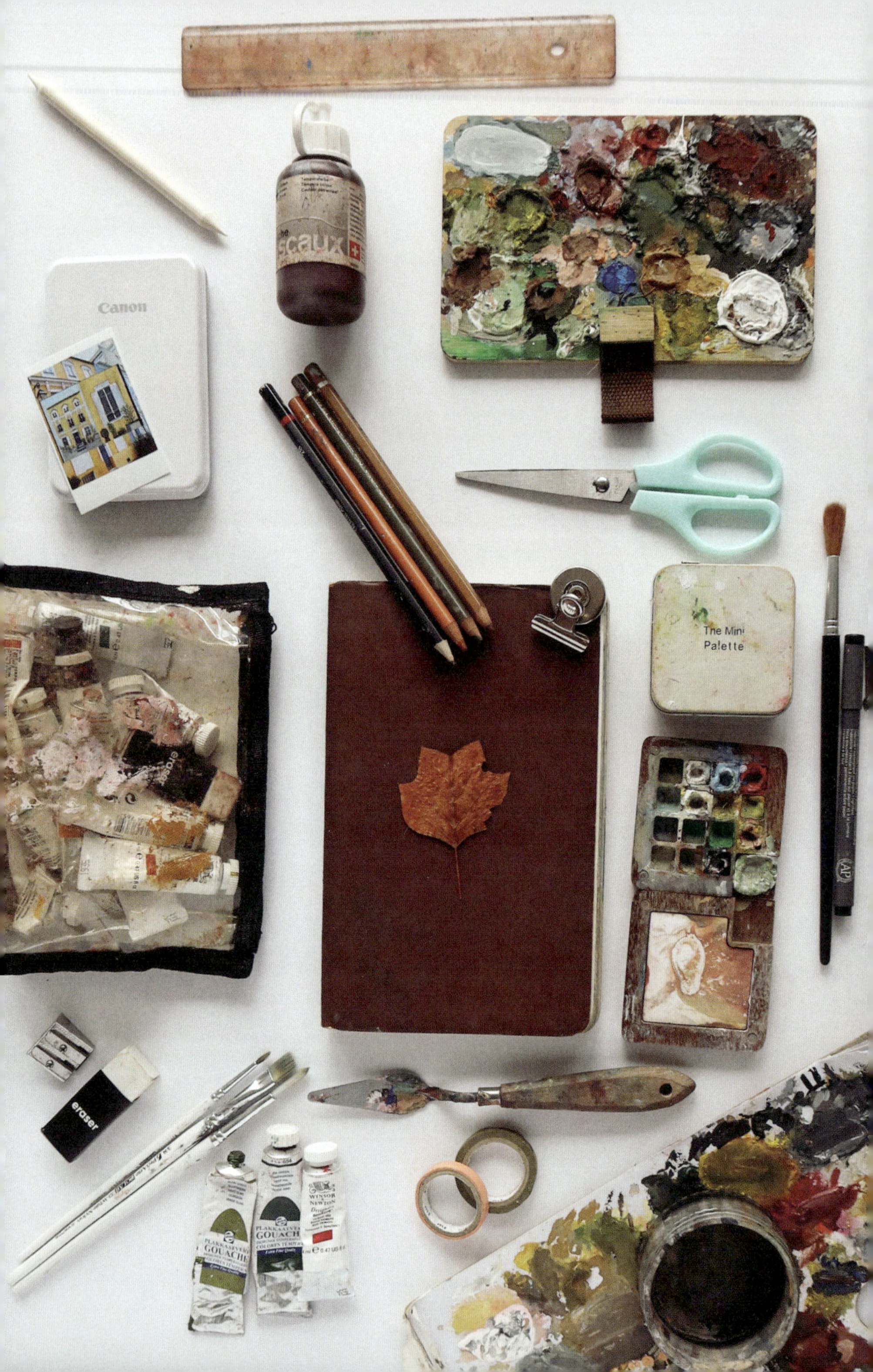

Canon
scaux
The Mini
Palette
GOUACHE
GOUACHE
WINSOR
NEWTON
eraser
AP

CHAPTER 3

WHAT YOU MAY (OR MAY NOT) NEED

Walking around an art supply shop can be overwhelming, as there is so much to choose from. How do you know which notebook, paint, or brush is right for you? Should you take a wide variety with you on your travels, or just select a few favourites before heading out? And how do you avoid regretting your choices later?

Generally, less is more. A pair of small scissors, a pencil, some glue, and a pen are must-haves. Do not bring anything that is too expensive or that takes up a lot of space, such as a big painting palette or a heavy magazine. If you intend to make collages, you can collect receipts and brochures along the way.

Notebooks

There are many different notebooks for various purposes.

(Creative) planning

A bullet journal is a good option if you want to mainly write and occasionally draw or scrapbook. The downside of bullet journals is that they are often not suitable for painting or working with alcohol markers. The brands Code&Quill and Leuchtturm offer good options.

Scrapbooking

I recommend looking into sturdy notebooks that will still be able to lay flat after you've filled the journal halfway through. Thick paper is recommended if you work with glue. If you use your journal intensively and take it on the road often, a stitched notebook works better than a glue-bound one. Although glue-bound journals are often more affordable, they are also more likely to come apart during your travels. Notebooks from the brand Ciak are suitable for scrapbooking. Their covers are flexible but sturdy. If you like to combine various materials in your scrapbook, I would recommend looking into mixed media books, such as those by Stillman & Birn.

Painting

Your safest bet for painting is to work in a mixed media sketchbook that can handle all kinds of liquids. If you're planning to paint in your journal, I would recommend working with at least 200-GSM paper. (GSM stands for "grams per square meter", and the higher the GSM, the higher its quality.) The mixed media sketchbook from Stillman & Birn's Delta series contains paper that is ivory, grainy, and textured, rather than white and smooth. For watercolouring, Hahnemühle is a suitable brand, as their thick, rough paper can handle a lot of water without becoming wrinkled or warped.

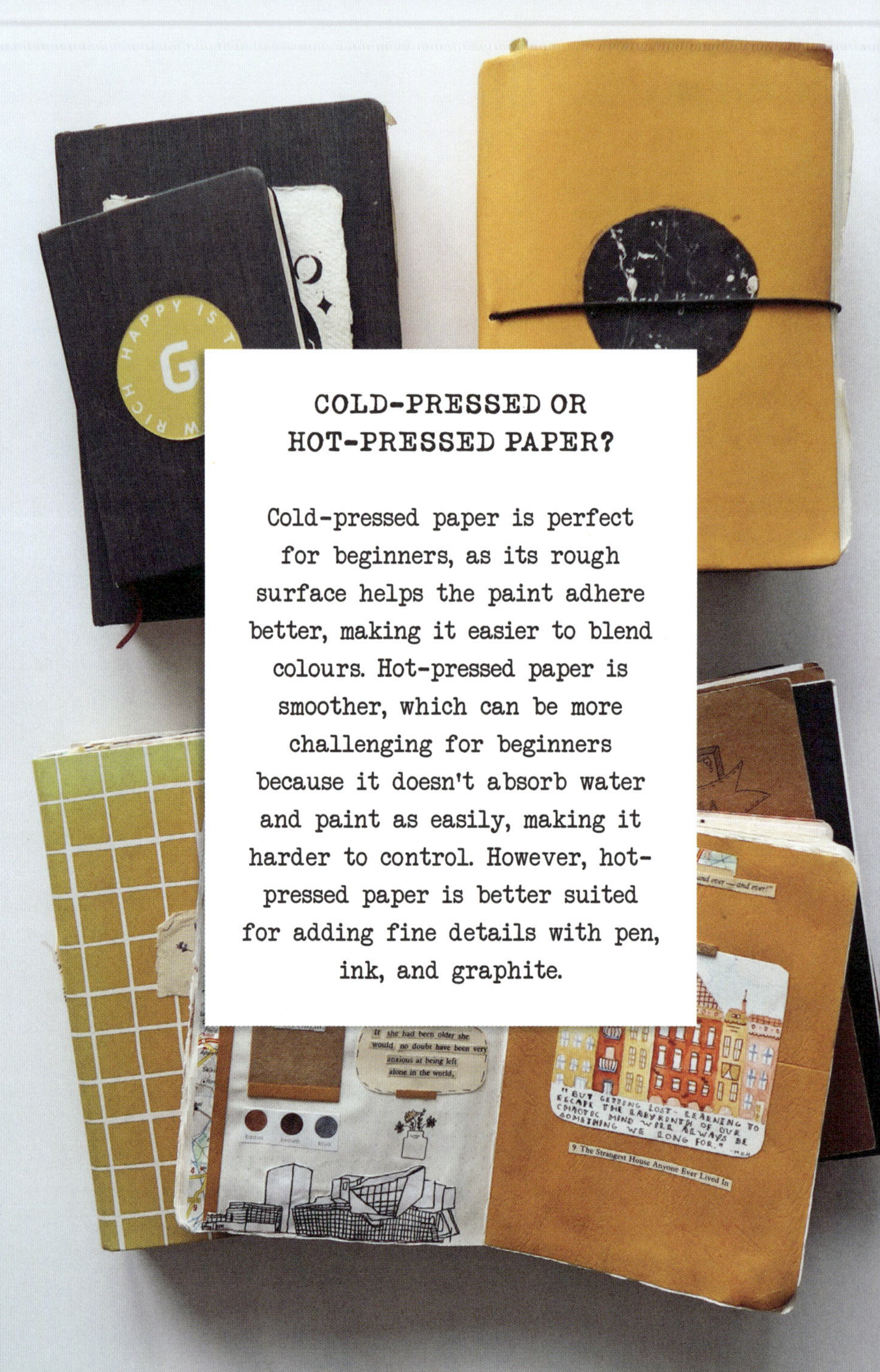

COLD-PRESSED OR HOT-PRESSED PAPER?

Cold-pressed paper is perfect for beginners, as its rough surface helps the paint adhere better, making it easier to blend colours. Hot-pressed paper is smoother, which can be more challenging for beginners because it doesn't absorb water and paint as easily, making it harder to control. However, hot-pressed paper is better suited for adding fine details with pen, ink, and graphite.

Paints

Are you just starting out with paint? To avoid getting frustrated, I would recommend getting a paint set from a good but affordable brand with just the primary colours: yellow, red, and blue. You can mix them to make other colours. Adding tubes of white and black can also be helpful.

Acrylic paint

Acrylic paint is the cheapest and easiest to work with. You can get it almost anywhere and it's available in both small and larger sizes. It works well on multiple surfaces and dries quickly. But once acrylic paint dries, you're not able to rewet the paint. Although the cheapest option might sound appealing, chances are that it's too watery for your liking. My personal favourites are acrylic paint tubes from the brands Amsterdam and Panduro.

Watercolours

Watercolours are ideal as lots of inexpensive kits are available, and you can easily remove stains. A good watercolour illustration is created by layering the work, using more water for highlights and less water (more pigment) for shadows. You can choose between tubes and pans. Watercolours in pans are easy to take with you. As the paint is not liquid, it will not stain easily and with just a little water, the paint is easily spreadable.

Most watercolour kits have an inbuilt mixing palette. Often, more expensive paint kits have better quality paints containing more pigment. You can't go wrong with brands like Daniel Smith, Winsor & Newton, and Van Gogh.

Gouache

You could say that gouache is the best of both worlds. It's as opaque as acrylics, but just as reusable as watercolours. A Himi Miya gouache paint set is well-suited for when you are just starting out with this type of paint. There are many different containers and colours to choose from. This paint is not expensive, yet well pigmented. Spray the paint cups regularly with some (distilled) water so it doesn't dry out. Use an electric paint mixer (or milk frother), toothpick, or palette knife to stir the paint. Don't close the paint box when the paint is still moist, as mould will develop more easily when oxygen cannot reach it. The brands Winsor & Newton, Talens, and Caran d'Ache offer good quality gouache as well.

Gouache paint in tubes is more convenient to bring with you during your travels. This is because gouache often remains liquid longer after you have used it, it stains more, and you have to stir it more often in separate pans or containers in order to use it. With tubes you can work more accurately, because the substance in tubes remains in good condition, and – unless you want to mix colours – the paint doesn't need to be stirred. Bigger containers, like Lascaux's gouache, are best suited for when you're working at home.

Check the packaging of paints and coloured pencils for lightfastness ratings. Lightfastness refers to how long your artwork will last over the years when exposed to sunlight. These range from I to V or 1 to 8, with I and 8 being the most resistant to fading and 1 or V the least.

I wouldn't recommend using oil paint, because it dries very slowly, and the oily substance of the paint is not beneficial for the lifespan of your journal.

Other materials

Glue

Glue sticks or rollers are the most user-friendly. For scrapbooking, I would recommend Mod Podge as glue as well as varnish to add a protective layer once you've finished your project.

Paint brushes

There are different brushes for each type of painting. For gouache paint, I would recommend round, synthetic brushes such as ProArte Polar brushes or Etchr Gouache brushes. It's also wise to have a few miniature brushes for adding details.

Coloured pencils

Faber-Castell Polychromos coloured pencils are my personal favourite, especially in combination with gouache (after the paint has dried). Crayons and pastels are also fun to experiment with.

Fineliners

For finishing touches or writing, I like the Sakura Micron waterproof fineliners. You need your fineliners to be waterproof if you want to use them before adding paint.

Portable photo printer

Using the Canon Zoemini printer, you can easily print photos from your camera roll and use them as stickers in your journal.

Markers

Water-based markers are best suited for working on paper, as alcohol-based markers easily seep through. For other surfaces, such as wood, metal, and fabric, alcohol-based markers are most suitable. Consider the Ohuhu Paint Markers or the Posca Paint Markers.

Masking tape / Washi tape

Washi tape is fun to decorate your pages with. You can also use it as masking tape, removing it after painting to frame your illustration. I often work with MT Slim Masking Tape.

Blending stump

Softening pencil lines can be easily done with your fingers, but this affordable tool is pretty effective as well when it comes to blending pencil lines with a lot of pigment and pastels.

As you have seen in this chapter, there are quite a few choices to make in terms of what tools to take with you on your trip. Start by considering what you want to achieve and then decide what materials to take with you. If you happen to forget something, chances are you will find it at your destination. Or you'll get creative and discover that you can put a different spin on things. For example, during my last trip I forgot to bring a glue stick, which I solved by using paint from a tube as glue. And always remember: less is more.

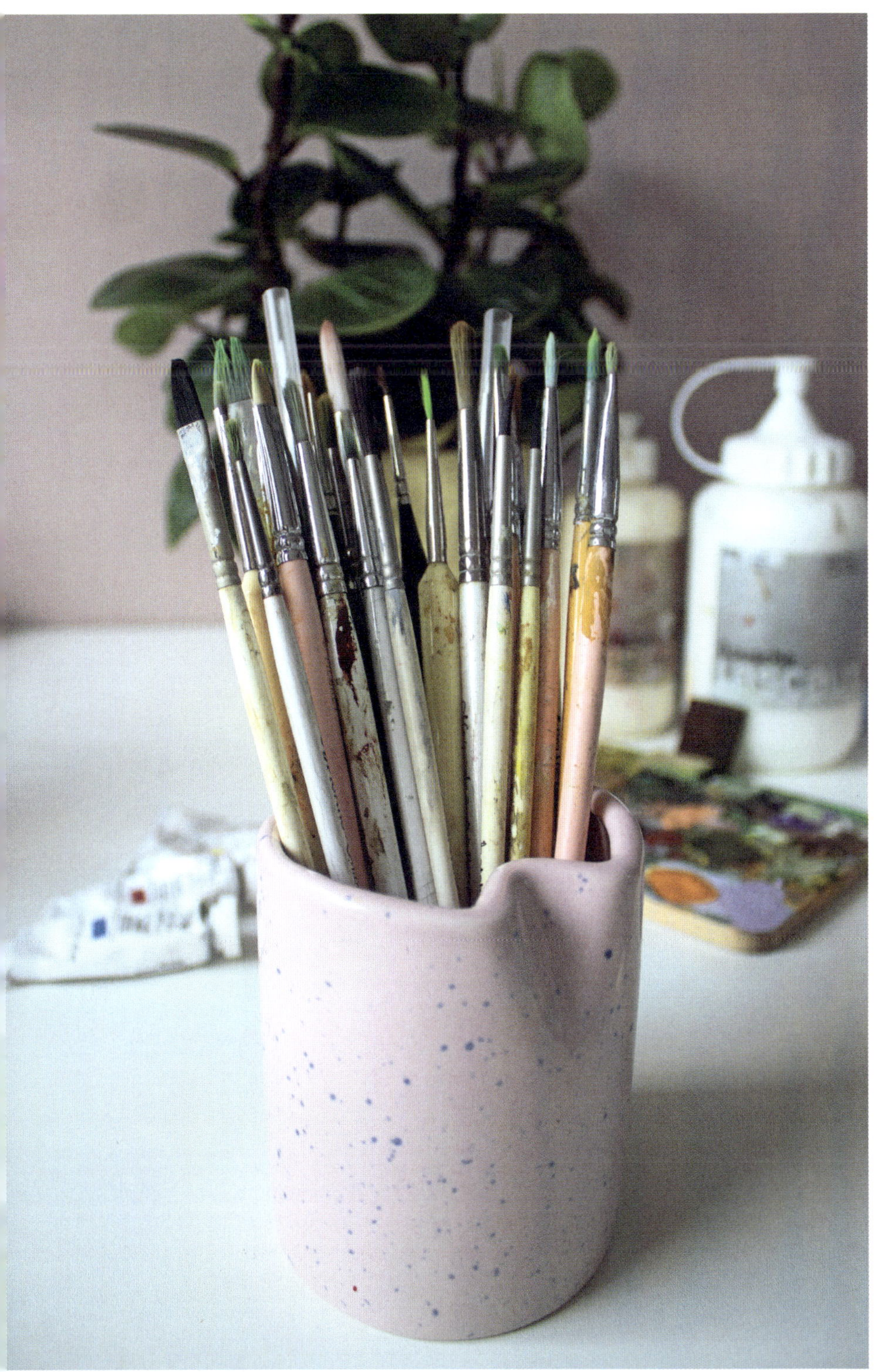

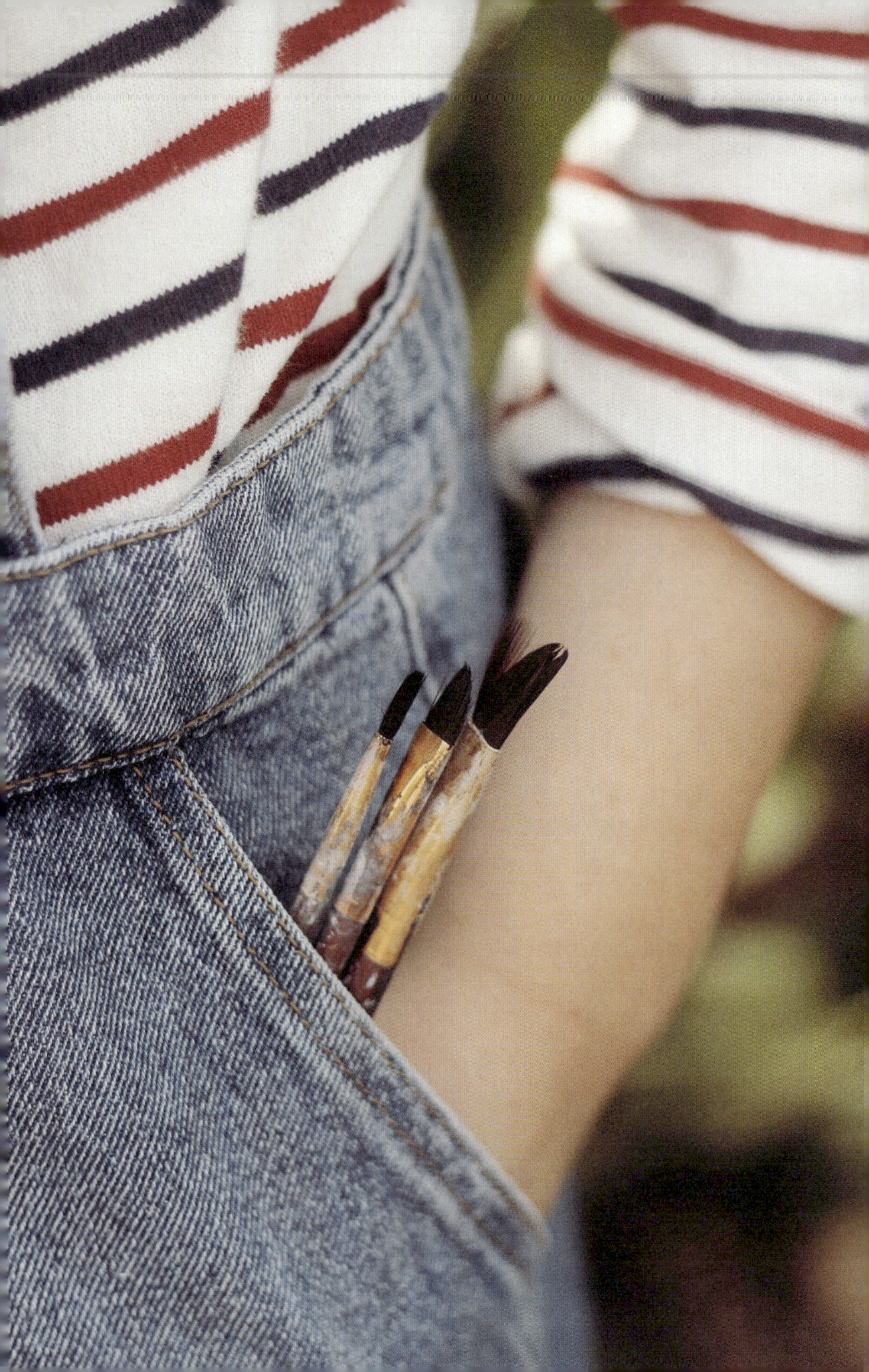

CHAPTER 4

COLOURS, PAINTBRUSHES, AND OTHER TECHNICALITIES

In this chapter, I'll explain the ins and outs of colours. You will learn the basics of colour mixing, various painting techniques, why these are ideal for your (travel) diary, and which brushes you can use. Keep in mind that your colours and brushstrokes don't have to exactly match real life. Just look at Van Gogh's paintings! He often painted cityscapes and flower portraits in his own way.

The theory of colour

Understanding which colours to mix to end up with a particular colour is best learned by looking at a colour wheel before you start drawing or painting.

Primary colours are the main colours – red, blue, and yellow. You can mix them to make other colours. Secondary colours are made by mixing two primary colours – examples are orange (red and yellow), green (yellow and blue), and purple (blue and red). When you mix a primary colour with a secondary colour, you get a tertiary colour. Think of red-orange or yellow-green. Complementary colours are opposite each other on the wheel, like red and green or blue and orange. They make each other stand out because they create contrast and intensity when placed next to each other.

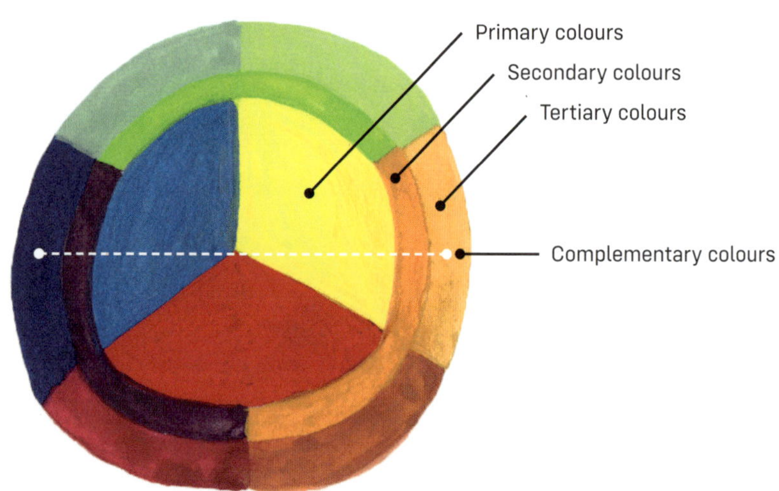

Mixing colours

Use a limited palette

To avoid overwhelming yourself, start with the primary colours plus white, and gradually add more colours as you become more confident.

Start light, go dark

When mixing colours, start with lighter shades and gradually add darker colours to achieve the desired hue. It's easier to darken a colour than it is to lighten it.

Mixing materials

Use a palette knife or brush to mix colours on a palette. Brushes are good for mixing and applying paint carefully, while palette knives are better for blending over a larger area and creating different textures.

Transparency and light

By adding water, you make a colour more transparent. The substance also becomes more liquid and dries faster. You can lighten a colour by adding white paint.

Experiment with different ratios

Mix colours in different ratios to achieve various shades and intensities. For example, mixing more blue than yellow will result in a different shade of green than mixing equal parts of both.

Keep notes

Keep track of the colours you mix and the ratios you use by jotting down notes or creating a colour chart. This will help you replicate the desired colours in future projects.

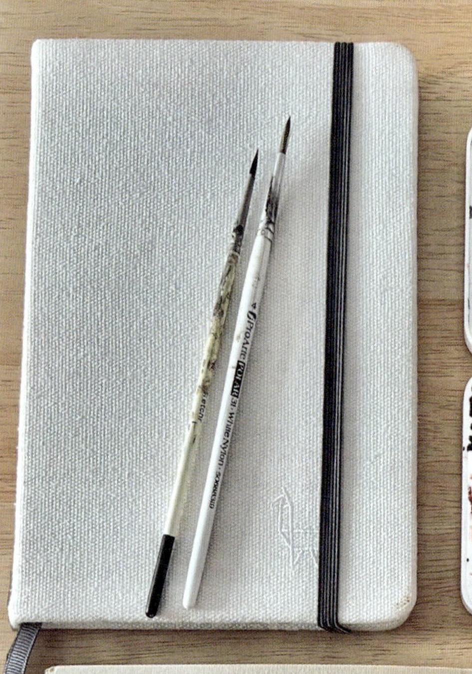

PIER LANE HOUSE
Pier Lane House, Whitby

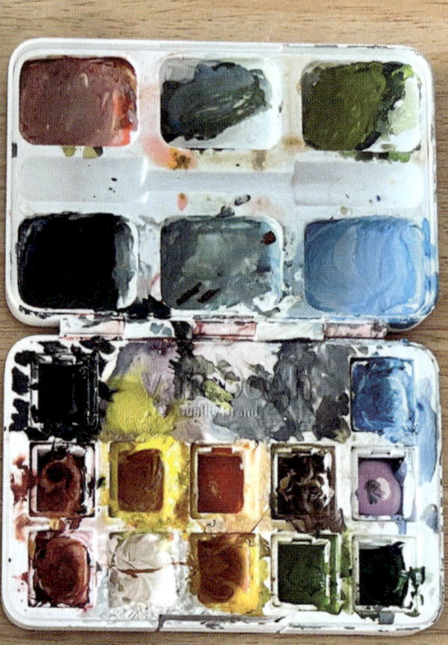

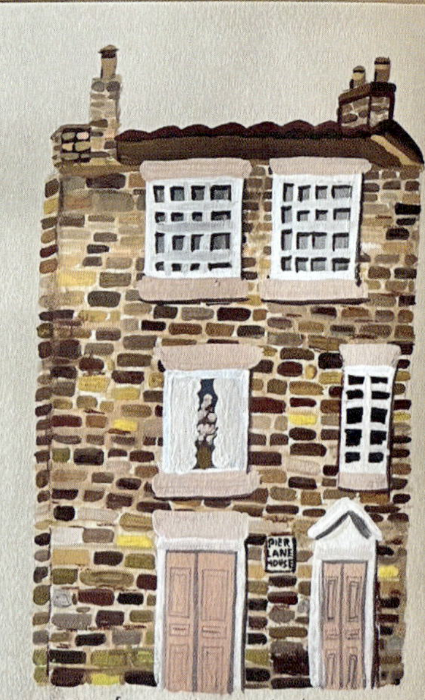

GASWORKS
WORK
VISCOSE
SILK QUALITY
NO. 75835
SOME RETRO PACKAGING
AND OTHER SIGNS I
SAW IN A SHOP WINDOW
RI RI
AERIAL
TUNING
BETTER
THAN
COILS
PHILIPS
Stonegate's
Teddy Bears
there is
A BLADON
LAMP
BLADON for
any
pur
pose
BLAD
ON'S
GAS
VALOR
ESSO
BLUE
I ate
Humble
Pie in
Whitby!
YORKSHIRE
TEA
VALLEY
BEETLE
BEETLE
THE TYPOGRAPHY IN
PARTICULAR
FASCINATES ME
sept. 03 2024

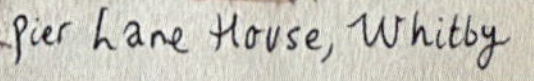

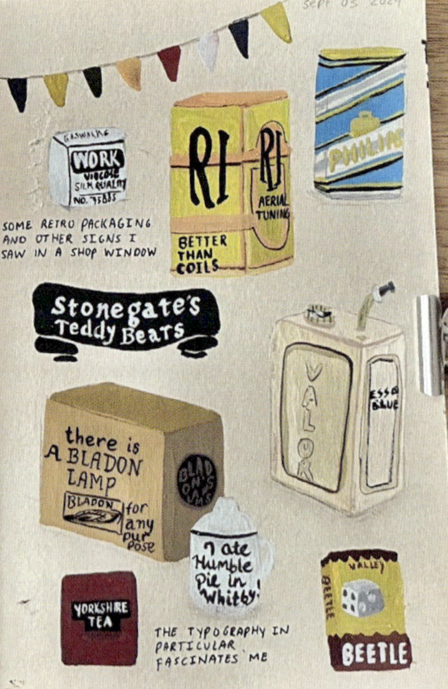

Colour mixing is a skill that takes time to develop. Be patient with yourself and practice regularly to improve your understanding of colour theory and your ability to mix colours accurately. Don't be afraid to experiment with different colour combinations to create unique and interesting hues. Sometimes the most unexpected combinations can result in beautiful colours. For example, adding a touch of pink in your painted sky can make a big difference. While travelling, earth tones can be used for painting landscapes as well as cityscapes. Use tubes of paint for consistent, ready-to-use colours without the need to mix.

How to fix mistakes

Picture this: you needed the perfect colour brown for wood, but it turned out muddy, or your sky looks much too green for your liking. Try to adjust by adding a bit of an opposite colour, such as blue or green for the brown mixture and red for the green mixture, to neutralise. You can also lighten the colours or add another paint layer once the first layer has dried. Sometimes, it's best to start over. Start mixing again with new paint, throw away your page, or stick another sheet of paper on top of it to cover it up.

Be careful with watercolours: if your first layer is too dark, it is difficult to make changes. Make sure that the first layer is as transparent as possible, and dab away some of the colour with water and a cloth. With acrylics, once the first layer dries, you cannot change it, but you can paint over it. Gouache works similarly, but be aware that this paint becomes liquid again when water is added to the mixture. Keeping the first layer a bit more transparent gives you freedom to build up your colours any way you want.

How to make dreamy colours (cold tones) using gouache

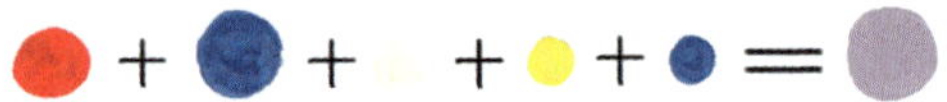

Lilacs

Mix equal parts of red and blue, and eventually add more blue and a little bit of white. If the mix is too red, just add more blue to the mix along with some yellow.

Light blue

Simply stirring some white into a blue base will create the light blue's soft hue. Don't start with too much blue paint to avoid having leftover paint.

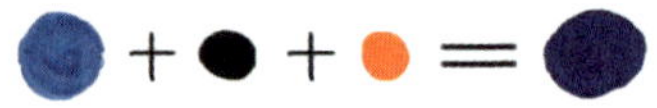

Dark blue

Add black or purple to blue to make dark blue. Add a bit of orange to make a darker blue.

How to make earthy colours (warm tones) using gouache

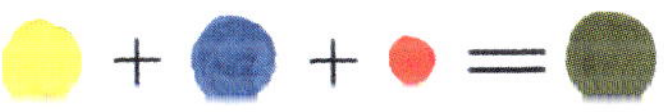

Olive green

Yellow base colour + blue + a touch of red to deepen the hue.

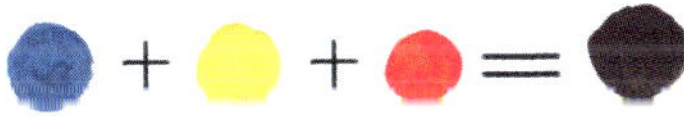

Burnt Umber

Blue base colour + yellow, and an extra amount of red.

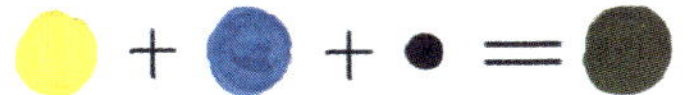

Forest green/dark green

Yellow and blue base (more yellow for a warmer shade, more blue for a cooler shade) + a bit of black to darken the green.

Burnt Sienna

Red base colour + small amounts of yellow and blue.

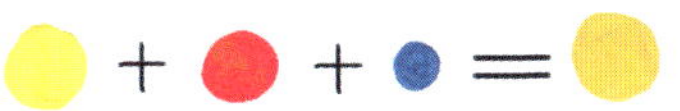

Yellow ochre

Yellow base colour + red and a little bit of blue.

Naples yellow

Add titanium white and a tiny bit of red to your yellow ochre.

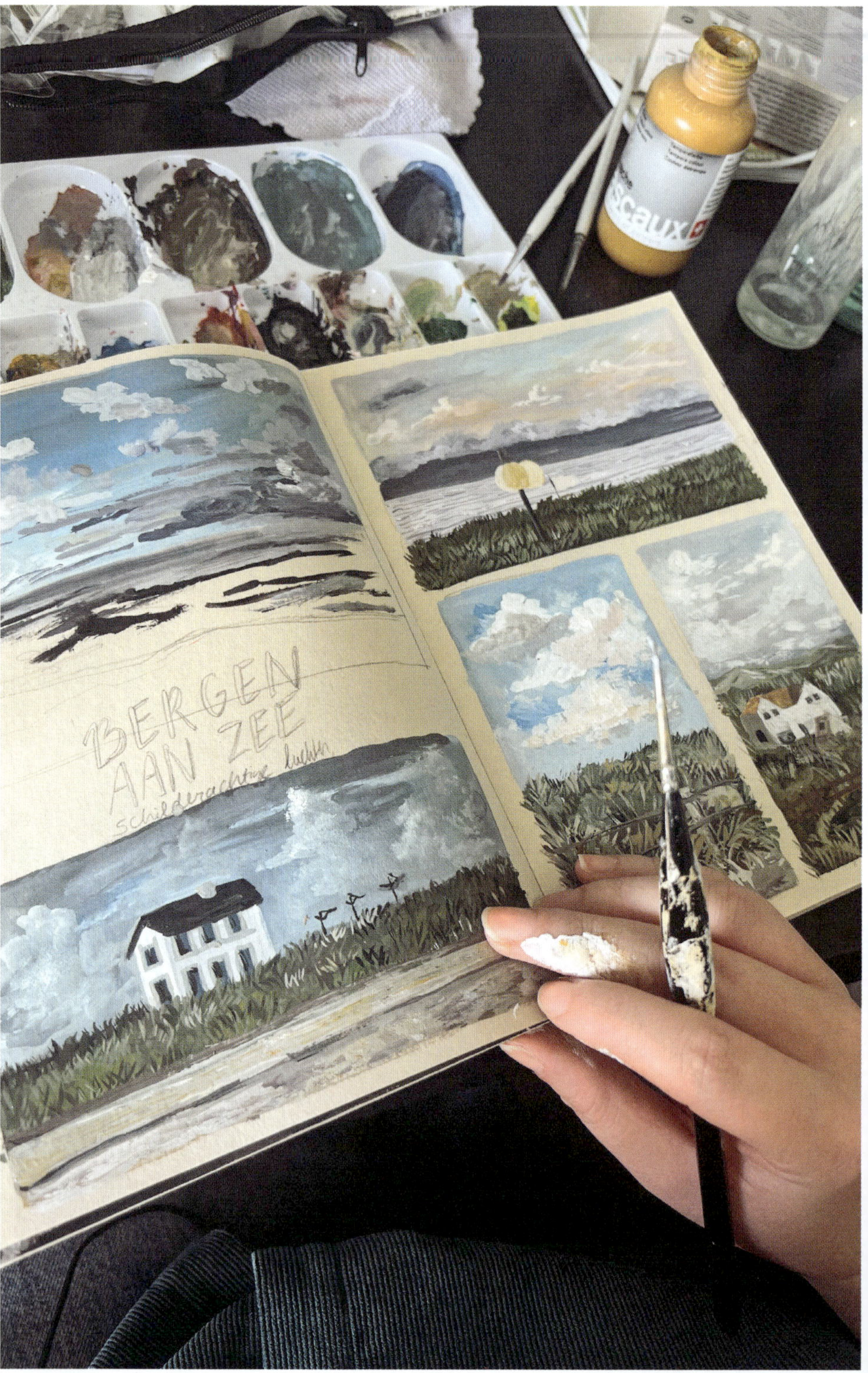
BERGEN
AAN ZEE
schilderachtige luchten

Different painting techniques

Wash

Create a background or underpainting by adding a wash with water colour. This is a thin, transparent layer of paint that establishes a base colour or tone.

Dry brushing

Use a dry brush with little or no water or paint to create a textured effect. This works great for adding details, for example when you want to add some highlights to an ocean wave.

Wet-on-wet

With this technique, you apply wet paint onto a wet surface. This is commonly used in watercolour painting to create soft, blended effects.

Scumbling

Apply a thin, opaque layer of paint over a dry surface with a dry brush or sponge to create a broken or irregular texture. It's often used in acrylic and oil painting for creating soft, atmospheric effects.

Glazing

Start glazing by applying thin, transparent layers of paint over dry layers to build up colour and create depth. This technique is often used in acrylic painting to achieve rich, luminous colours.

Impasto

Apply thick layers of paint with a palette knife or brush to create texture and three-dimensional effects. Note that the paint needs a long time to dry.

Different brushes

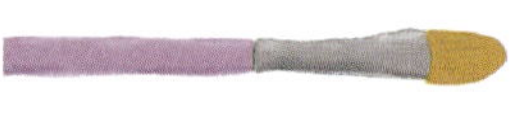

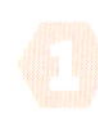

Round brushes

Round brushes are suitable for general painting, details, and lines. They are available in various sizes, from fine to large.

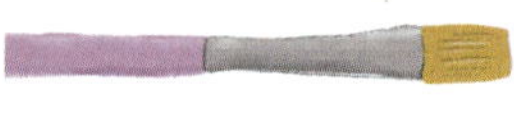

Flat brushes

Flat brushes are ideal for broad strokes, washes, and filling large areas. Long bristles make for smoother strokes. They come in various sizes.

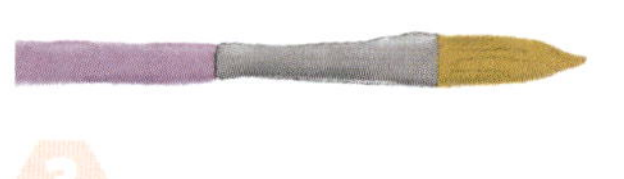

Filbert brushes

Filbert brushes combine the characteristics of round and flat brushes. Useful for blending, soft edges, and creating rounded shapes.

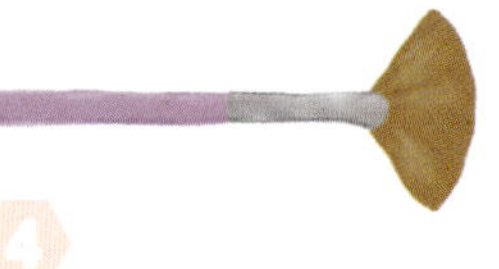

Fan brushes

Fan brushes create textured effects like foliage, grass, or fur. These brushes are used for blending and softening edges.

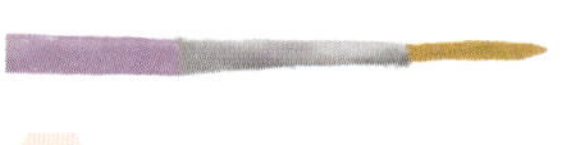

Detail brushes

Detail brushes have very fine tips for intricate details and fine lines. They come in various shapes, such as liners, riggers, and spotter brushes.

Practicing your techniques

Observing colour hues

Have you noticed that the sky is not just blue with clouds, and the grass is not just green? Take a good look and try to recreate the colours with paint or coloured pencils. By paying more attention to the colours you see in everyday life, you will understand colour theory better.

Warm meets cool

Make a colour swatch of only cold colours (like blue, green, and purple), and one with warm colours (red, orange, and yellow). Add a warm accent to your cold colours and vice versa. What do you see, what changes? Would you apply this more often (in an illustration), or not?

Dots, drips, and dabs

Try the following painting techniques: stippling (apply several dots of varying sizes and spacing to create a larger image), pouring (mix paint with water and let it flow or drip), splattering (flick or splash paint mixed with water onto your pages using a paintbrush or toothbrush), and dabbing (instead of moving the brush slowly, dab it quickly and lightly on the paper).

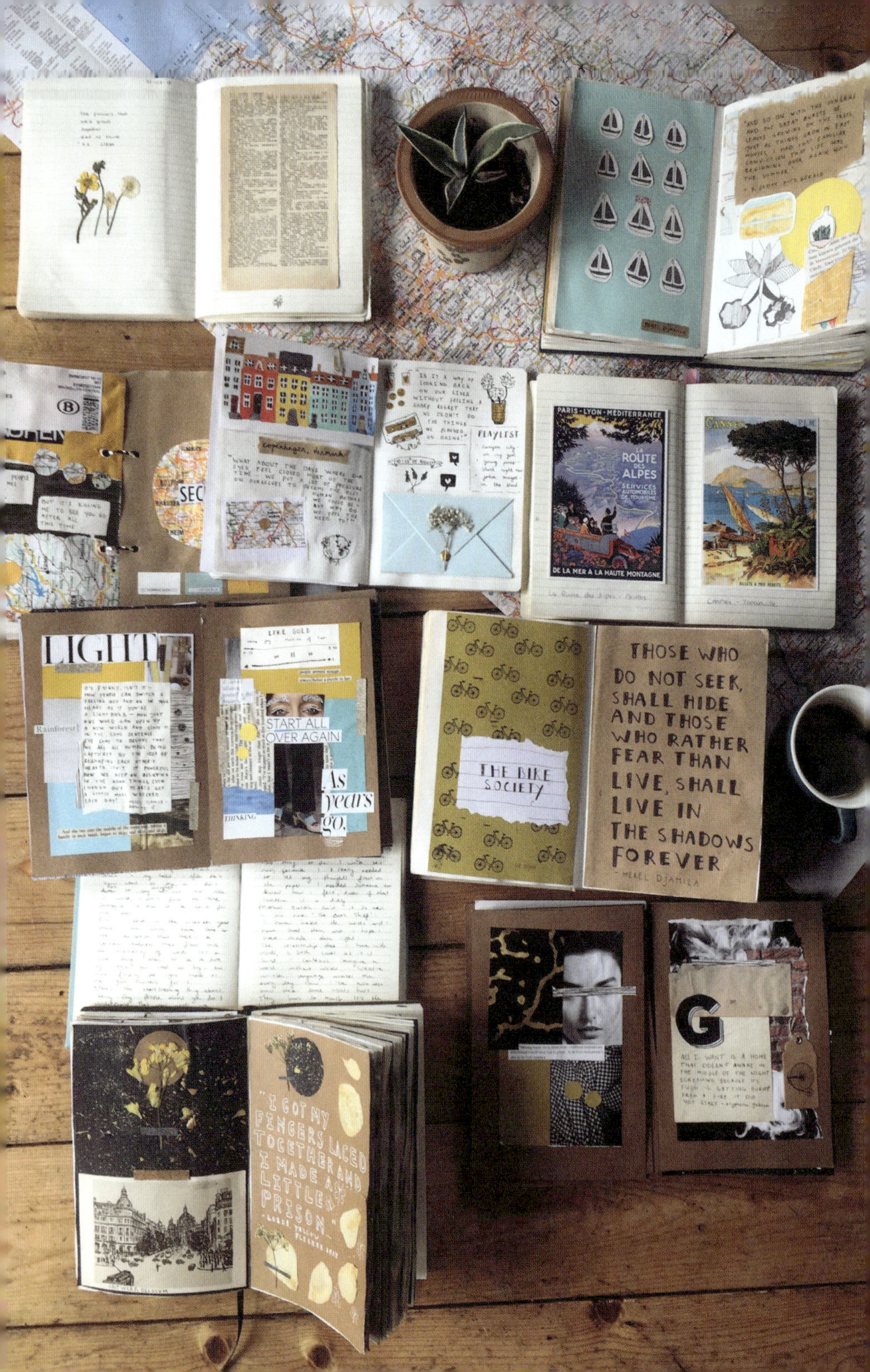

CHAPTER 5

TURNING SCRAPS INTO STORIES

Do you already have an idea of what you want to create, but do you feel intimidated by the wide range of materials available? Translating your travel memories into journal entries doesn't require much – you can simply work with what you have collected along the way.

With scrapbooking, you combine various elements (such as pictures, paper cuttings, and washi tape) to tell a story, usually about a specific theme or event. It allows you to visually summarise your trip in your travel journal.

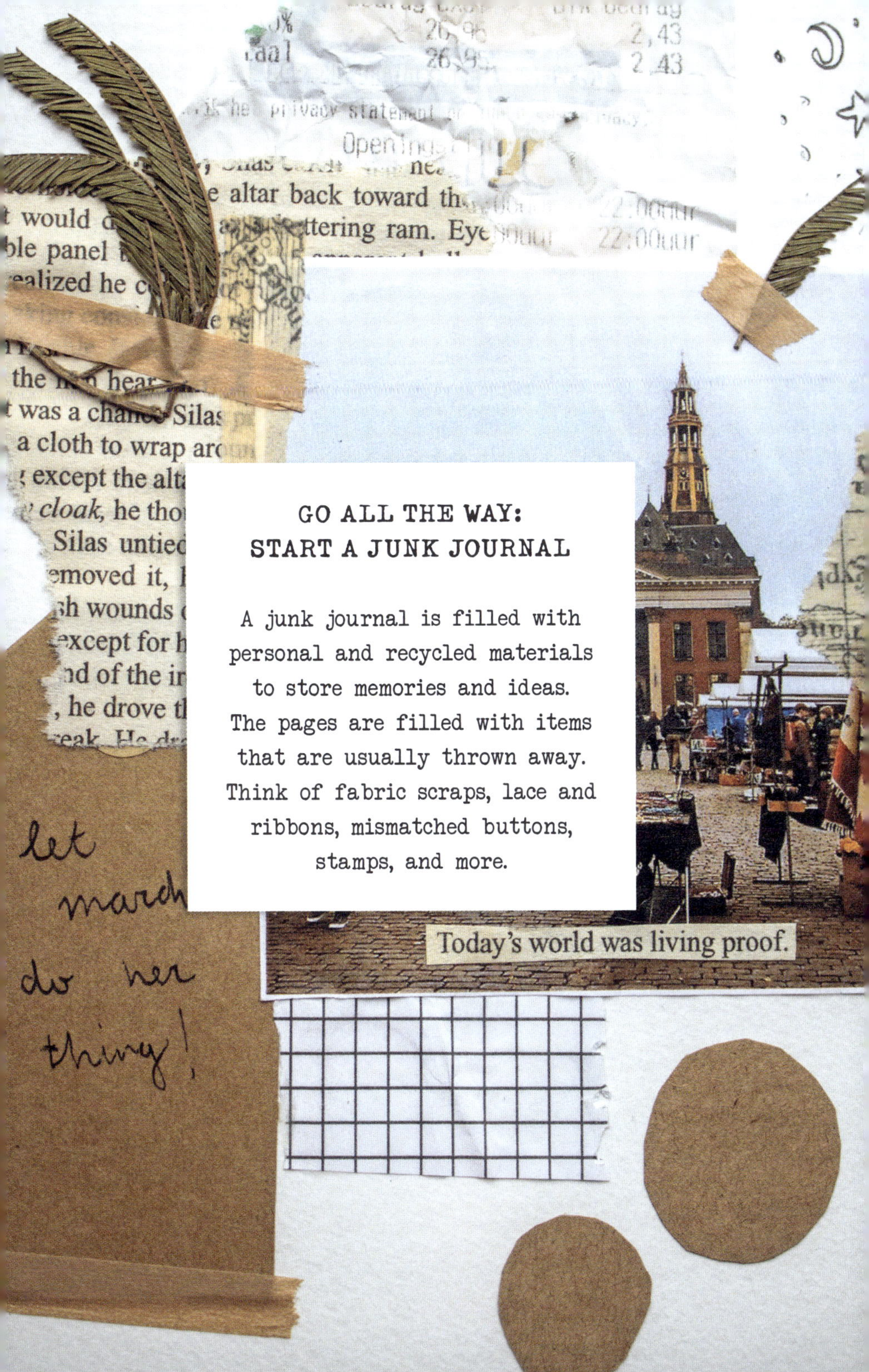

GO ALL THE WAY:
START A JUNK JOURNAL

A junk journal is filled with
personal and recycled materials
to store memories and ideas.
The pages are filled with items
that are usually thrown away.
Think of fabric scraps, lace and
ribbons, mismatched buttons,
stamps, and more.

Filling your scrapbook

Focus on an overarching theme
When travel journaling, you might focus on your favourite holiday or country to visit. You can also focus on a specific colour palette. Find one to three colours and only use matching pieces, or do the opposite and look for contradictions. Other ideas include journaling about music that evokes memories of a place or time, favourite artworks from a museum, or birds you spotted on a nature excursion.

Combine the old with the new
Create surprising new fictional worlds by combining retro photos with modern elements, black-and-white photos with a touch of colour, or by alternating photos with drawings. While travelling, you can easily achieve this by finding a vintage postcard at a souvenir shop and adding colourful elements: draw or cut a funky pair of sunglasses for a person on the postcard, or add coloured dots or just a sun shining brightly in the left corner.

Add text to your collage
Write your own words or cut them from a printed sheet of paper or a magazine. Think of your favourite song lyrics, poems or words that describe the collage well. For inspiration, flip through a magazine and see which words stand out to you. You can also cut out letters in different fonts to form a word.

CHAPTER 11

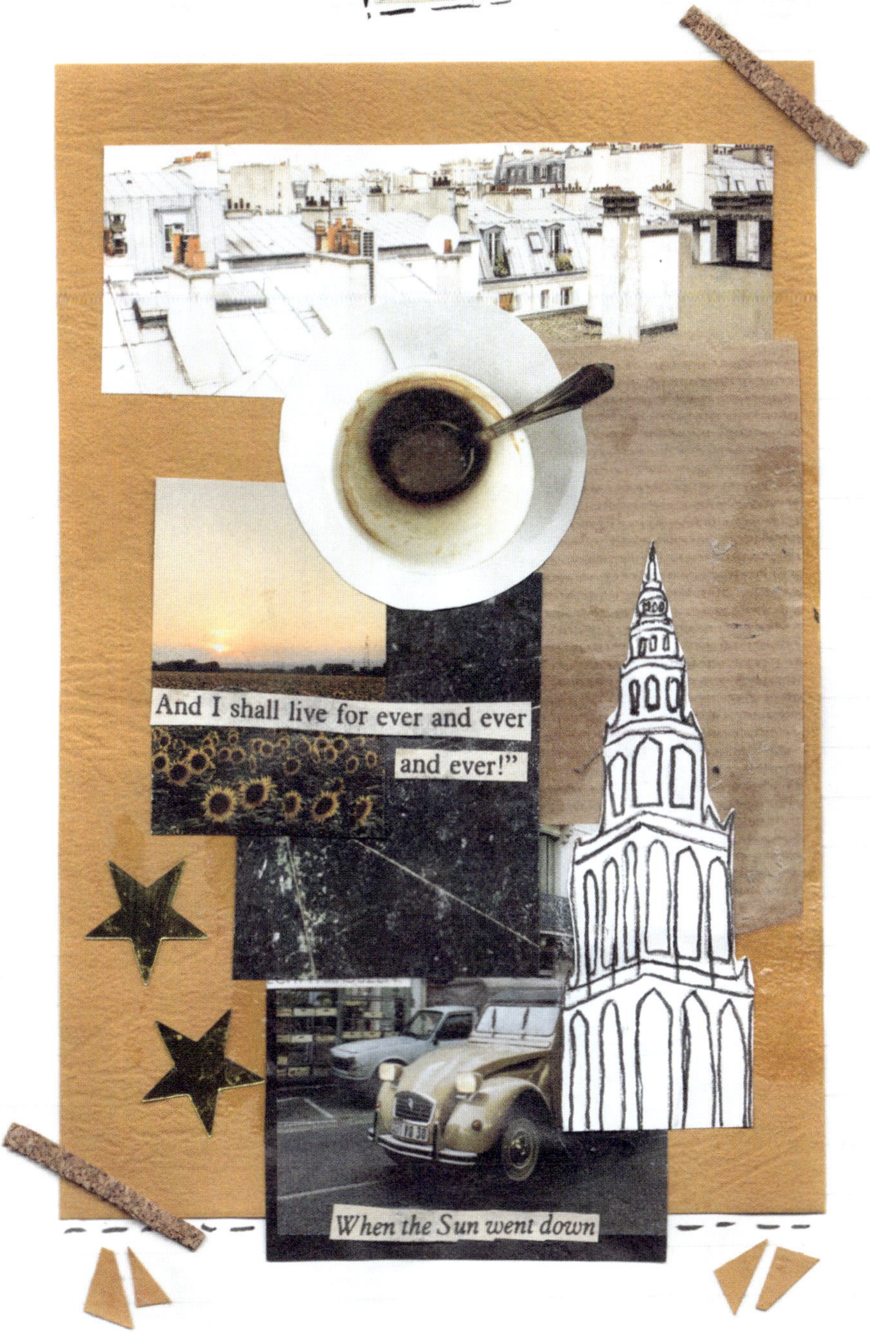

And I shall live for ever and ever
and ever!"

When the Sun went down

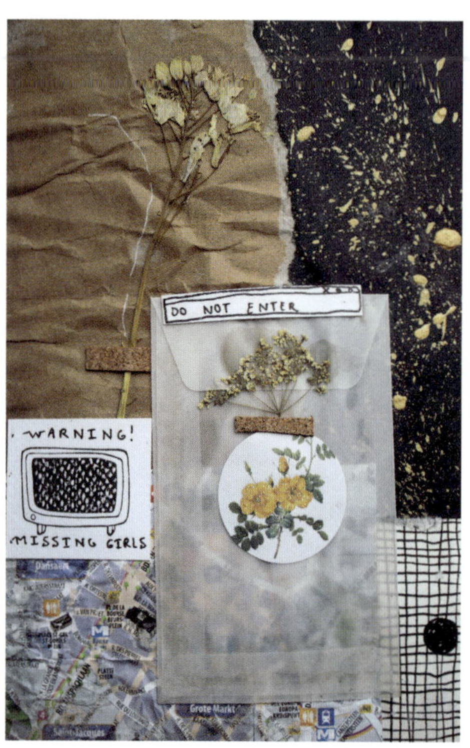

DO NOT ENTER
WARNING!
MISSING GIRLS
Grote-Markt

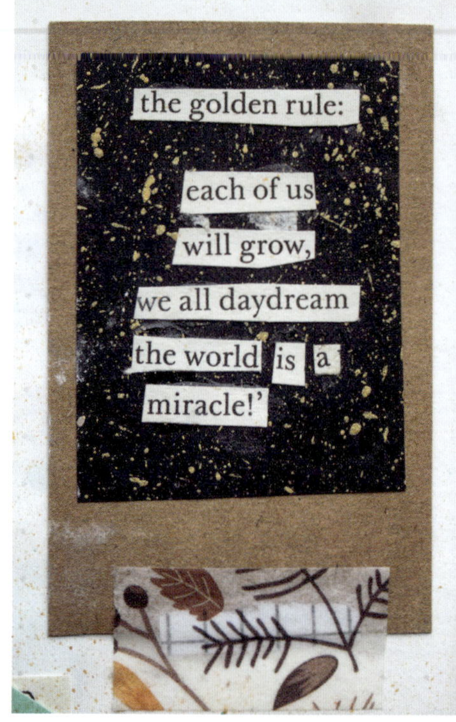

the golden rule:
each of us
will grow,
we all daydream
the world is a
miracle!'

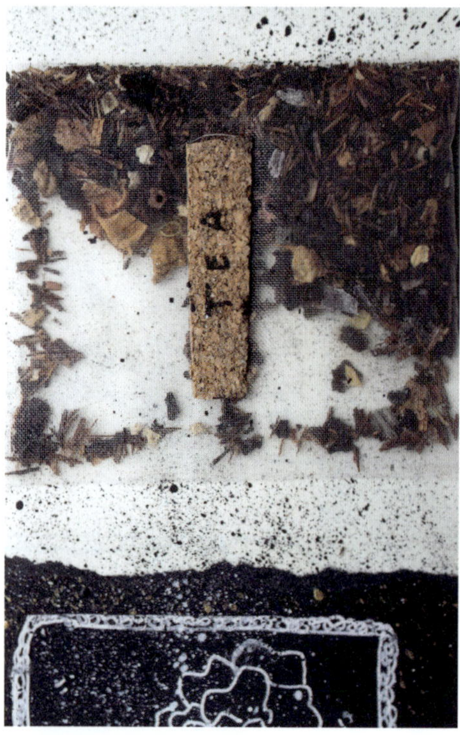

TEA

FOR
ALOUD
PROJECT
MINI
PAINT
BOX
WATER
BOTTLE
BOOK
WHAT
IS IN
MY BAG?

**Include an unexpected
(3D) object**
Pick something that stands out but
is still part of the whole. Add an
envelope (and place a note in it),
tea bag, or a piece of card. Other
options are cardboard coasters,
flowers or leaves (press them between the pages of a heavy book for
a few weeks first), pages of books
you can get for next to nothing in
second-hand shops or at markets,
different types of paper (crumpled,
torn, holographic, black, tissues),
photos (with and without border),
washi tape, and excerpts from (old)
newspapers and magazines. In
Chapter 8, I will show you how to
make a 'zine' (mini magazine) as
an addition glued to your journal
pages, or placed in an envelope
attached to the page.

**Look for easy drawings
to (re)create**
If you're a beginner and you would
like to add drawings to your
journal, start by looking up some
easy drawings. Practice them a
few times. Always remember that
most drawings are built from basic
shapes such as triangles, squares,
and circles. For travel-related
illustrations, experiment by drawing your travel gear (such as your
backpack or suitcase) or vehicles
(cars, trains, airplanes, caravans,
campers, or bikes).

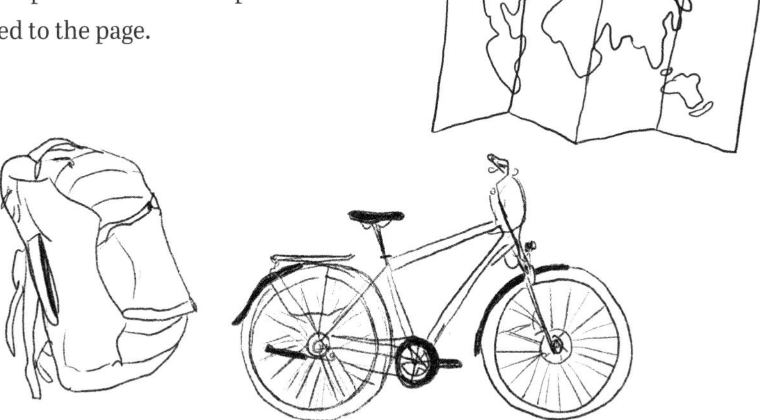

The kraft paper on the left mirrors the paper tag on the right, while the word *Antwerpen* ties in with the photo of the train station in Antwerp.

The colour pink is repeated, from the paper clip and circles to the star confetti from a concert in Antwerp.

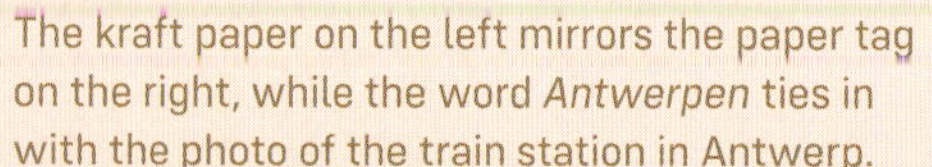

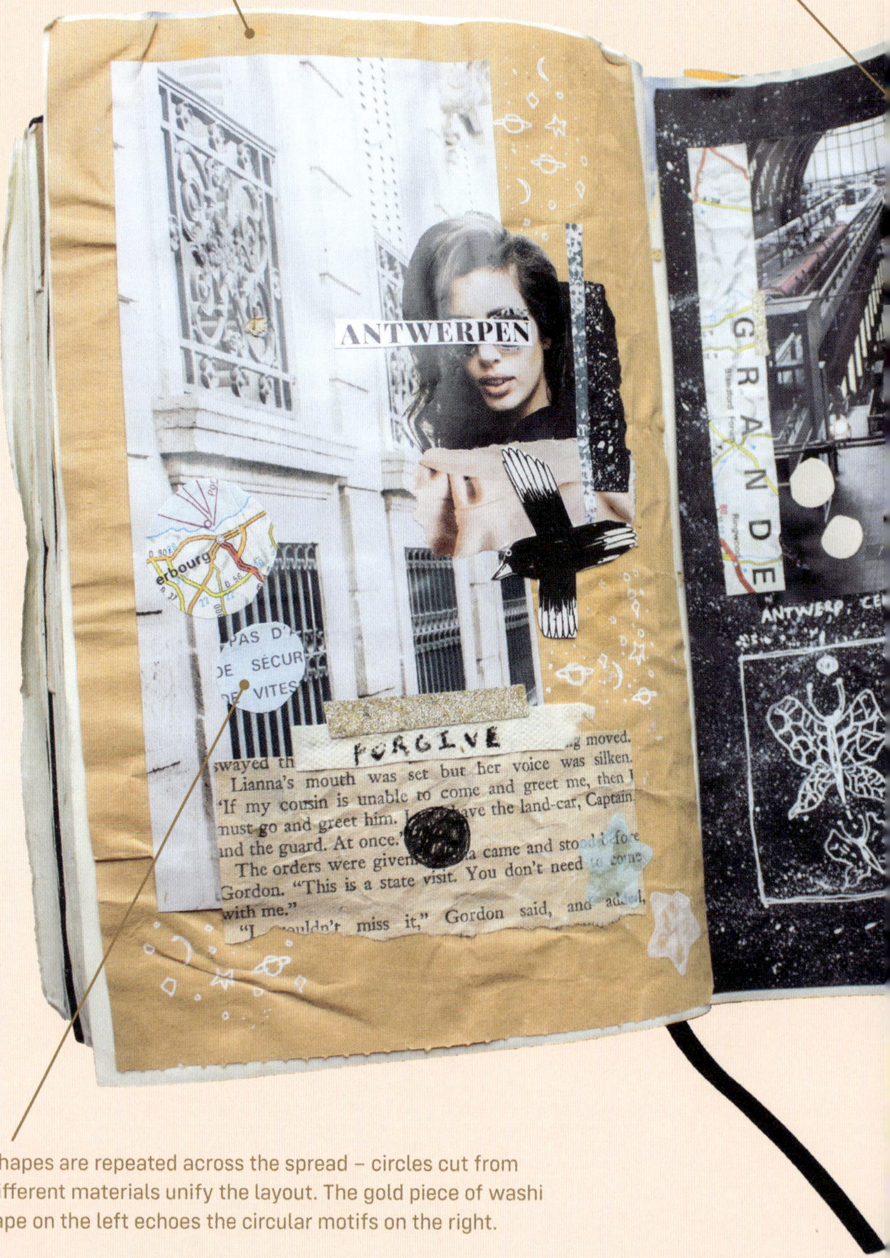

Shapes are repeated across the spread – circles cut from different materials unify the layout. The gold piece of washi tape on the left echoes the circular motifs on the right.

Life in Antwerp

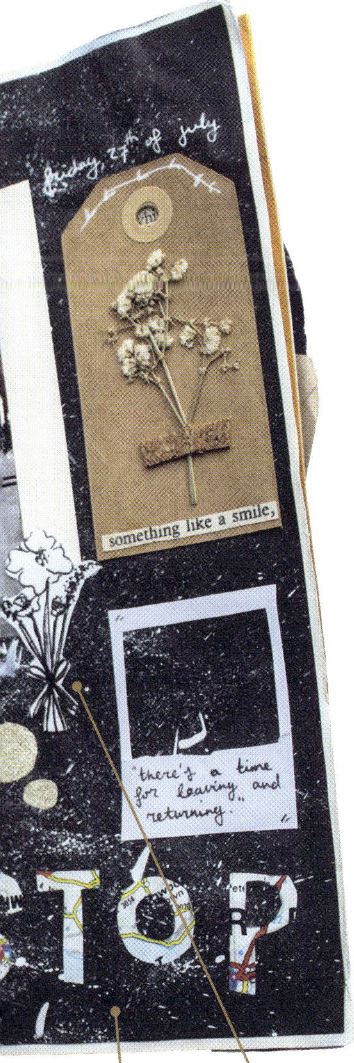

I created this scrapbook spread when I lived in Belgium for a few months. I used a map, photos of Antwerp (including one of the city's beautiful train station), and a book excerpt. During this time of living and studying abroad, journaling helped me to reflect on my experience, create my own visual archive of the cities I called home, and add structure to my weekday evenings. I used brochures and newspapers from school and my internship at a magazine editorial office.

Looking at the individual items, you might think that they would overwhelm the pages. However, the overall composition of this spread works because the elements on the pages complement each other in colour, shape, and simplicity.

Even the floral theme recurs, by adding a pressed flower as well as hand-drawn ones.

The paint-splattered black background on the right page complements the bird and the black dot on the left.

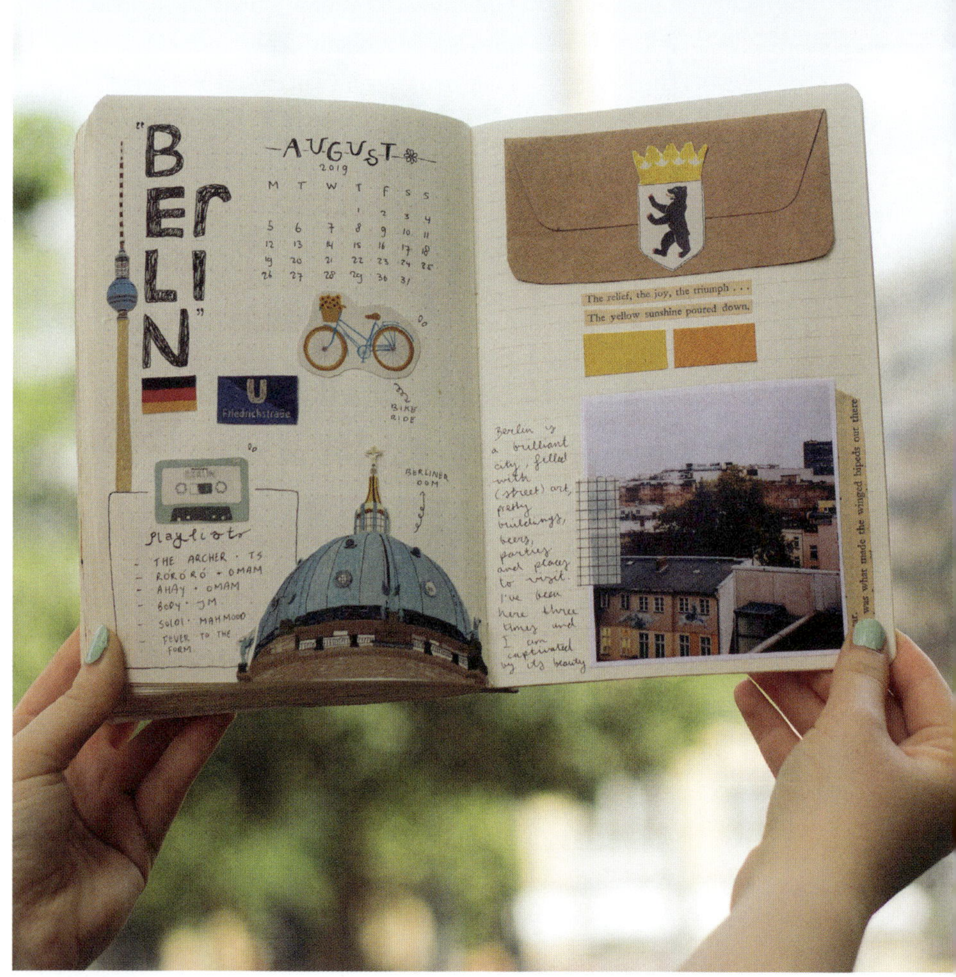
"BERLIN"
AUGUST
2019
M T W T F S S
1 2 3 4
5 6 7 8 9 10 11
12 13 14 15 16 17 18
19 20 21 22 23 24 25
26 27 28 29 30 31
Friedrichstraße
BIKE RIDE
BERLINER DOM
playlist
THE ARCHER · TS
RORÓRÓ · OMAM
AHAY · OMAM
BODY · JM
SOLDI · MAHMOOD
FEVER TO THE FORM.
The relief, the joy, the triumph . . .
The yellow sunshine poured down,
Berlin is a brilliant city, filled with (street) art, pretty buildings, beers, parties and places to visit. I've been here three times and I am captivated by its beauty
was what made the winged bipeds out there

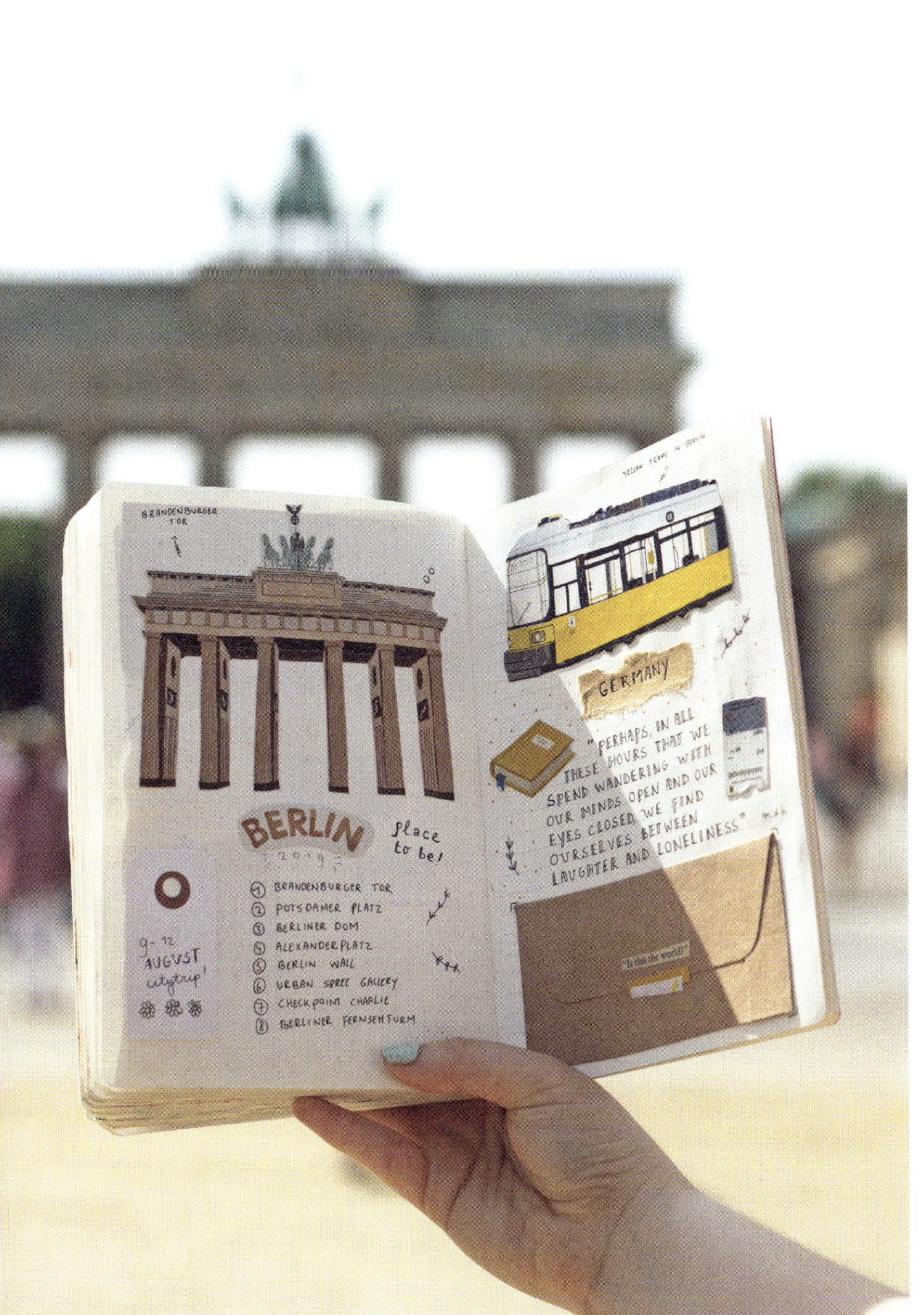
BRANDENBURGER TOR
BERLIN
2019
place to be!
9-12 AUGUST citytrip!
1 BRANDENBURGER TOR
2 POTSDAMER PLATZ
3 BERLINER DOM
4 ALEXANDERPLATZ
5 BERLIN WALL
6 URBAN SPREE GALLERY
7 CHECKPOINT CHARLIE
8 BERLINER FERNSEHTURM
YELLOW TRAMS IN BERLIN
GERMANY
"PERHAPS, IN ALL THESE HOURS THAT WE SPEND WANDERING WITH OUR MINDS OPEN AND OUR EYES CLOSED, WE FIND OURSELVES BETWEEN LAUGHTER AND LONELINESS"
"Is this the world?"

Maps and Magritte

This collage includes many of my favourite elements: different shapes (circles made of a glittery background and an old map), a pressed flower stuck on the page with a piece of washi tape, a galaxy background (that I create by gently running my finger over an old paintbrush or toothbrush covered in white paint), and at the bottom right I added a few samples from a free colour guide.

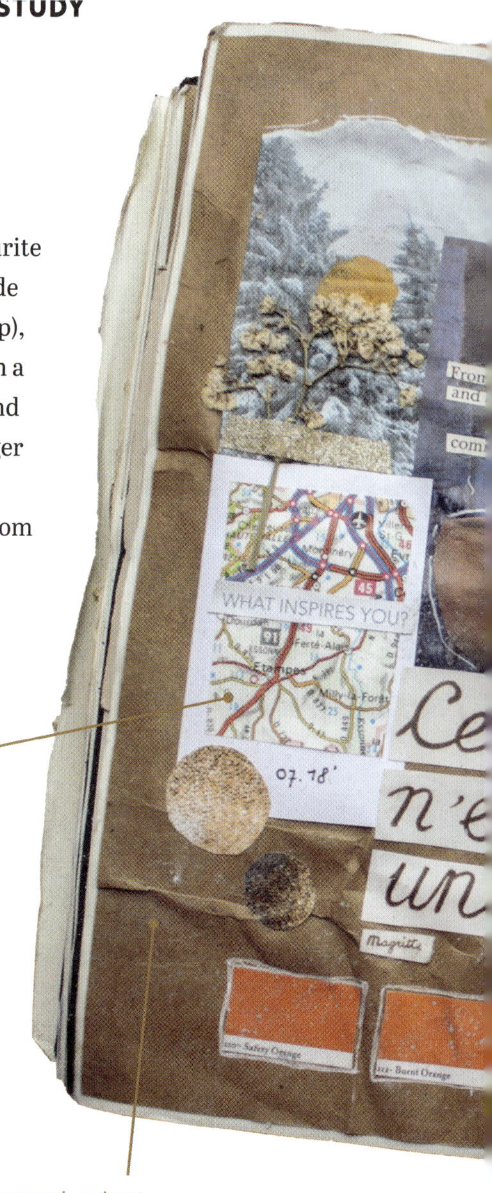

I once asked my dad if I could use his old maps for scrapbooking and, since his collection had been in the loft for a long time, he agreed. I rarely use maps in their entirety. More often, I cut out shapes to use as decorations on my pages.

You might notice that the background, a sheet of card, has a crease in the bottom left. I can't quite recall if it was there originally or if I added it intentionally, but I find it rather charming.

"HEARTBREAK, PAIN, LOSS AND SADNESS ARE UNDERSTOOD DIFFERENTLY THROUGH EACH BRAIN. THEREFORE, YOU ARE NOT IN THE POSITION TO CALL SOMEONE WEAK FOR WHAT A PERSON ENDURES. IT IS NOT IN YOUR NATURE TO UNDERSTAND SOMEONE ELSE'S PAIN." - MEREL DJAMILA

65

Scrapbooking your travels

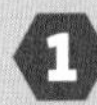

Local cuisine

Document your culinary adventures. What local dishes did you try? Which were your favourites? Include recipes or restaurant recommendations. It's even more fun when you add receipts from the restaurants, or pictures of the food you tasted.

Travel friends

Celebrate the people you travelled with by sharing anecdotes, inside jokes or heartfelt moments spent together. If you document your travels after your return, make sure to note these important moments on your phone before recording them in your journal.

Souvenirs

Showcase the souvenirs you collected during your travels. Describe their significance and why you chose to bring them home. You can include photos or drawings of your souvenirs, or simply write about what makes them special to you.

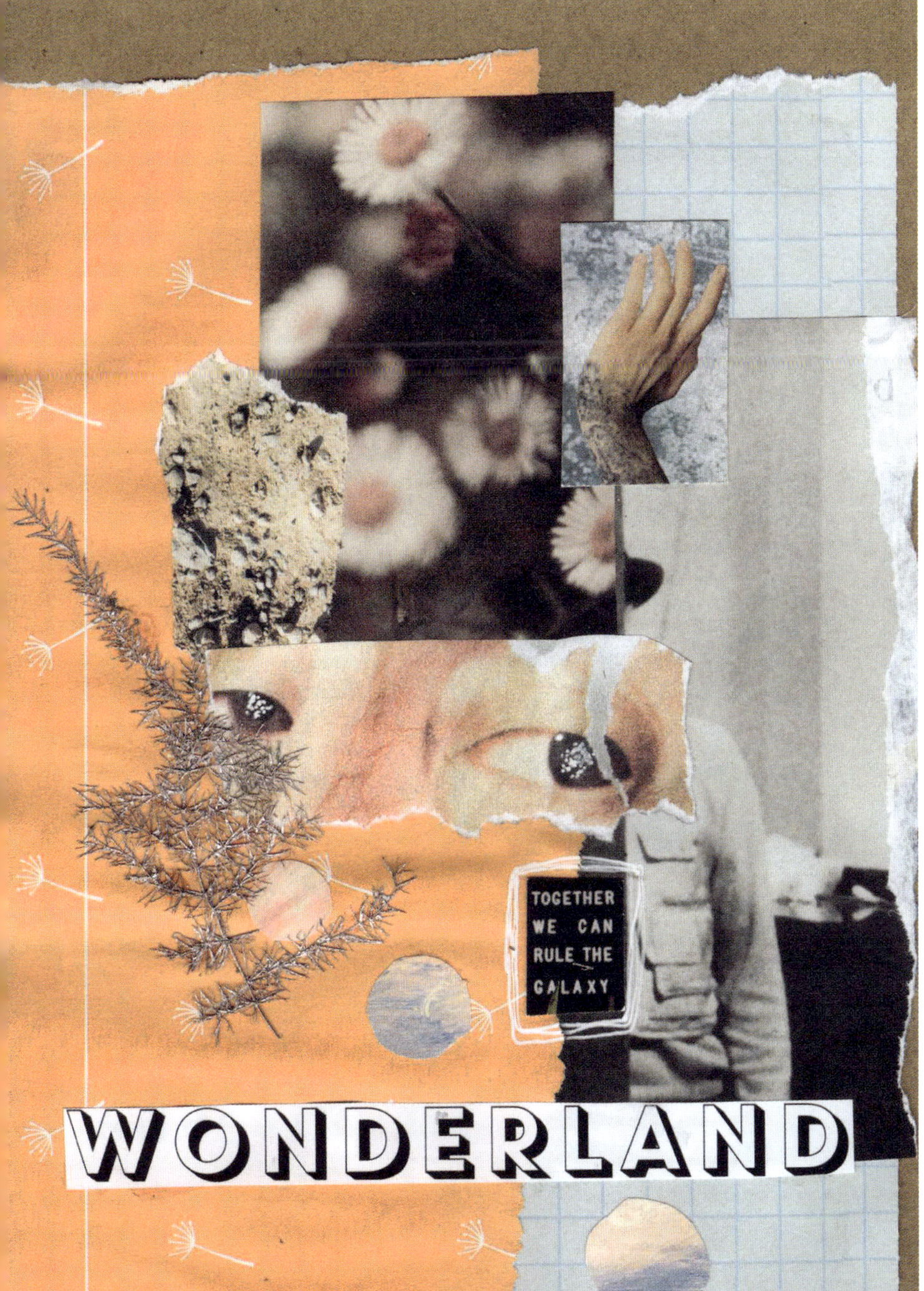

TOGETHER
WE CAN
RULE THE
GALAXY
WONDERLAND

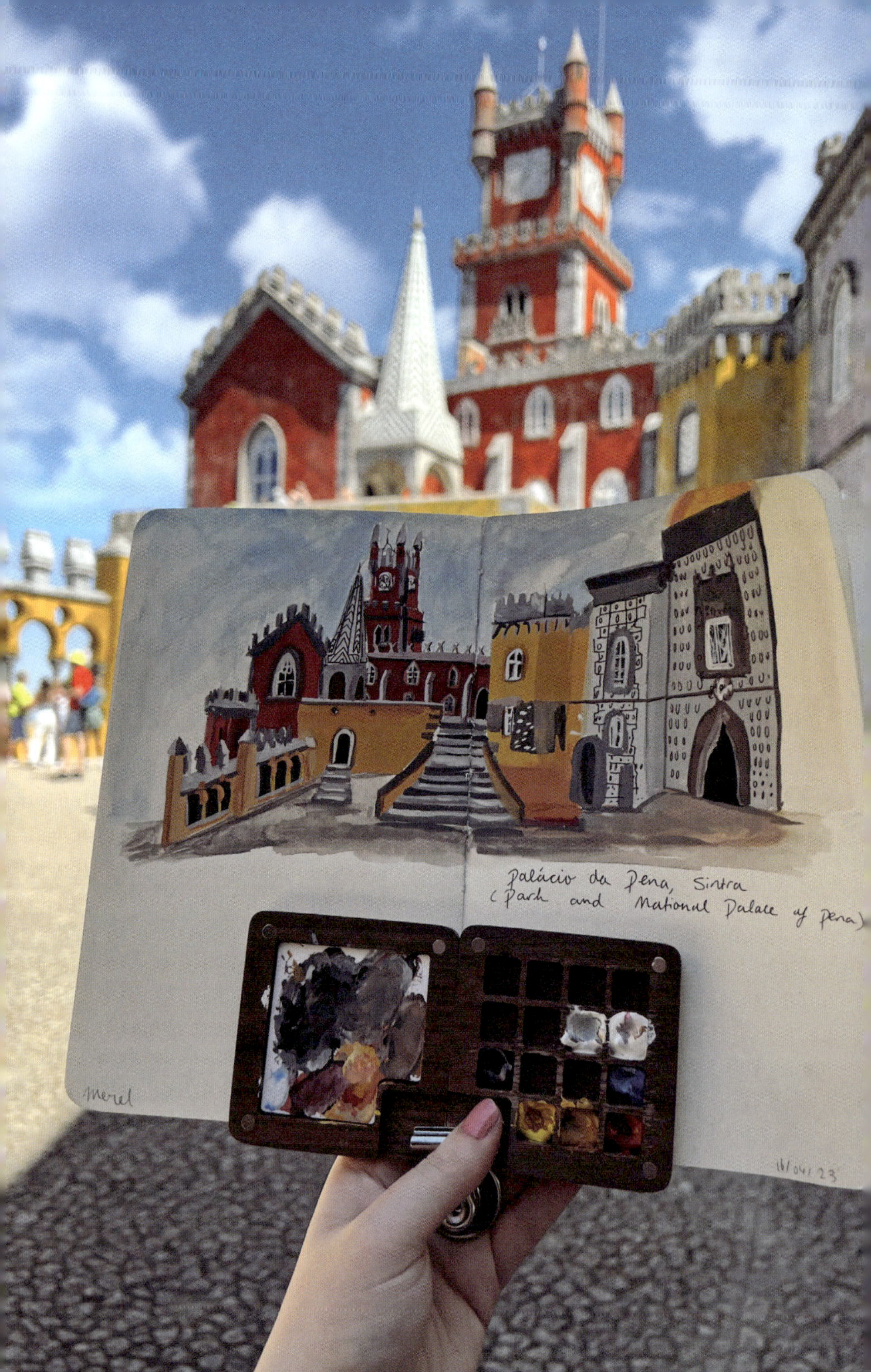

Palácio da Pena, Sintra
(Park and National Palace of Pena)
Merel
16/04/23

CHAPTER 6

STREETSCAPES AND SKYLINES

A city trip is all about exploring! Imagine the narrow streets of Venice, the canals of Amsterdam, the artistic flair of Madrid, and the romantic charm of Paris. I will show you how to capture this beauty using paint and paper.

Some of my most treasured memories are of people approaching me as I paint, sharing the history of the city I'm capturing. Their stories allow me to see the city from a completely different perspective.

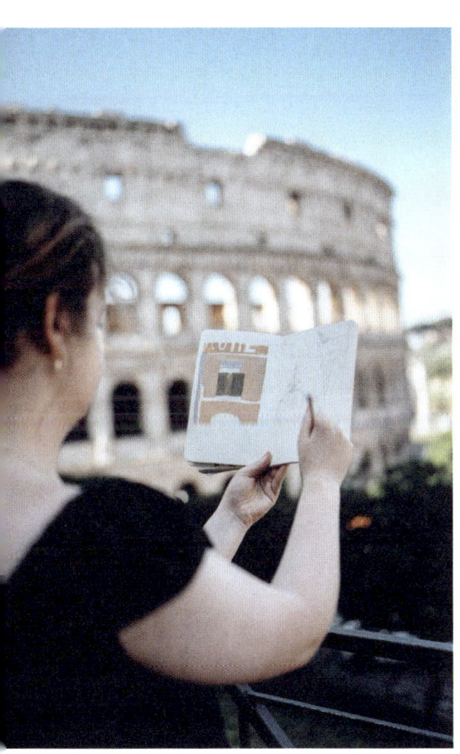 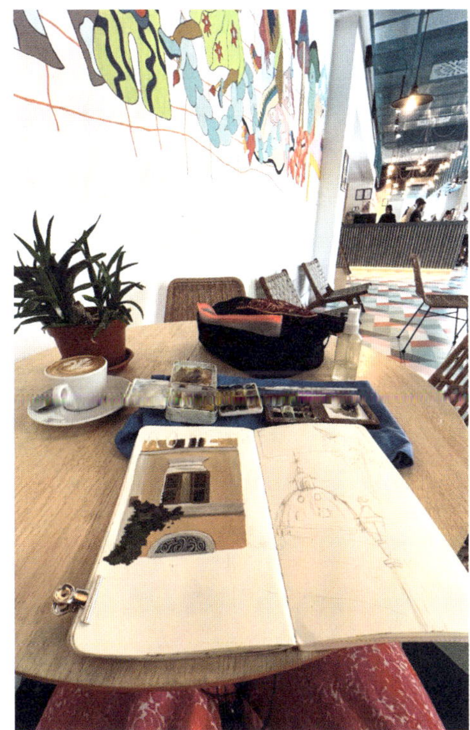

First things first: a suitable location

When choosing the right spot, think about what you need. If you want to be close to what you're capturing, you might have to settle for a less-than-ideal seat, like a small table or an uncomfortable chair. If you work quickly and can finish within 15 to 20 minutes, any spot might do. If your work takes longer and requires more detail, it might be better to start on location to absorb the surroundings, then move to a more comfortable place, like a nearby café, to finish. Tip: bring earplugs if you want to focus.

Painting on location: pros and cons

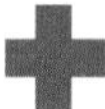

You're not dependent on a still, two-dimensional photo. This allows you to take in your surroundings well and from different angles, too. Capturing nuances of light, colour, and atmosphere is much easier in person than through a photo. Observing these elements on location instead of through a screen often results in a more accurate and more vibrant depiction of the scene.

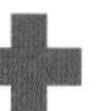

Overcoming the challenges of painting outside (such as changing weather, shifting light, and the unpredictability of the environment), helps you develop your skills and grow both technically and artistically at a fast pace.

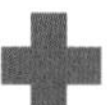

Immersing yourself in the outdoor environment can spark spontaneous inspiration and creativity. It might be a unique hat you spot on your city stroll, a street musician playing nearby, or simply the calm of being surrounded by forests or a lake that ignites your imagination.

You are dependent on the weather. Painting in a sudden thunderstorm is less than convenient, and so is painting in the scorching sun. But if you bring an umbrella, you can shield yourself from all kinds of weather.

It can be difficult to find a suitable spot for your painting session, especially when the scene you want to paint is a busy street and you might need to bring a stool or chair. It's more difficult to take a break when you're by yourself because there's nobody to watch your belongings while you're away, whether it's for a toilet break or to change your paint water.

Painting on location can take a long time. When your trip is fully planned out, it might be hard to dedicate your precious time to painting on location. This doesn't have to stop you, because you can take photos during your trip and paint them afterwards. It may even be just as fun, because you can linger in that holiday spirit a little longer!

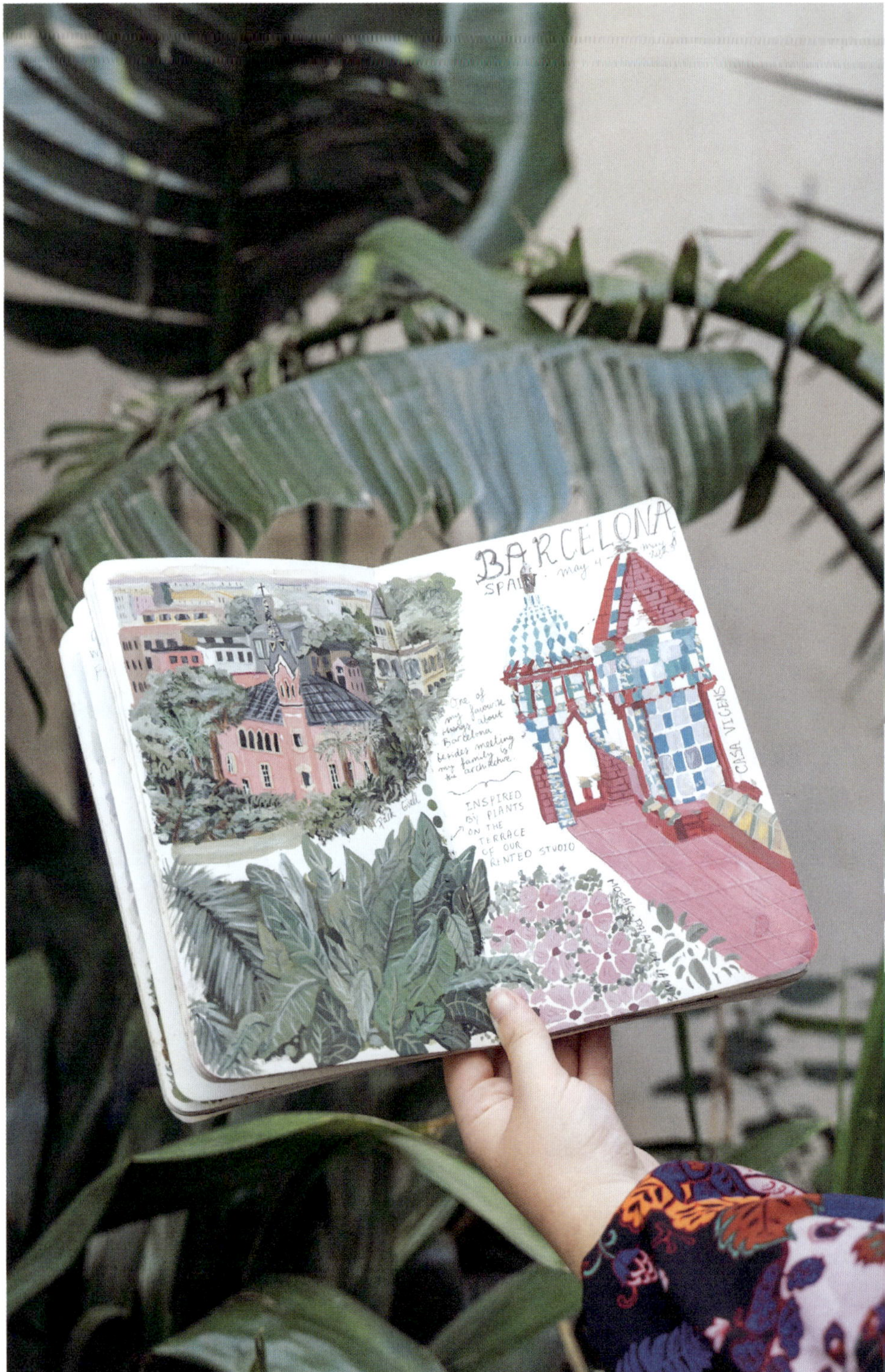

BARCELONA
SPAIN . may 4 — may July 3
One of my favourite things about Barcelona besides meeting my family is the architecture.
INSPIRED BY PLANTS ON THE TERRACE OF OUR RENTED STUDIO
Park Güell
CASA VICENS
MOSAIC DETAIL

My rules of thumb

As the historic centre is usually my favourite part of a city, I often include
it in my travel journals. I like to add recognisable landmarks too. For
example, in Copenhagen, I featured the colourful houses of Nyhavn. In
Rome, I captured the artsy and culinary district of Trastevere. During a day
trip to the Swedish island of Hönö near Gothenburg, I painted the typical
red houses. In Zadar (Croatia), I drew a pink house that looked like a doll's
house. In Barcelona, I was inspired by the beautiful Art Nouveau details and
devoted several pages to the works of the famous architect Gaudí, including
Park Güell, a magical urban park with buildings, sculptures and tile work.
Casa Vicens, the first house he designed, also features stunning details and
vibrant colours that would deserve a spot in your travel journal.

In short, let the city inspire you and capture what you love. Whether it's
amazing architecture or a great jazz café, journaling these experiences
helps you cherish your fondest memories. Ultimately, the only rule when
it comes to painting your travels: include only what inspires you and what
you wish to remember.

« Park Güell and Casa Vicens, Barcelona, Spain

I painted the windows and the flowers in front
of the Gamla Stan houses with a small brush.

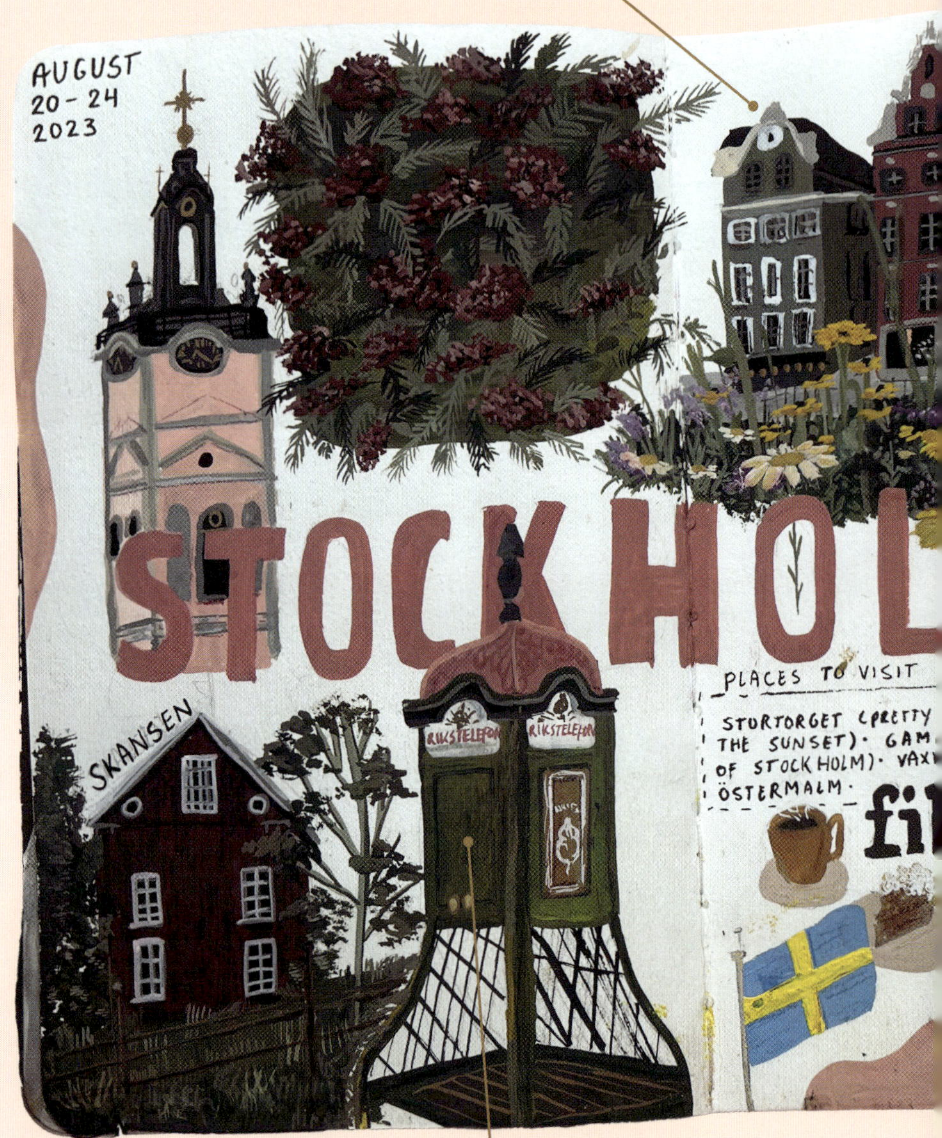

These old Rikstelefon booths can be found across the city.
Although the Swedish government agency Televerket, that
was responsible for telecommunications, no longer exists,
you can still find these phone booths and the Rikstelefon
logo on manhole covers and markers around the city.

Fika in Stockholm's Gamla Stan

As you stroll through Stockholm's old town (Gamla Stan), you'll spot colourful houses and cafés perfect for a 'fika'– a coffee break with a tasty treat. I aimed to capture this vibrant atmosphere in my illustrations, using pastel colours and bold letters to create a cheerful and lively representation of the Swedish capital. Since these pages about my time in Stockholm include many illustrations, I chose not to depict the sky. The white space gives the illustrations room to breathe.

How do you know you're finished?

The Stockholm pages were complete after I added the final details (like the Swedish flag and colour scheme), wrote my final notes, and painted pink blobs to fill the empty space at the bottom right and middle left.

Space left on your pages? Add your colour scheme, as I did with circles, or the flag of the country you're visiting.

I focused on specific details that caught my eye rather than my surroundings. For instance, with the illustration of the pan of soup, I could have included the café's awnings, but I left them out to make space for other Stockholm memories.

A walk through Nyhavn, Copenhagen

Nyhavn is one of Copenhagen's top tourist spots in the city centre, and it was too charming to leave out of my journal. No matter how many photos you've seen, this colourful harbour is even better in person. You can take a boat ride on the canal, stroll past the lively restaurants to the mermaid statue, or sit on the quay with your journal, like I did. For this spread, I focused on certain details and left out others to make it manageable. For example, I did not include any people at the harbour.

I used my portable mobile printer to print photos from my phone and to use them as stickers. I highly recommend taking it with you on the go!

I painted daisies in the lower left corner. In reality, they were purple flowers; painting them white kept the pages from looking too busy.

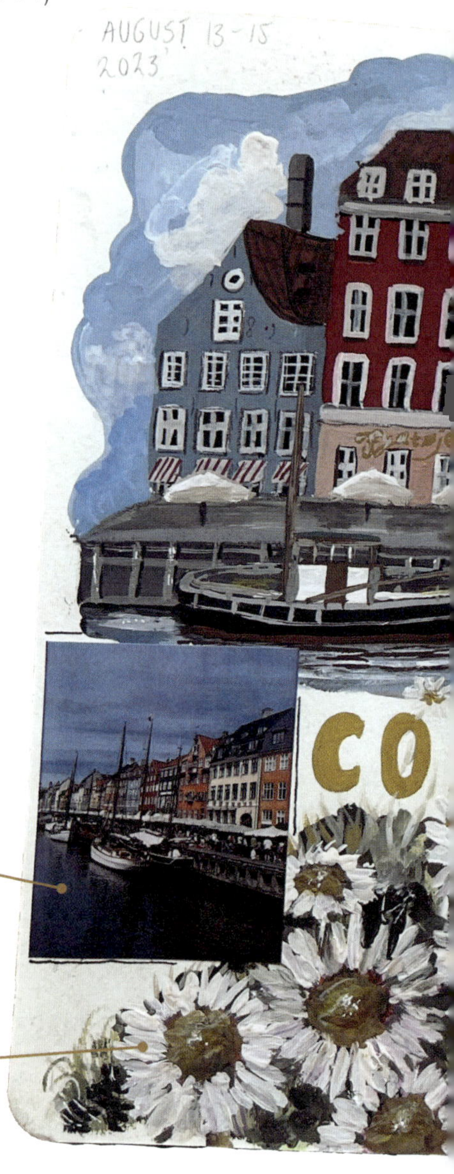

Adding a side façade to a building is easy and enhances your drawing. It's simpler than drawing in perspective but makes a big difference because the building looks more three-dimensional. Use a different shade for the side, lighter or darker depending on the time of day.

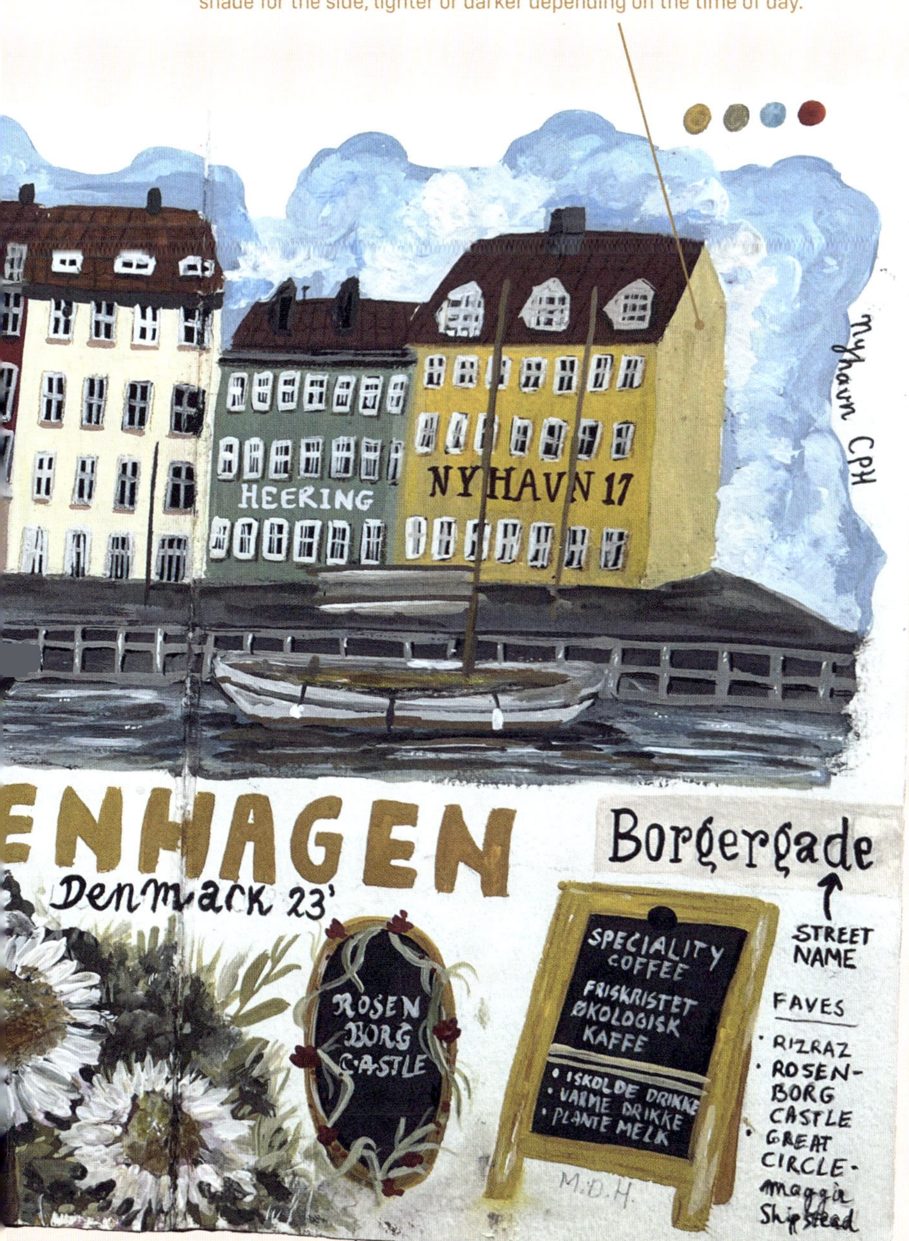

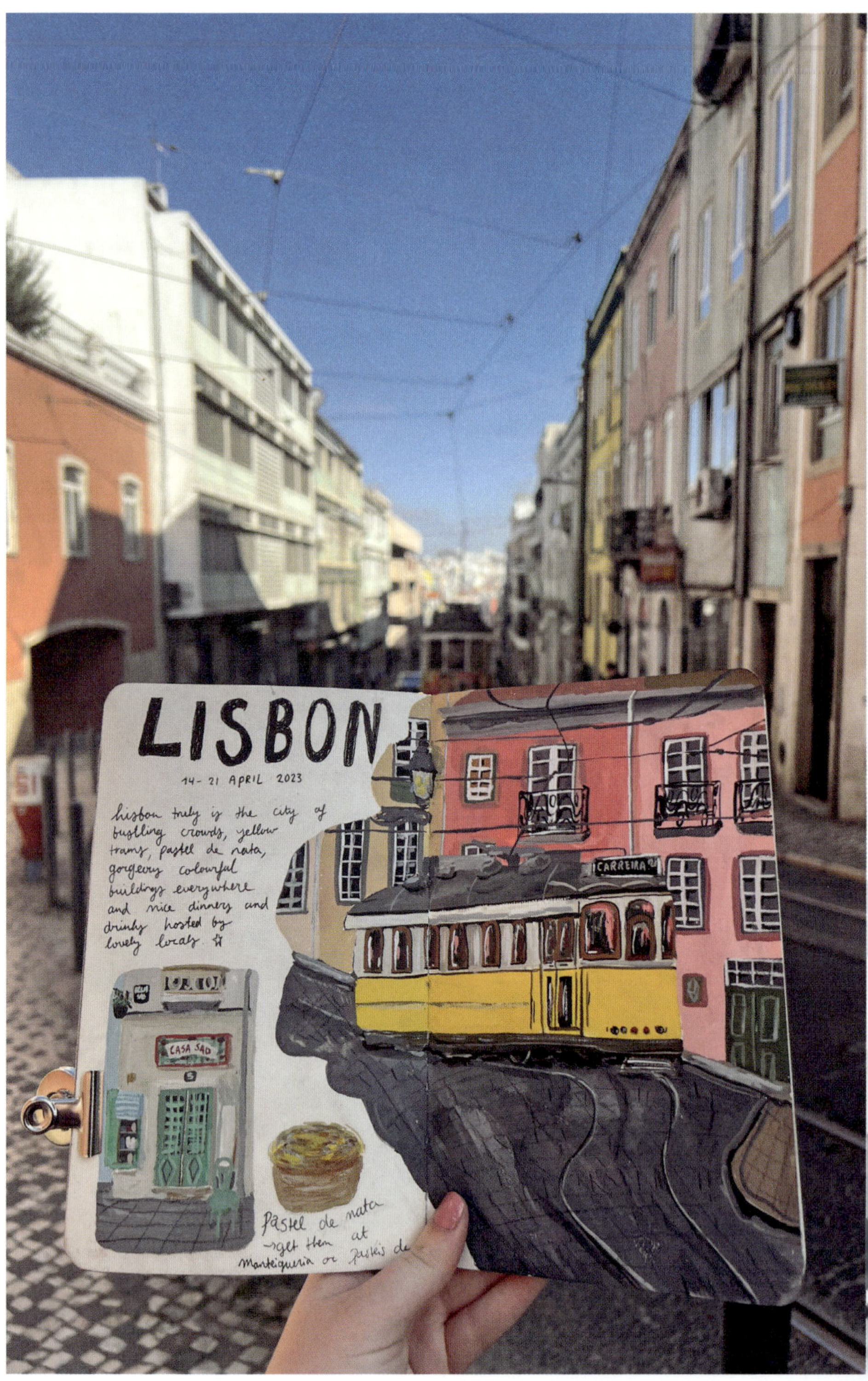

LISBON
14 - 21 APRIL 2023
lisbon truly is the city of
bustling crowds, yellow
trams, pastel de nata,
gorgeous colourful
buildings everywhere
and nice dinners and
drinks hosted by
lovely locals.
CASA SÃO
CARREIRA
Pastel de nata
→ get them at
Manteigaria or Pastéis de

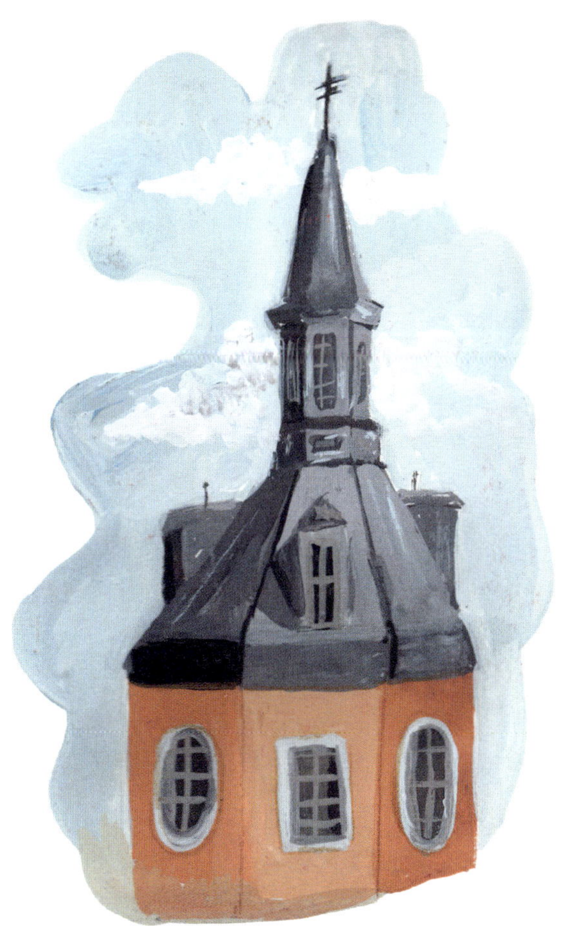

Unusual shapes

One of my favourite ways to fill travel journal pages is by painting within unusual shapes. Instead of sticking to square frames or circles, I sketch a 'blob' and start painting inside it. For example, my painting of a yellow tram in Lisbon lightly resembles the silhouette of a face, and the white space next to this illustration allows the page to breathe. On my pages of Madrid, the playful shape of the outline complements the church tower (as seen above).

Classic and contemporary buildings

Usually, a city's buildings and architectural style are its defining and unique traits. Whether you're painting modern or classic buildings, there are different techniques you can apply.

For drawing the outlines of both modern and classic buildings, you can use simple shapes, such as rectangles, squares, triangles, and circles, as a base. Use clean lines and fewer colours to capture the sleek look of modern buildings. For classic buildings, you can use varied brushstrokes, layering, and more colours to show the intricate detailing and historical charm.

I prefer buildings that stand out, whether through their colours, unique façade, or beautiful details. Think of the cube houses in Rotterdam, Hundertwasser House in Vienna, or the dancing house in Prague.

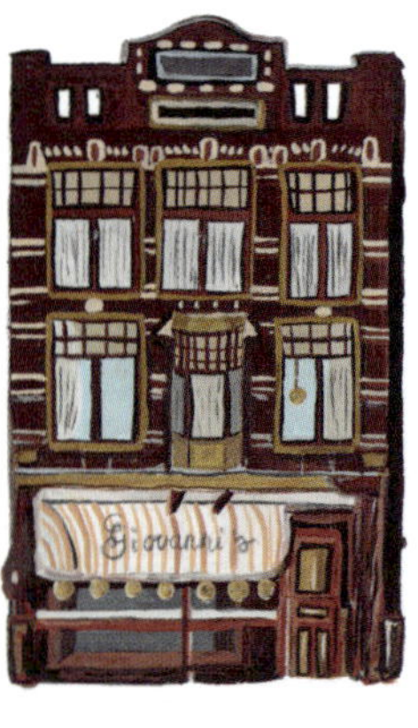

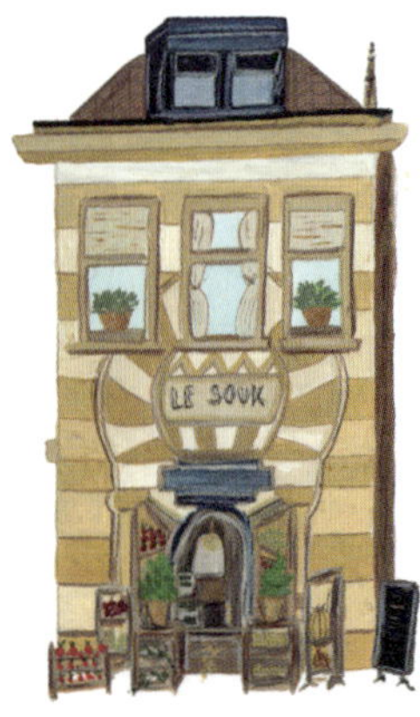

Vurnik House,
Ljubljana, Slovenia »

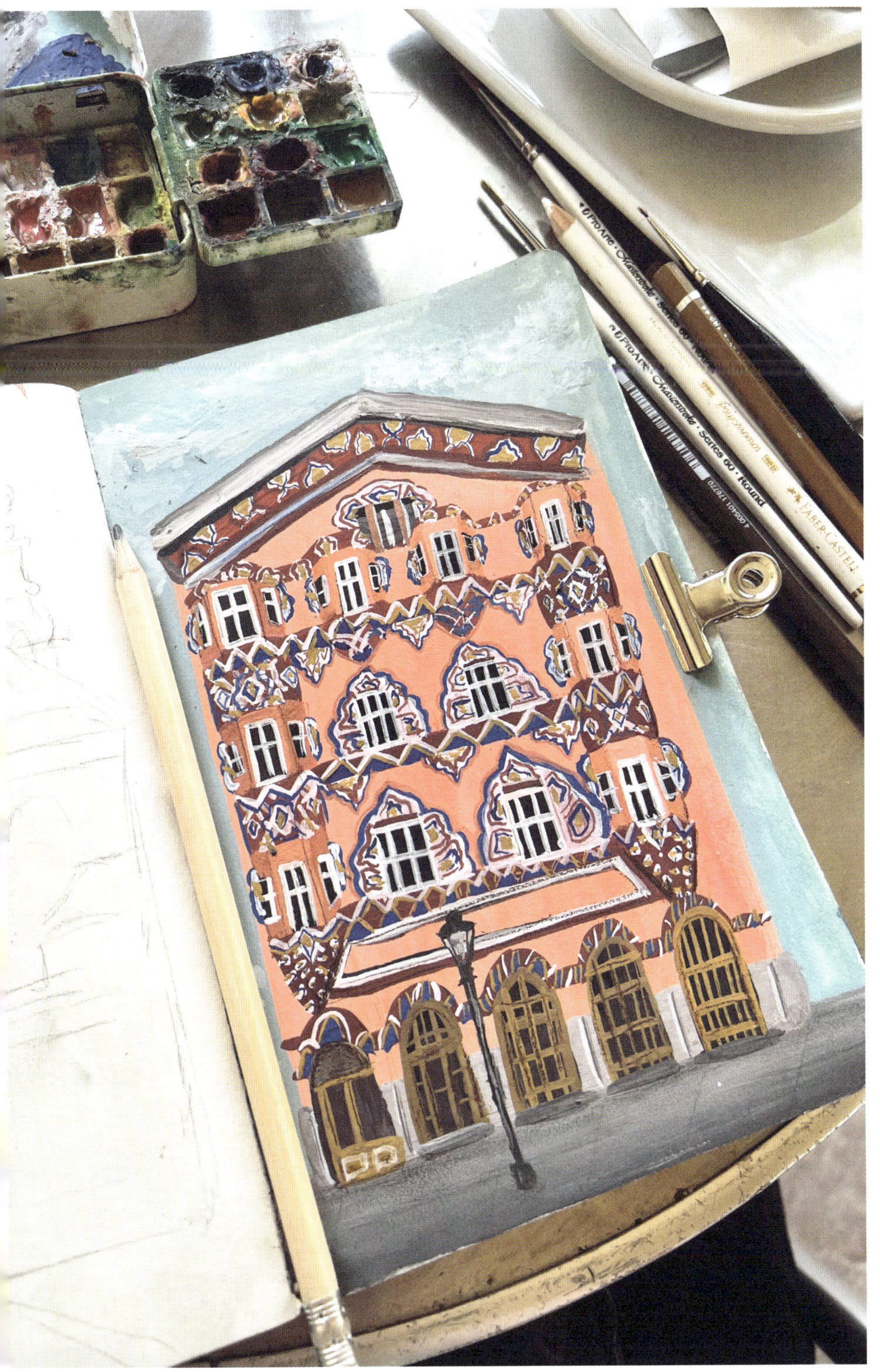

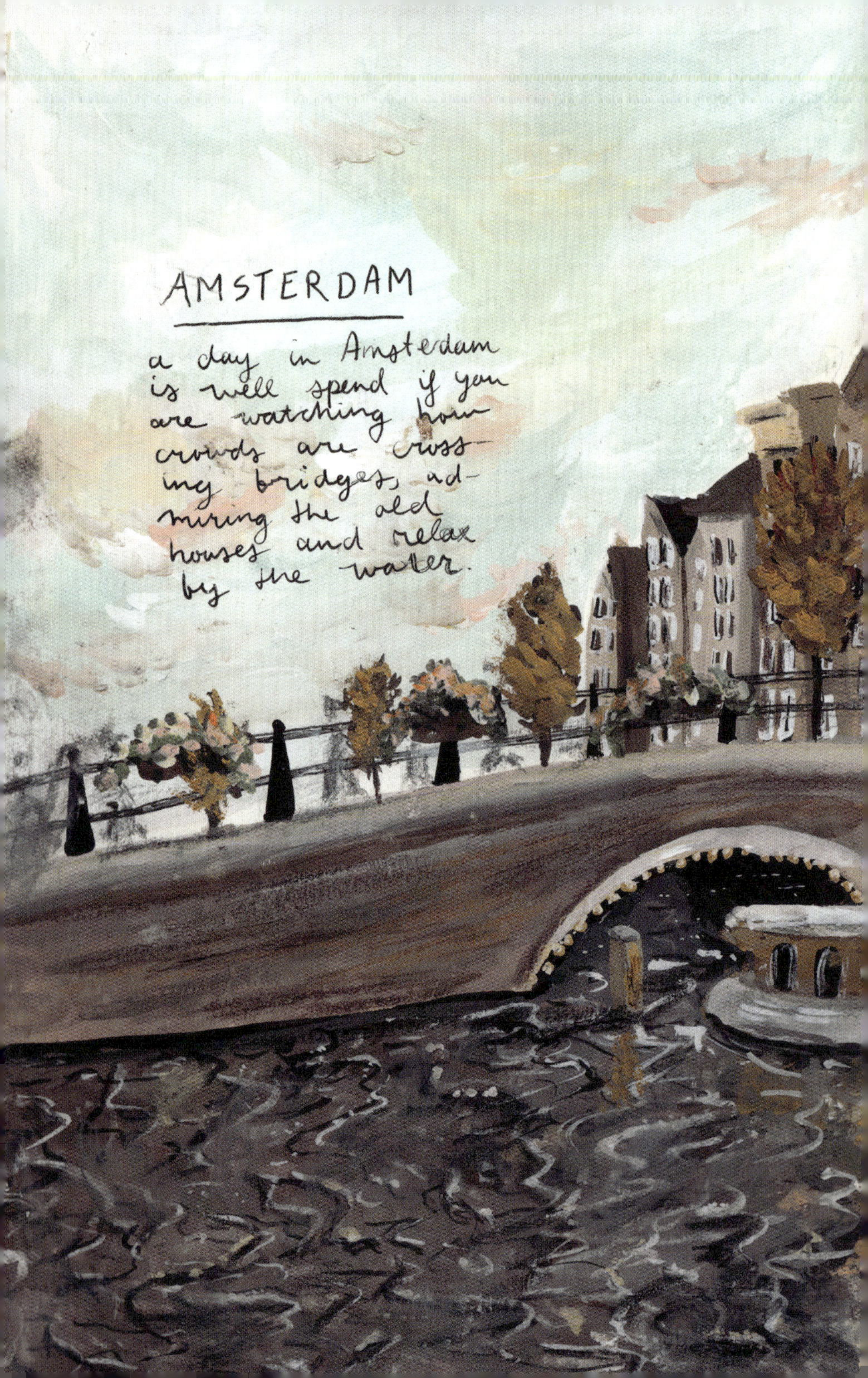

AMSTERDAM

a day in Amsterdam
is well spend if you
are watching how
crowds are cross-
ing bridges, ad-
miring the old
houses and relax
by the water.

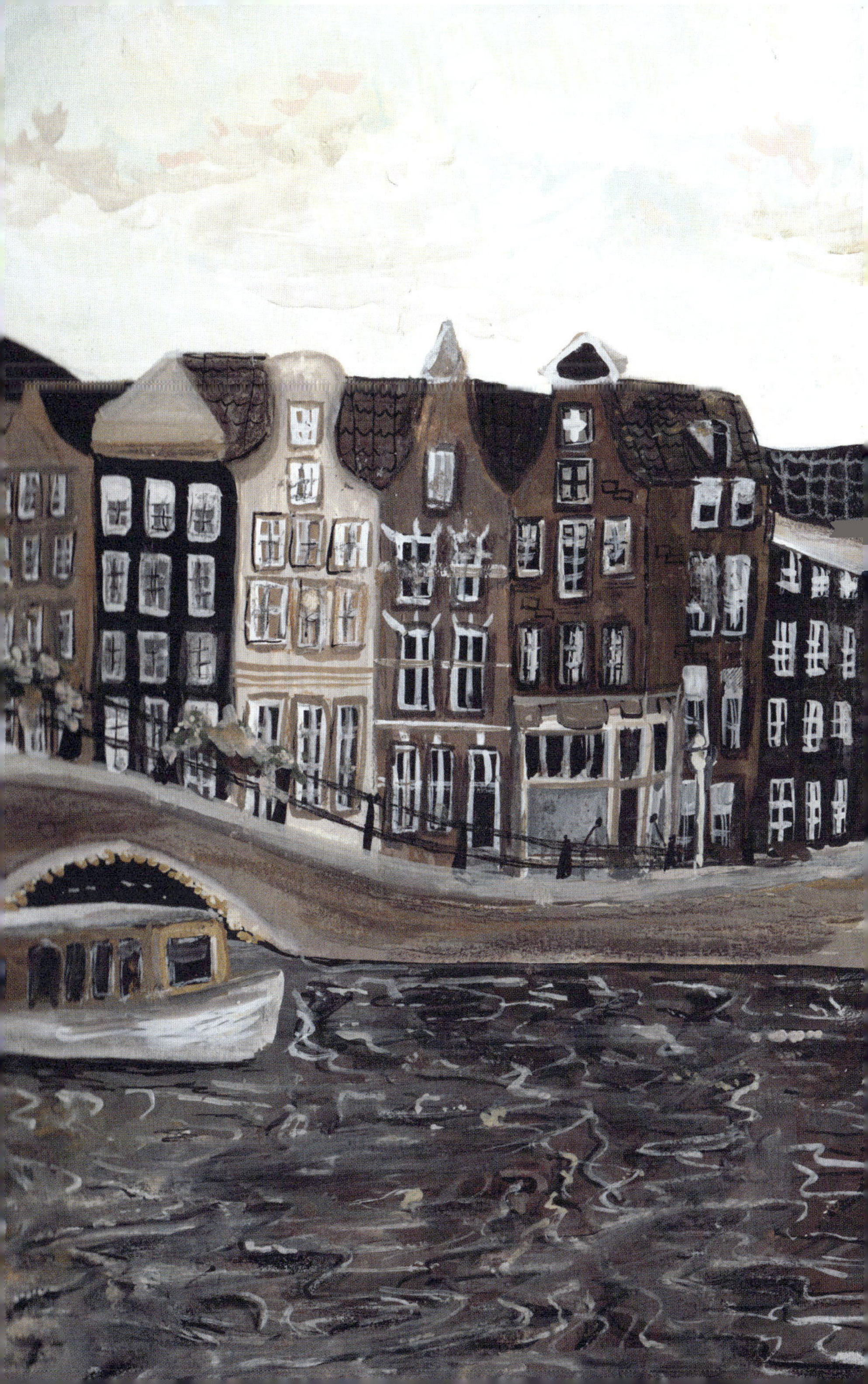

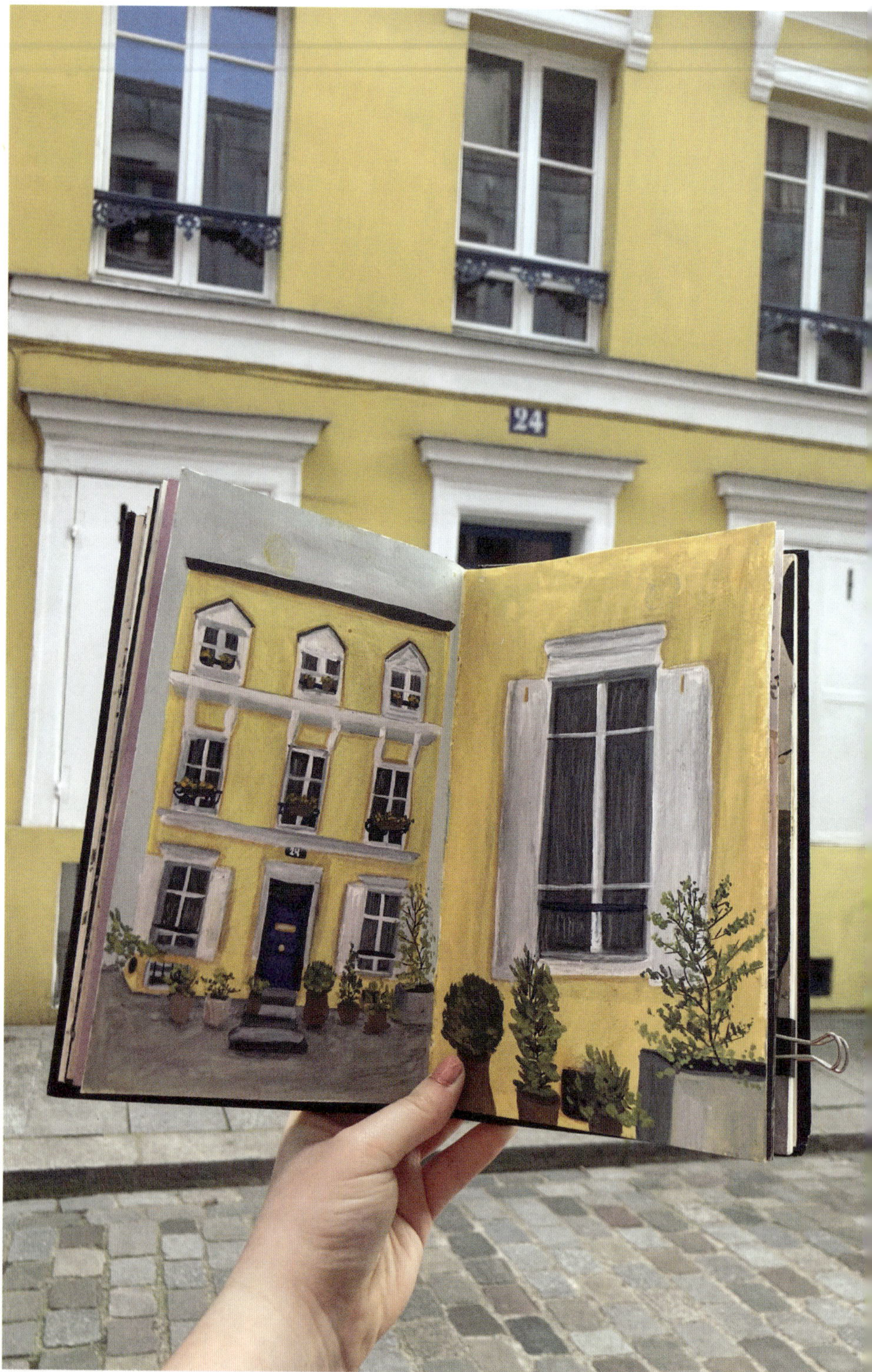

How to paint a house with gouache

Look carefully at the building you want to capture

Whether you are observing it in real life or painting it from a photograph, take time to absorb all the details and colours. If you want to refresh your observation skills, you can refer back to Chapter 2.

Make a pencil sketch

Figure out what you want to depict, how you want to capture the building, where it will be located on the page, and to what extent background elements such as the sky, pavement, and road play a role. Choose whether you want to depict the building straight on, or make it more playful by drawing it slightly askew. To switch things up a bit, try sketching with a red or blue pencil. Painters do this so they can see the lines better when painting over them. This is especially useful for when you're painting a building, as you can still clearly see the outline of the windows. Note that if you work with opaque paints, the lines become more difficult to see.

Choose techniques, materials, and colours

Think about the colours you'll need, and if you don't have the exact shades, refer to the colour wheel in Chapter 4 for mixing guidance. Ensure you have the correct brushes, a cup of water, and tissues at hand.

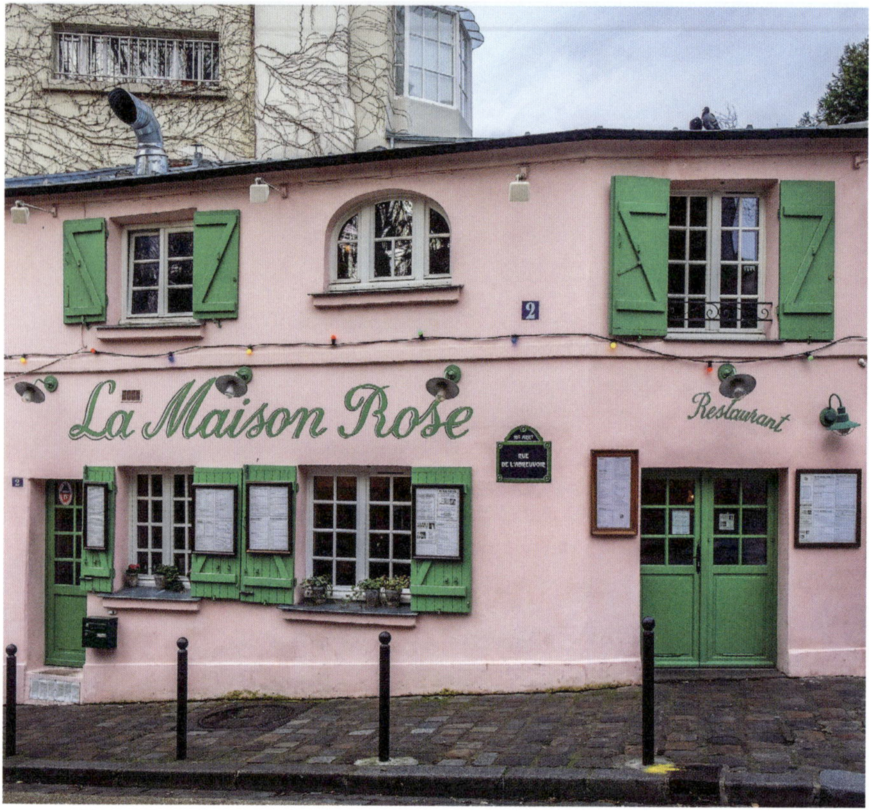

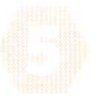

La Maison Rose, page 92–93

Apply the first layer of paint, which forms the base of your building
You will be able to build more depth into your work if you add multiple transparent layers (by combining paint with a lot of water) on top of each other.

When the first coat of paint is dry, you can add windows, frames, and a door
Paint the key elements without focusing on details. Elements like windows often appear many times in a house illustration, so it is mainly a repetition of moves.

Time for details!

Add shutters and curtains, for example. Make paintings look more realistic by adding shadows with a dark pencil and/or brush. Be subtle, and soften it with your finger or a blending stump, if necessary. Add it wherever you like, at the bottom of a building or several buildings, to lampposts, flowerpots, and next to and under window frames. Add accents and highlights to the places that deserve the most attention or where you want to capture the glare of the sun (such as in the window reflections). Add bricks by placing rectangles in different sizes with a white pencil or paint. Decorate the roof with a dark pencil or fineliner. Draw a lot of Us back-to-back or upright, like a simplified wave. Or make diagonal lines and draw straight lines through them to create a block pattern.

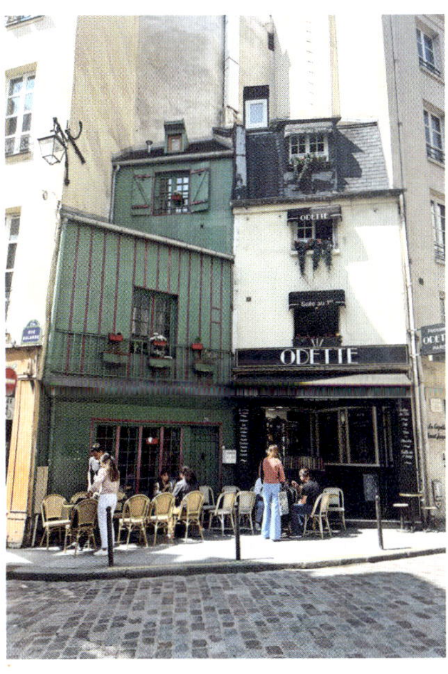

Odette, page 95

Add a background

When painting buildings, it's best to wait until the end to add a background. Whether you want to do this depends on how colourful and crowded the pages are. Adding a blue sky or a sunset may enhance your painting, but by leaving out the background you do have more space for other illustrations or notes. Wait until the paint on your pages has dried to prevent it from smudging or mixing.

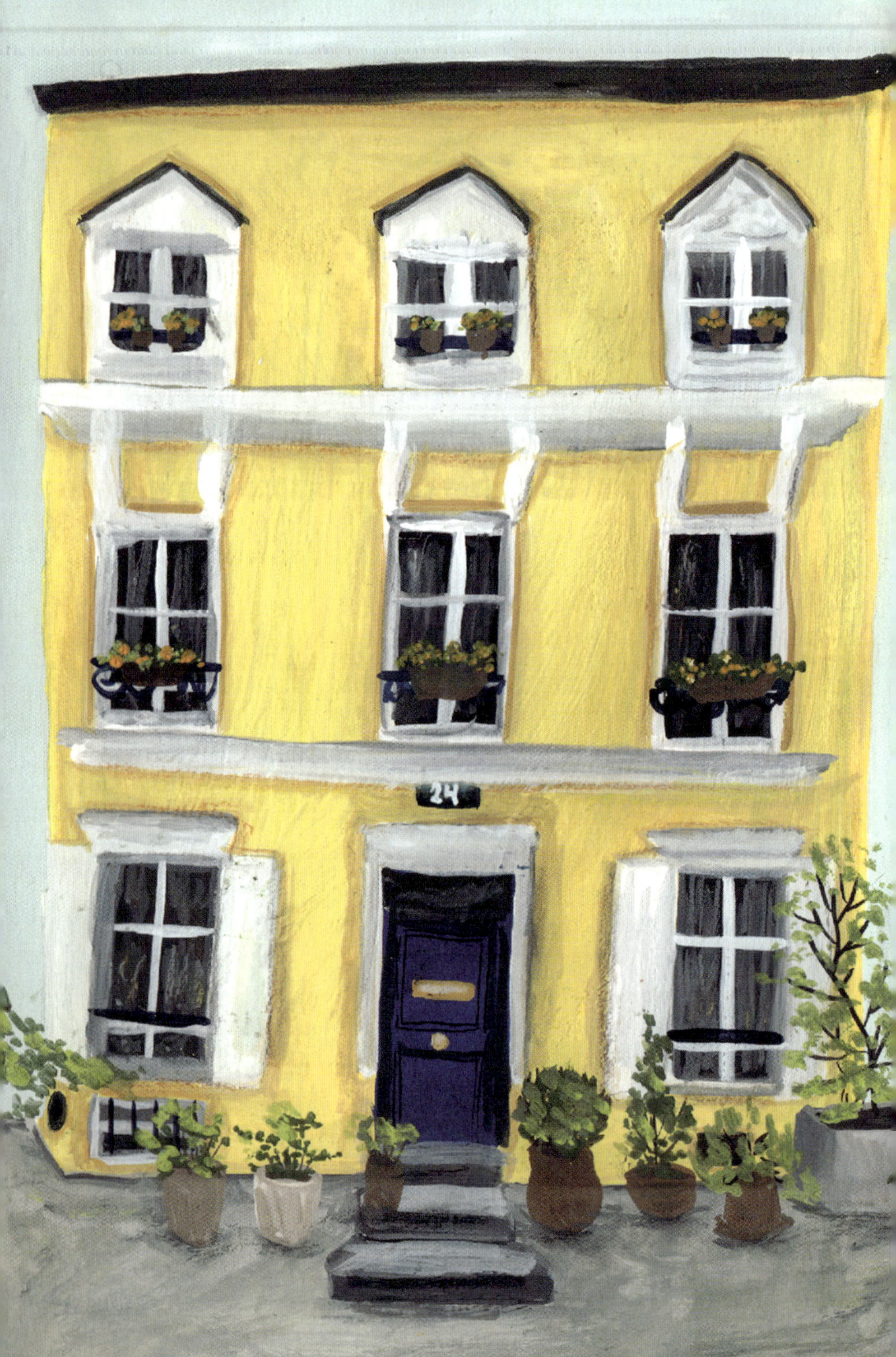
24

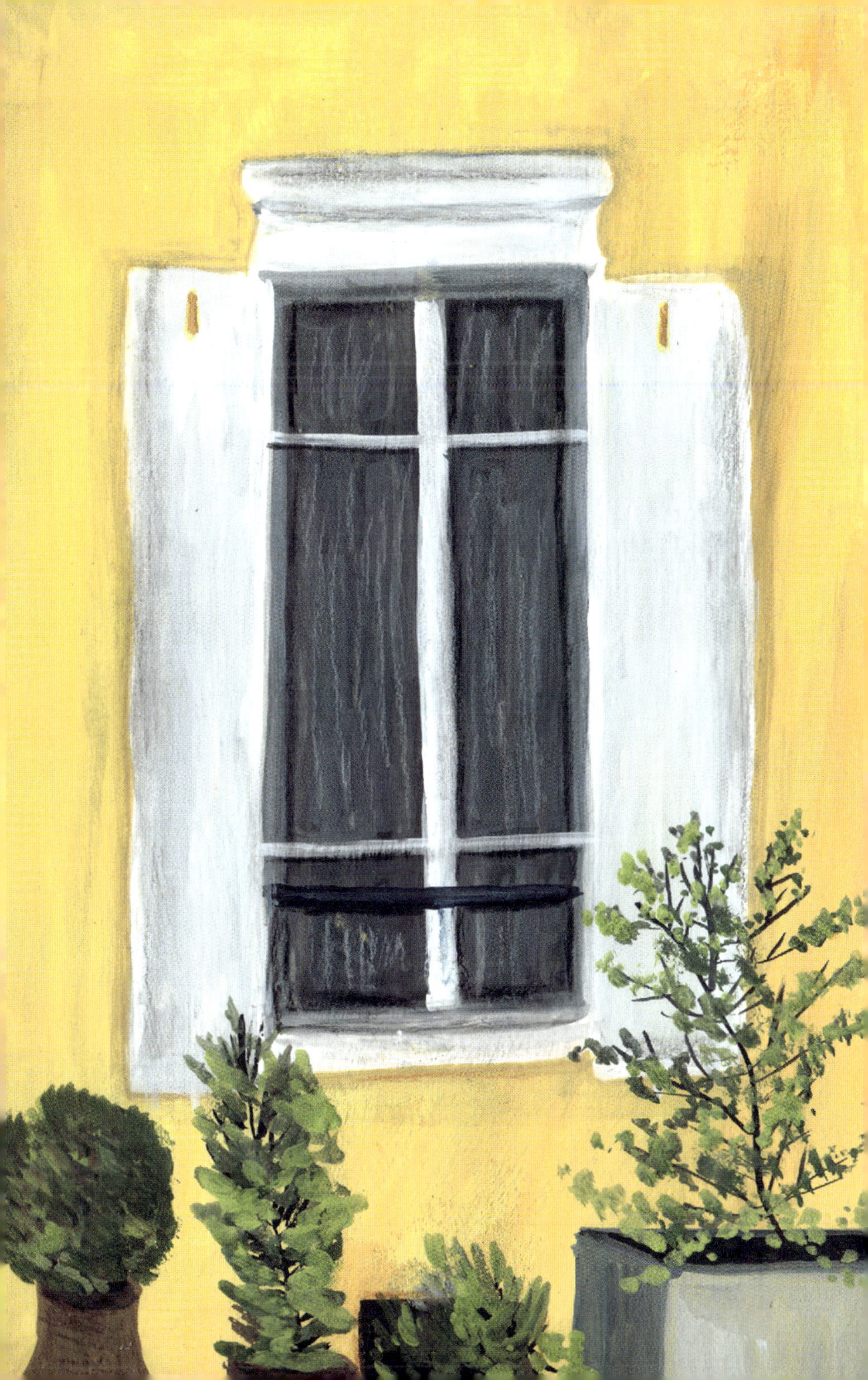

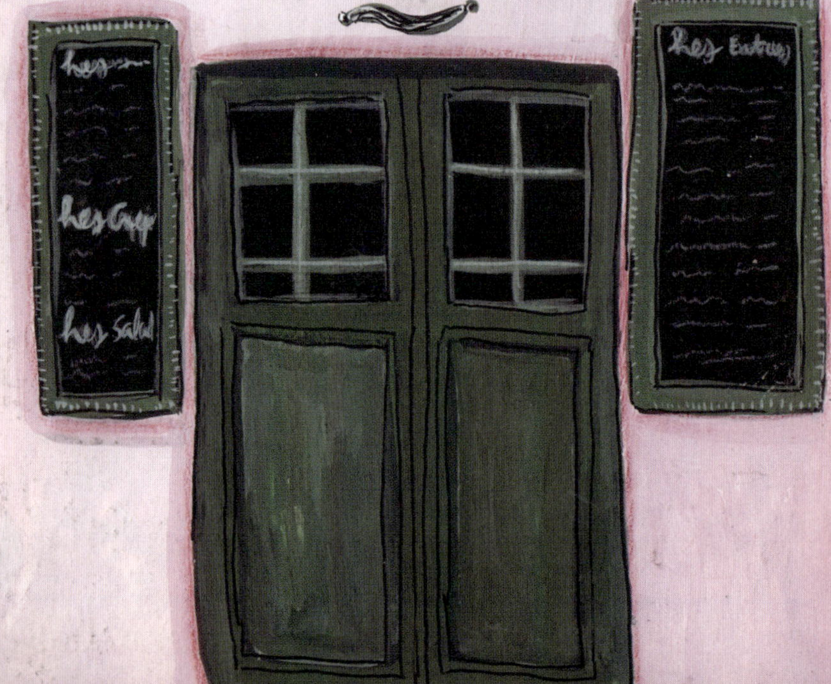

Café Restaurant
les Entrées
les Sal

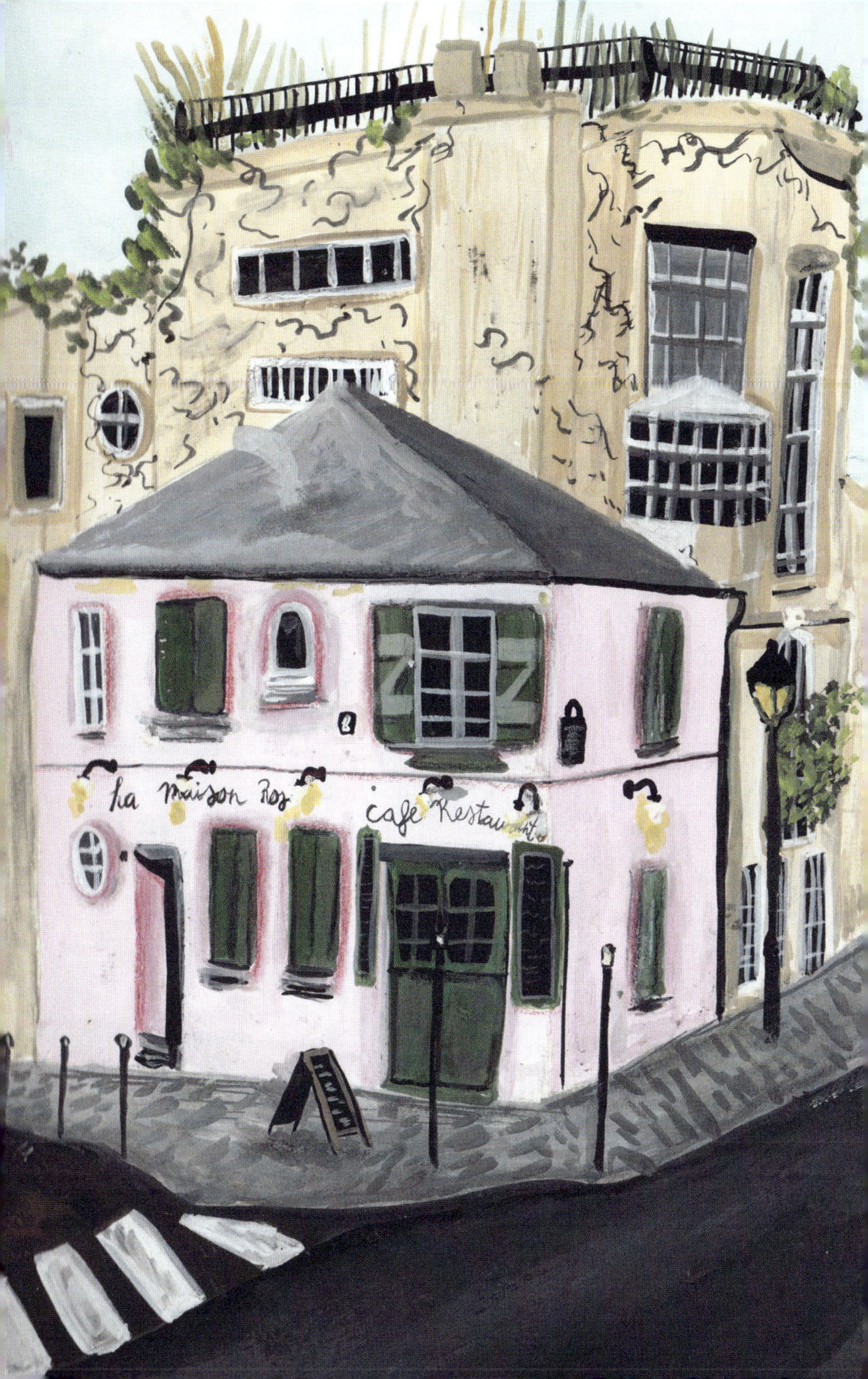
la maison Rose
café Restaurant

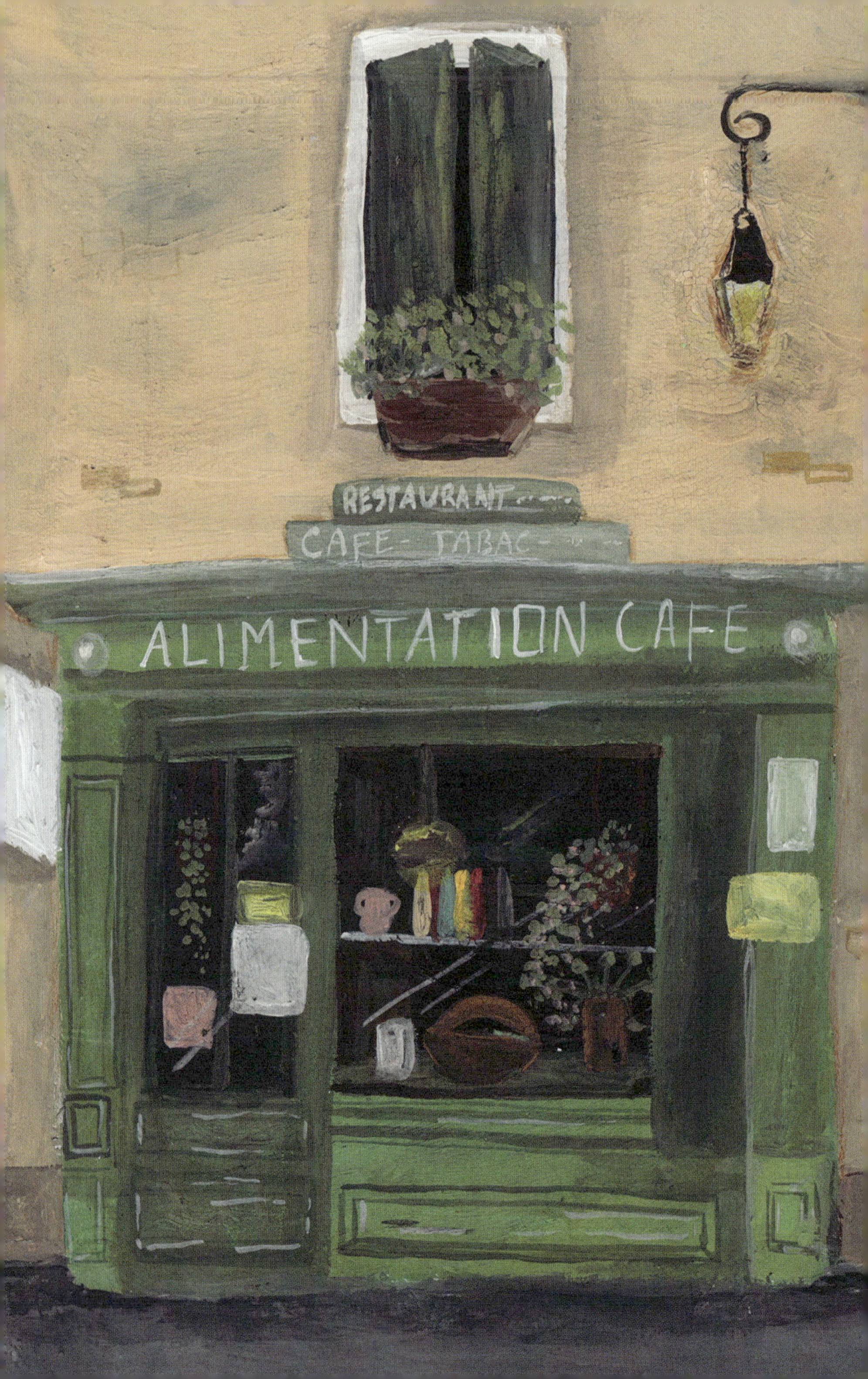

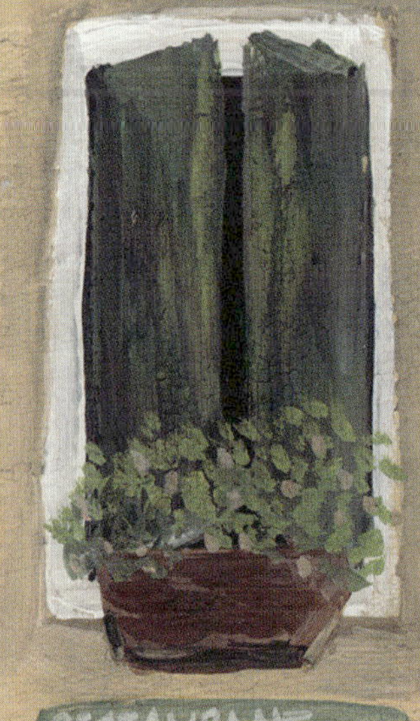

RESTAURANT
CAFE - TABAC
ALIMENTATION CAFE

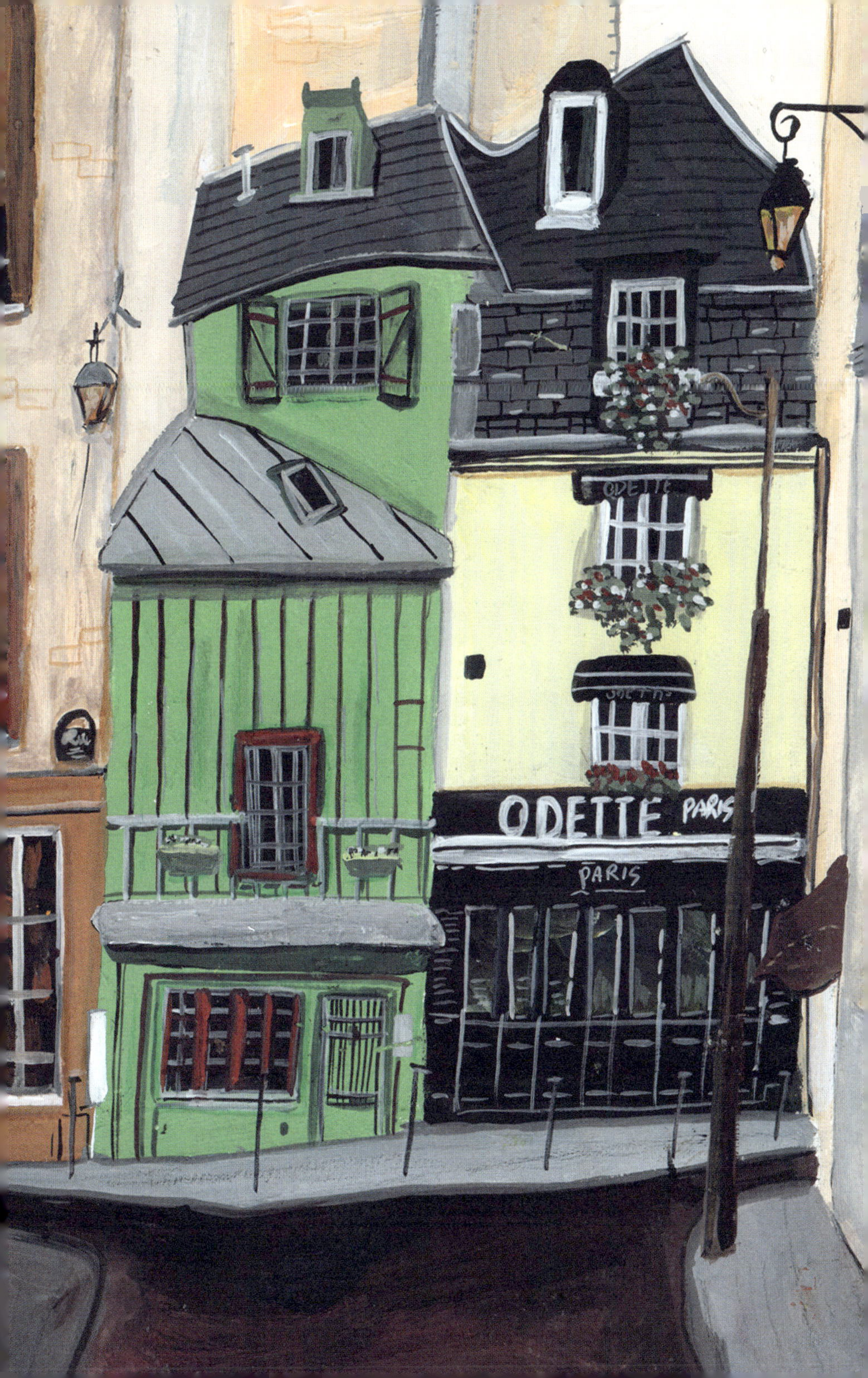

ODETTE PARIS
PARIS

Painting people

Your travel pages become more personal when you add people. They make scenes livelier. Focus on capturing a person's essence rather than trying to make an exact copy.

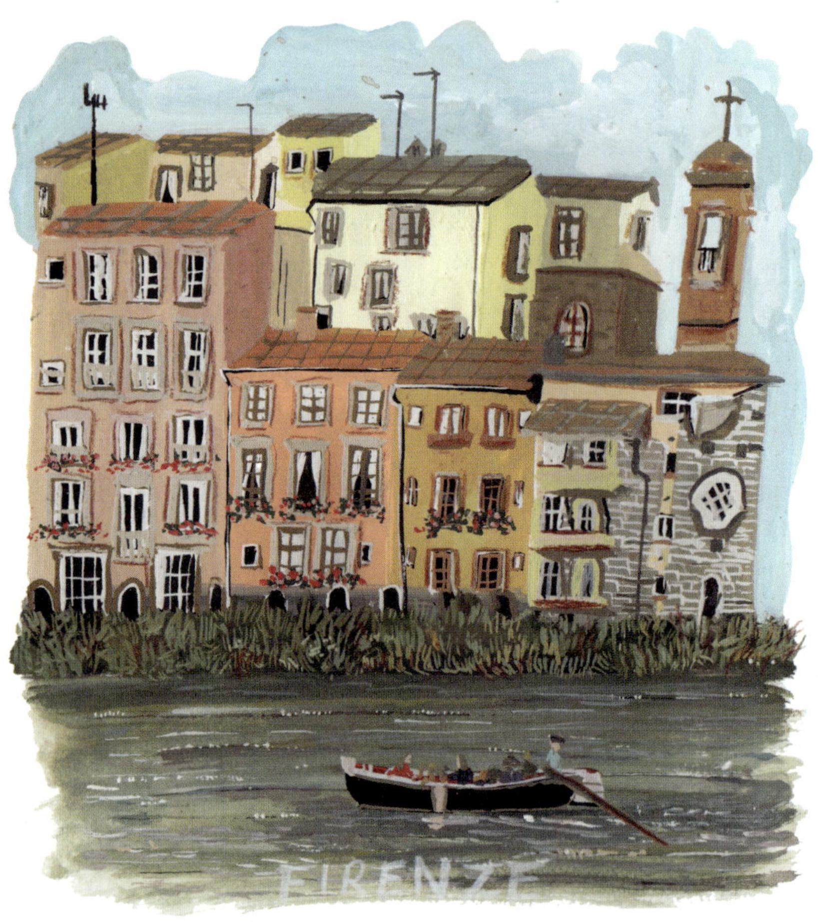

Stick figures

The easiest way to draw people is by creating stick figures. Use basic shapes like circles, ovals, and rectangles to outline the head, torso, and limbs. Connect these shapes with lines to form the body structure. Make this even easier by drawing the outline of a person's shape. It is best to use a thin brush or pencil to work as precisely as possible. If you want to give people more character and make them more recognisable, you can add more colour by continuing with the next steps.

Add colour

Start with light washes to block in the main colours. Use watercolours or gouache, and add a lot of water to cover larger areas like skin, clothes, and backgrounds. Add several layers to build depth and dimension. Let each layer dry before adding the next to prevent colours from muddying.

Identify the light source

Use darker shades for shadows and lighter tones for highlights. Blend edges to avoid harsh transitions.

Add details

Use smaller brushes and/or coloured pencils to enhance the details of the face, hair, and clothes. Focus on key features like the eyes, nose, and mouth. You can use a pen or fineliner to add outlines. This helps define the figure as well. If a figure you have drawn is moving, you can add two dashes to the legs or feet. It is a quick addition you often see in comic books.

Context

Include environmental elements to give your figure(s) context. Add a background, such as a café or a street scene. You can also start with the background and add the people last. This makes it easier to add shadows without accidentally removing details like a scarf or hat.

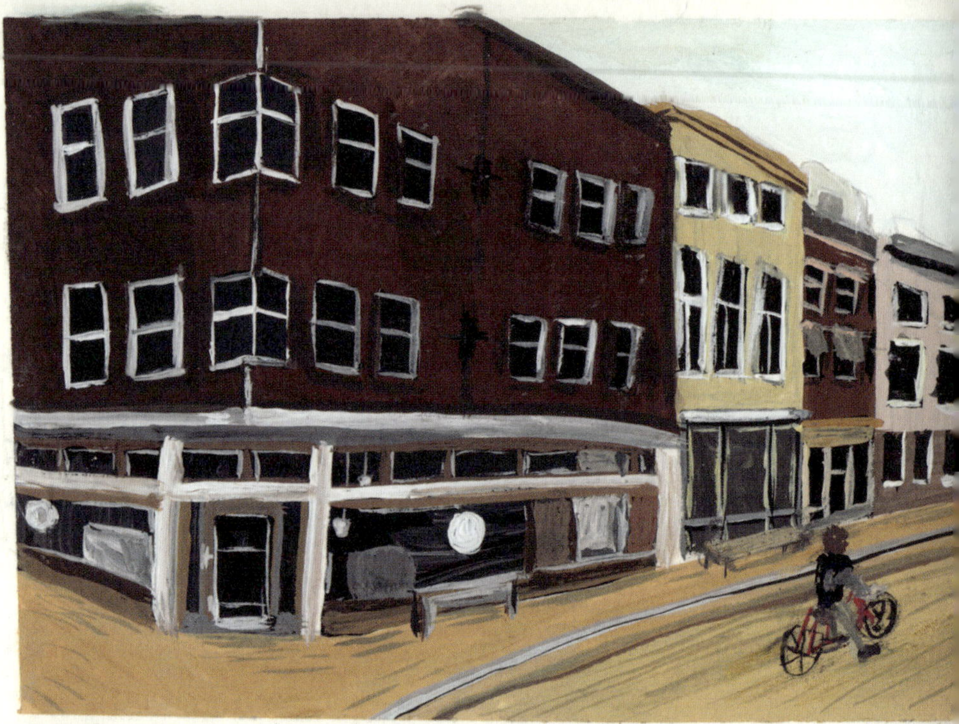

Oude Kijk in 't Jatstraat

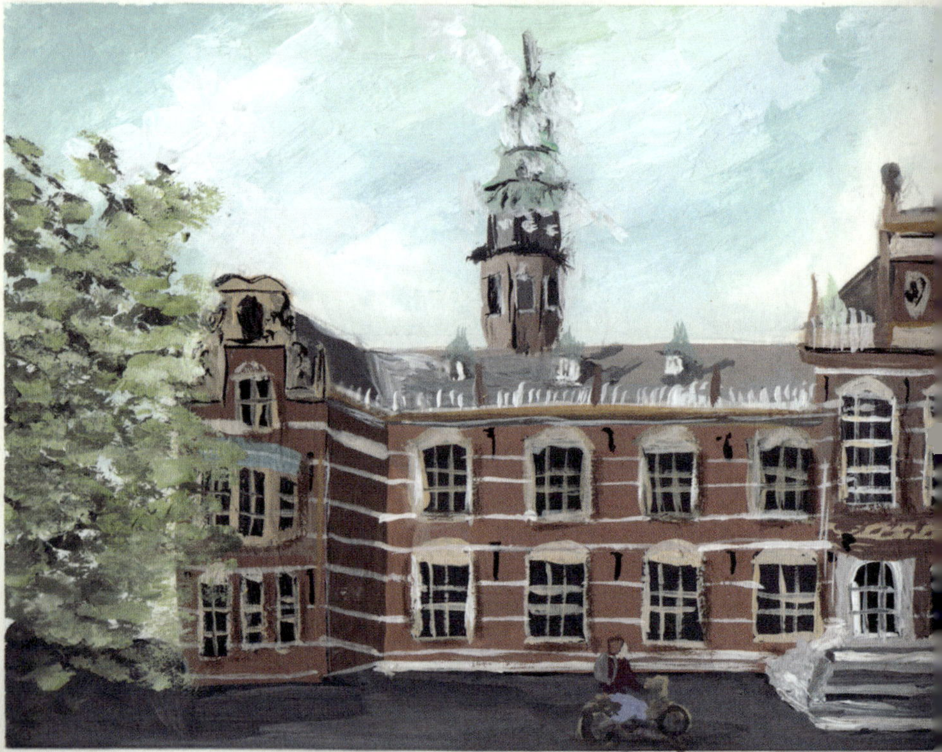

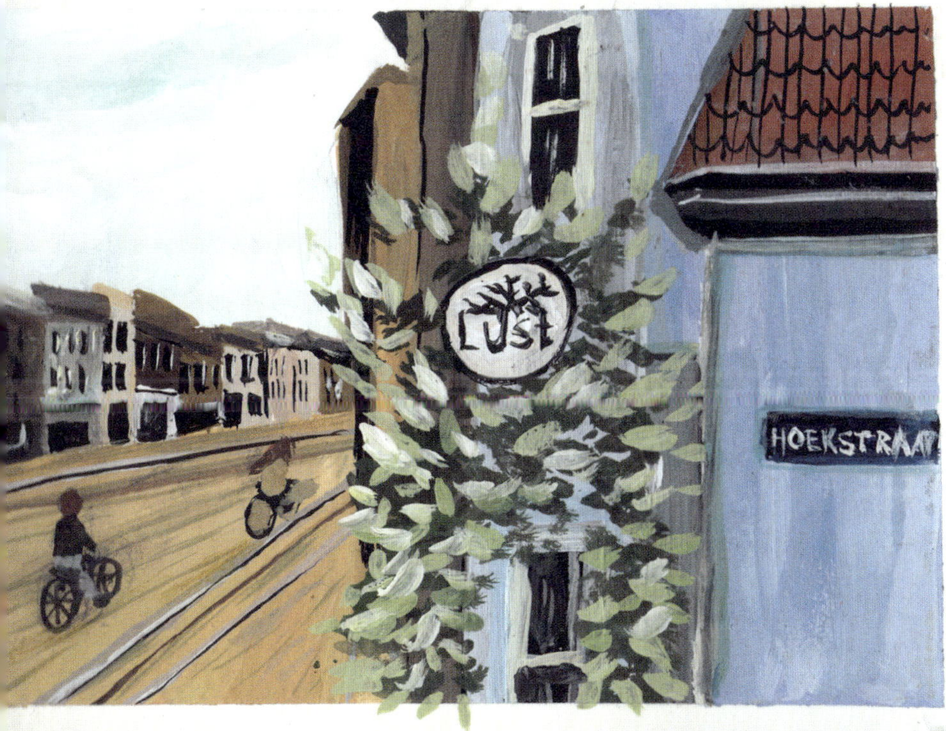

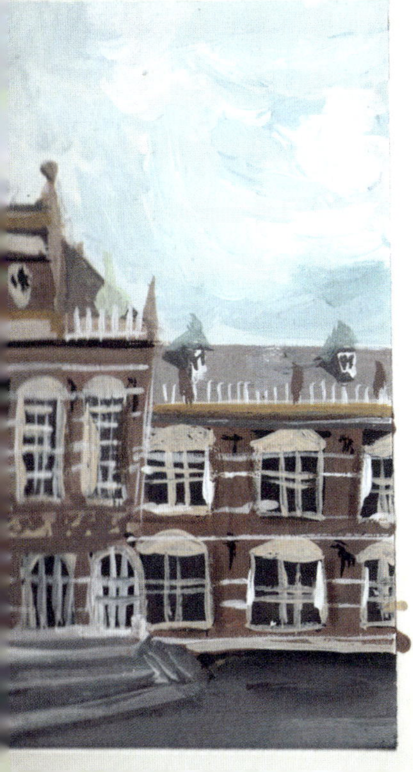

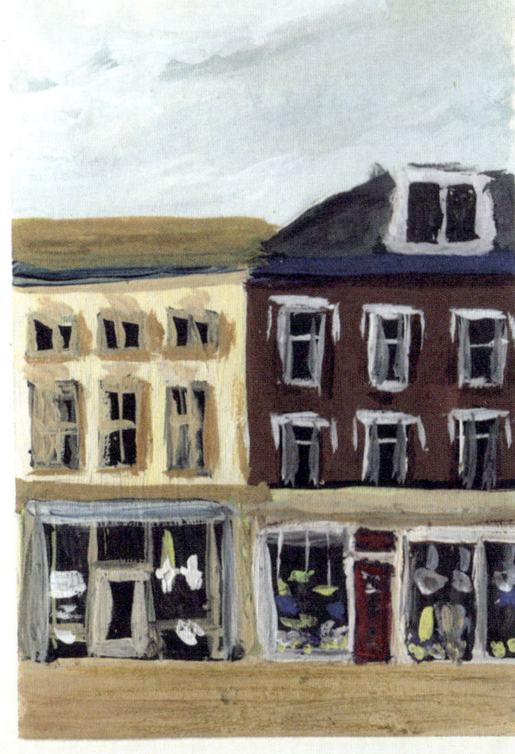
LUSt
HOEKSTRAAT

Painting cityscapes

On the Italian coast, you will see beautiful cityscapes
where houses seem to be stacked like building blocks.
In many shapes and with beautiful pastel colours,
they attract a lot of attention and admirers from all
over the world. But how can you capture their essence
with paint?

Start with a loose sketch
Start by sketching the outline of
the houses, and indicate where
the windows and doors approxi-
mately will be. Make sure there is
variety in the shapes by drawing
the front as well as side views.
You don't have to sketch buildings
from top to bottom; experiment
a bit with a house here and there
and eventually fit them together
so that they become united. Then
draw the houses more accurately,
so that by the time you're painting
them, it is simply a matter of just
colouring in the different boxes.
Keep to reality. Keep looking at
a picture of the houses or look up
often when drawing on location,
but also repeat certain figures to
make it easier on yourself.

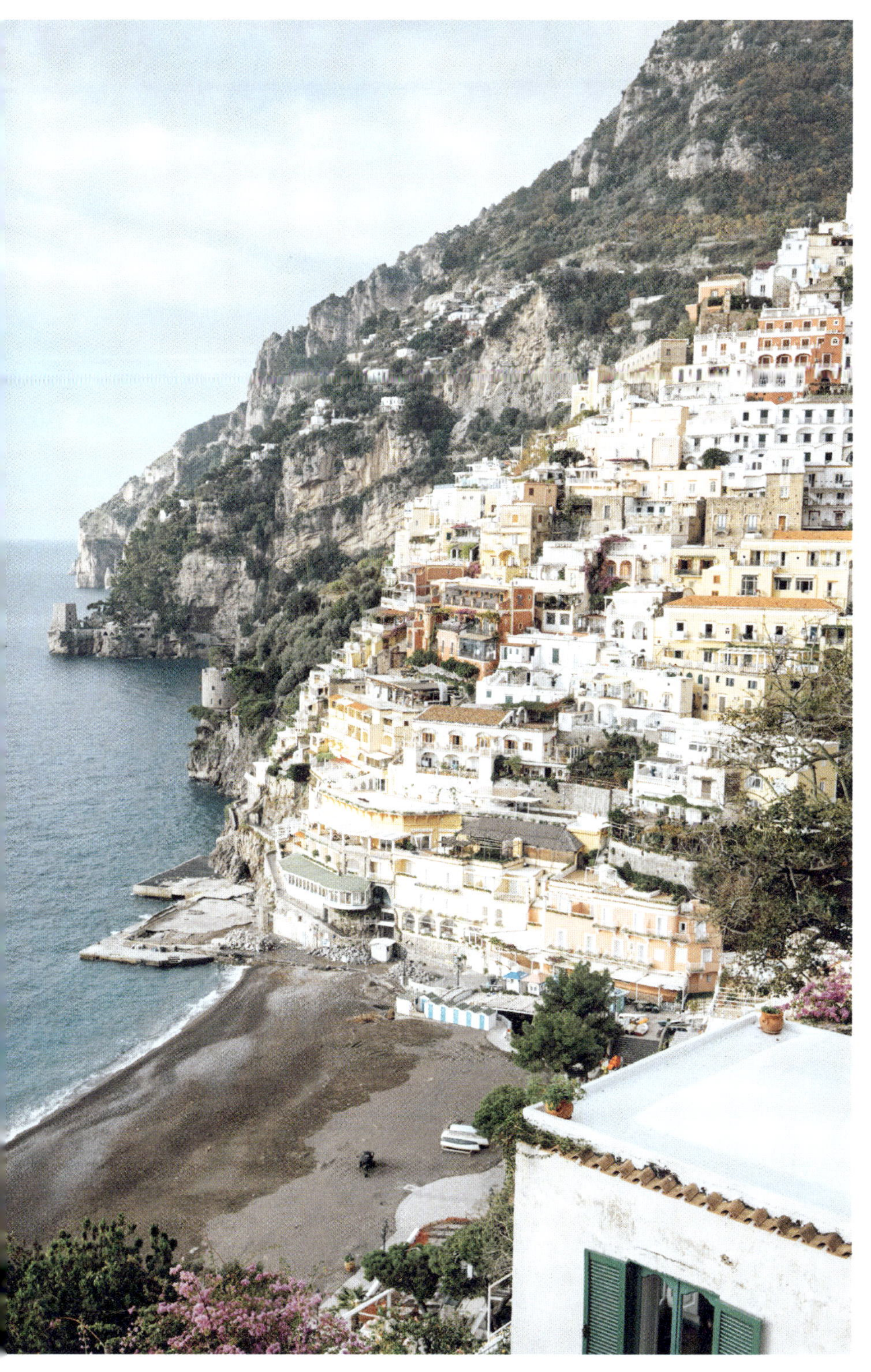

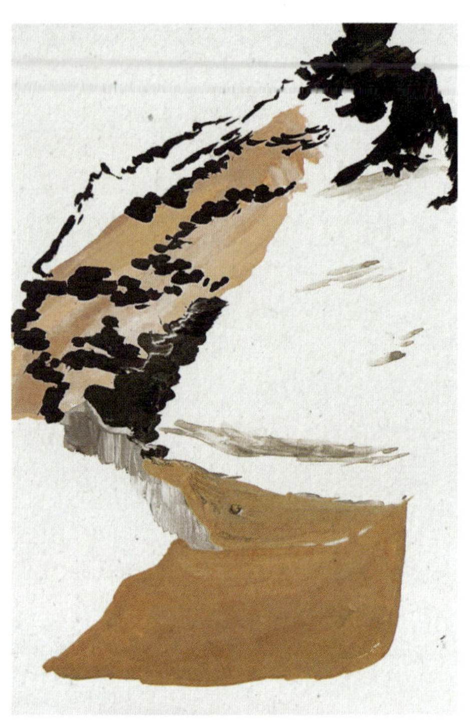 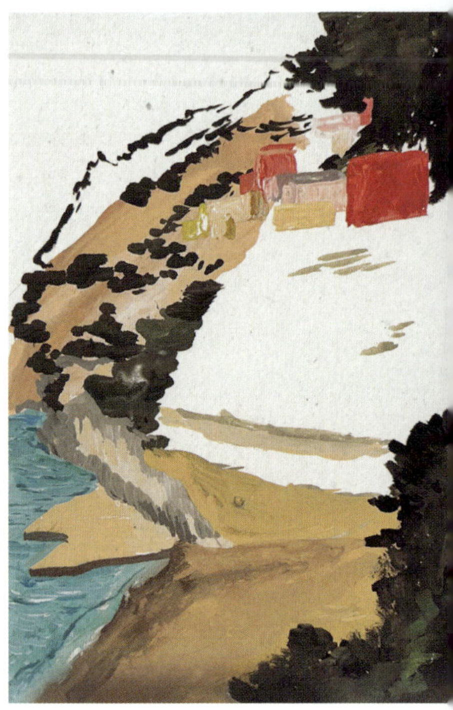

2

Pick your colours

Mix paint into the colours you have in mind. Houses on the Italian coast are often characterised by their pastel colours. Soften a colour by adding a drop of white, or make it warmer by adding red and/or yellow paint.

3

Paint the surroundings

Think of the ground, or any surrounding rocks or the beach. Combine various shades of grey for rocks. If there are hills to be seen behind the houses, you can paint those as well. I often use dark colours, so I can add accents and details such as (light) green brushstrokes later in the process. Sometimes, I switch steps 3 and 4, depending on what fits the painting best.

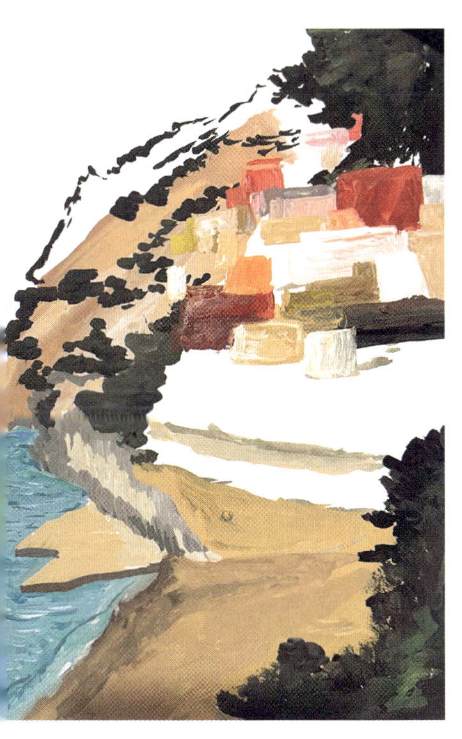 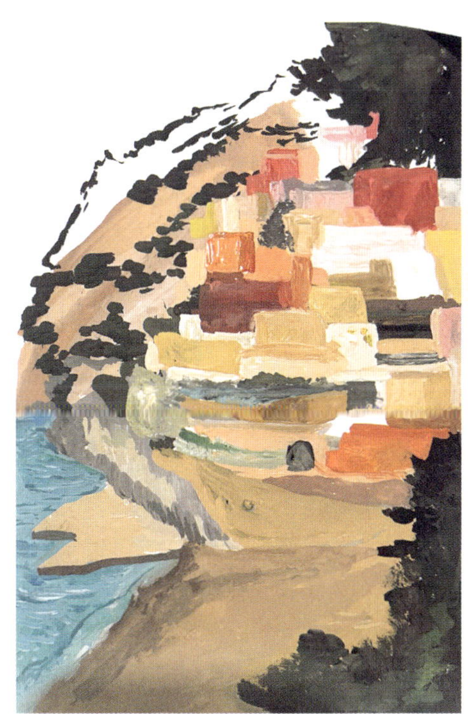

Start colouring the houses

Make a cheerful, colourful ensemble, or keep it more subdued by working mostly with pastel colours and adding a drop of white to each colour. Paint water at the bottom or the side (depending on where it is in reality). Try to match the colours of the actual lake or sea water as closely as possible. In Chapter 7 you'll find more about painting water.

Add windows

Use a thin paintbrush and black or dark grey paint. As you have more control with pencils, you can try a black pencil to work more precisely. Paint windows as rectangles and add a curve at the top if you feel like it. Place around three windows in a row and three underneath each other, depending on the amount of space there is. To add character to a window, you can paint another frame around it with a thin brush, fineliner, or pencil after the paint on the windows has dried. Add an additional border with a dark brown pencil to give a window more shade and character. Finish by adding curtains using a light colour, a single stripe to represent a washing line, and add a few vertical and horizontal lines in the windows for reflections.

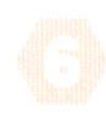

Paint the sky
Make sure that if you paint a sun or if your sky contains shades of pink, reflections in the water match this. If you already painted the water, you can add these pastel shades to it later. If you work with gouache or watercolours, you can add some extra water to reactivate the paint and blend the colours. If you work with acrylic paint, it works best to add water reflections with pencils or pastels. Gently blend the colours with your finger or a blending stump.

Add final details
Think of sparkles in the water (a few small white dots next to each other and under each other), blades of grass, flowers, and/or patterns as decoration on an awning or on the church tower.

Positano, Amalfi Coast, Italy »

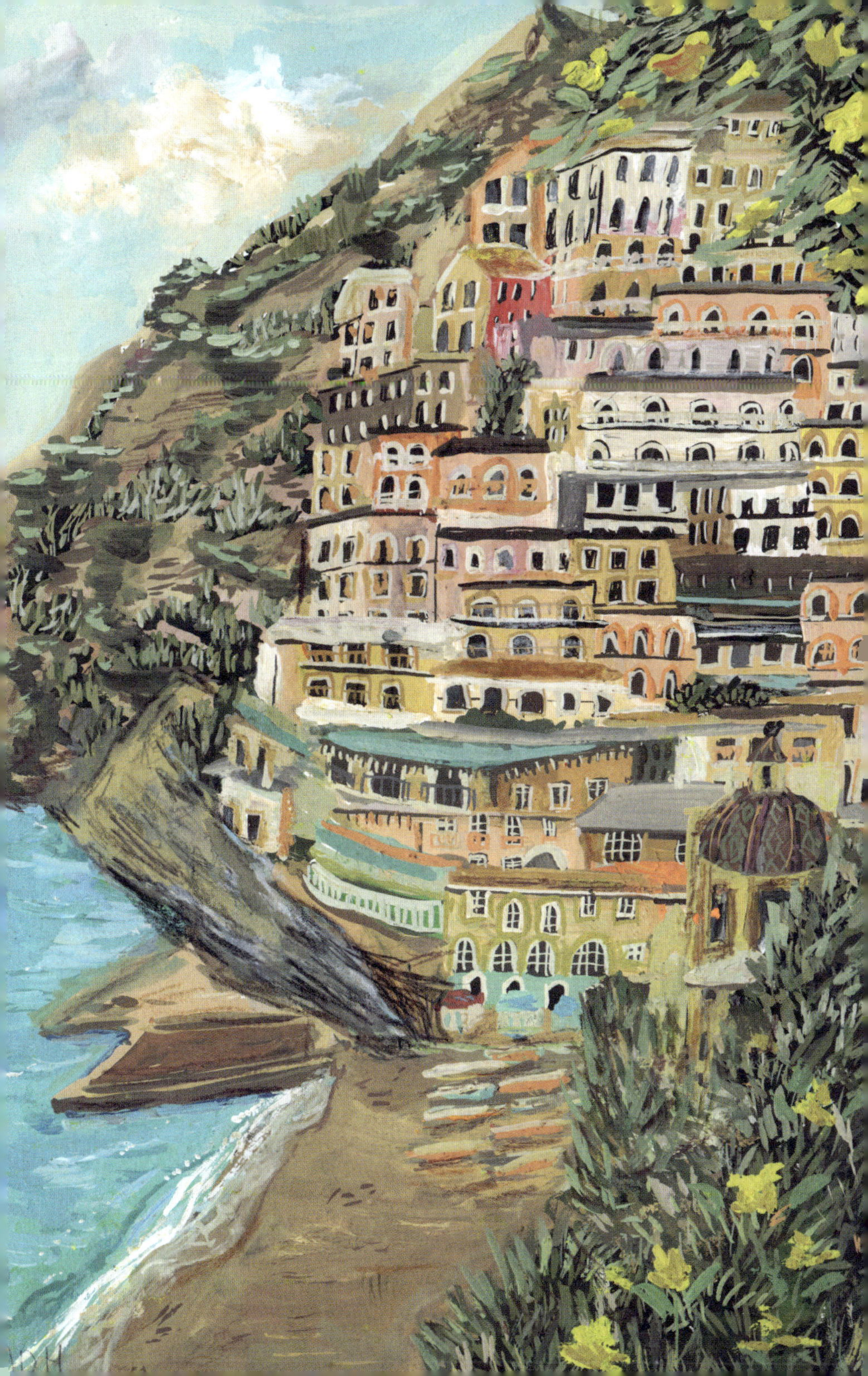

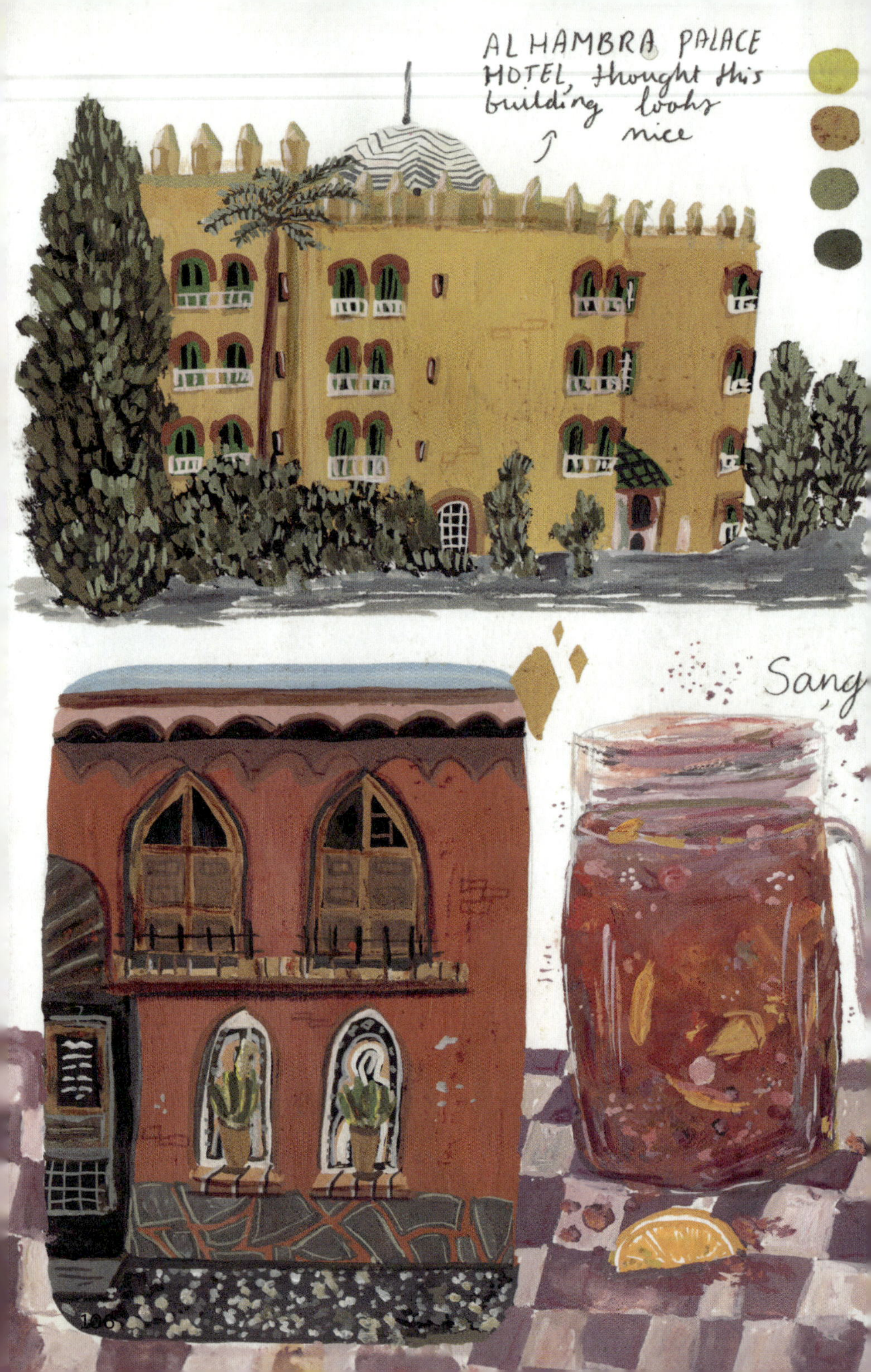
AL HAMBRA PALACE
HOTEL, thought this
building looks
nice
Sang

Painting food

One of the best ways to experience a new country is by trying the local food. Food says a lot about the culture, people, and the history of a place. I typically decide beforehand what I want to capture: the entire restaurant, people in the background, or just my table with food and drinks.

I take a picture of my food or immediately start sketching once my plate arrives. Although the dimensions might vary slightly from reality, I still want to ensure my coffee cup isn't three times the size of my plate (unless that's exactly how it is, of course!). A dish depends significantly on the lightning. In dim or fluorescent-lit settings, it might not look as appetising or atmospheric. I improve this by slightly adjusting my reference photo, such as lowering temperature and colour saturation.

To fill the pages, I like to add the name of the restaurant, the people I'm dining with, details of my order, the receipt, and a short review about my experience on the same page. As a last step, I like to add details, such as a highlight on a cherry or the cutlery, decorations on my plate or table, ice cubes, or steam billowing out of a hot drink.

« Granada, Spain

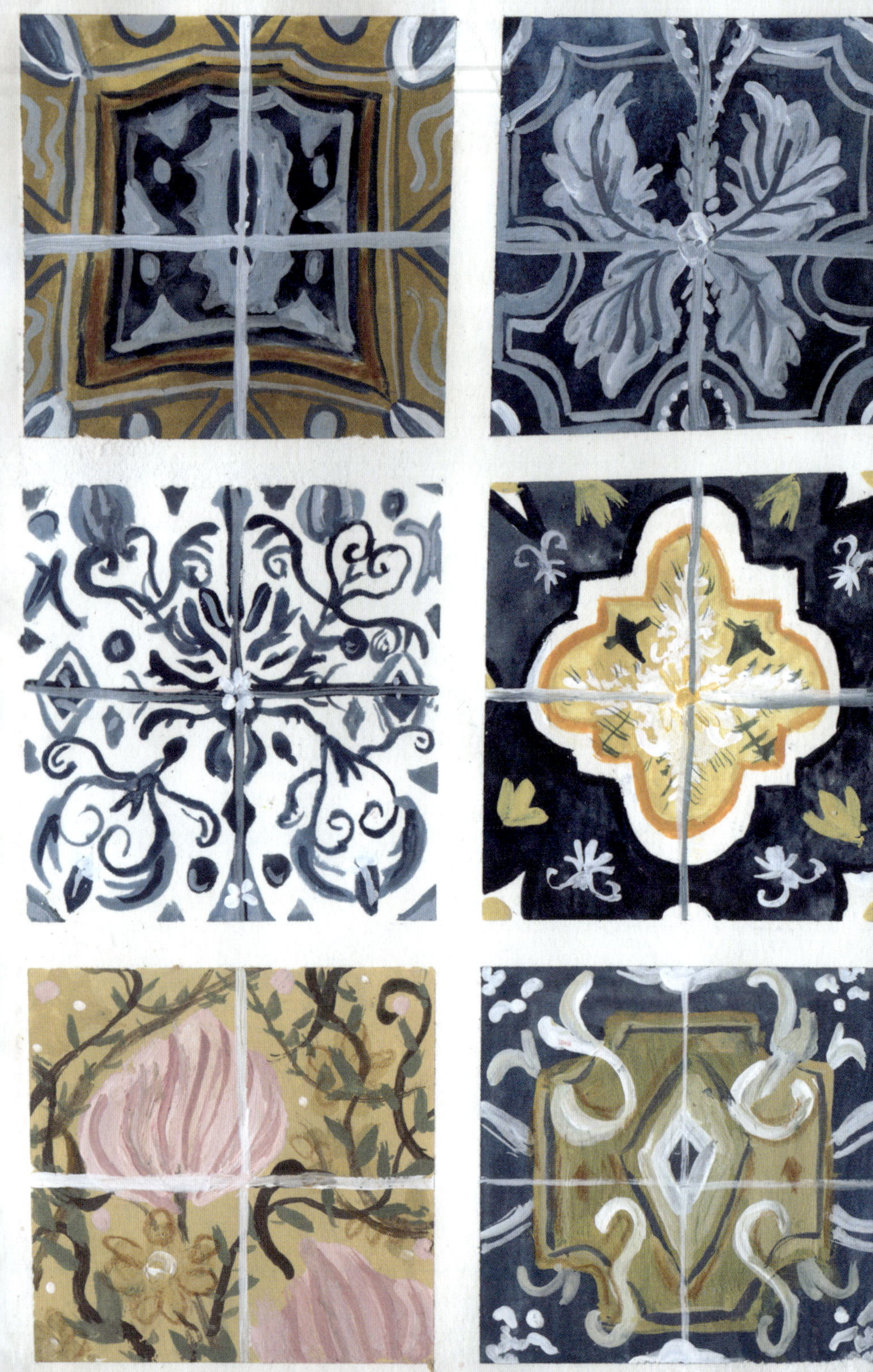

Painting Portuguese *azulejos*

Capturing an environment can be done by recording patterns or icons that characterise a city. Here's how to paint Portuguese tiles, or *azulejos*, in your travel sketchbook.

Gather inspiration for your tiles
Start by collecting images of tiles that appeal to you. Choose the colours you wish to use. Make sure the colours of tiles that you paint go well together.

Separate tiles with masking tape
Use masking tape to get nicely aligned boxes in your sketchbook. Make sure you use tape that you can easily remove without tearing the paper. Another option is to draw boxes with a ruler, but this requires more precision and often does turn out messier.

Divide each tile in fours
Draw a vertical line in the centre, and add a horizontal line. The lines will not be visible when you have painted the tiles, but will help you achieve symmetry while working. At this point, you should have four boxes per tile.

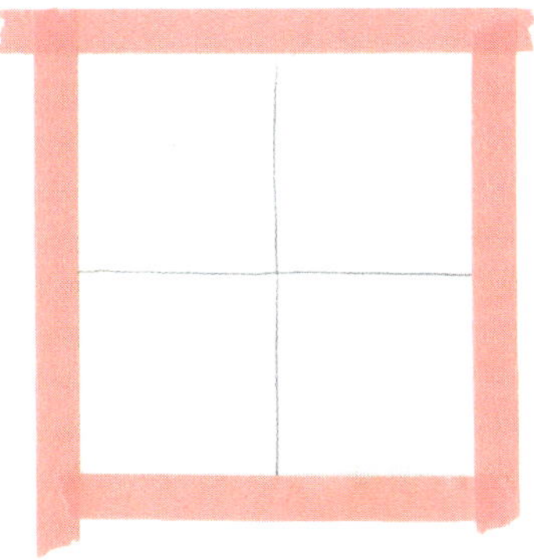

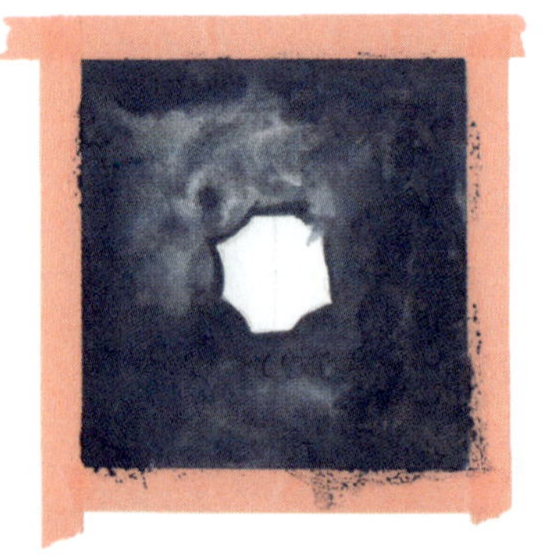

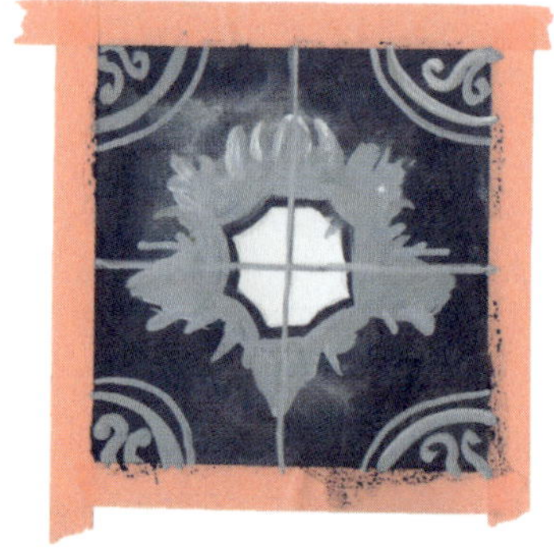

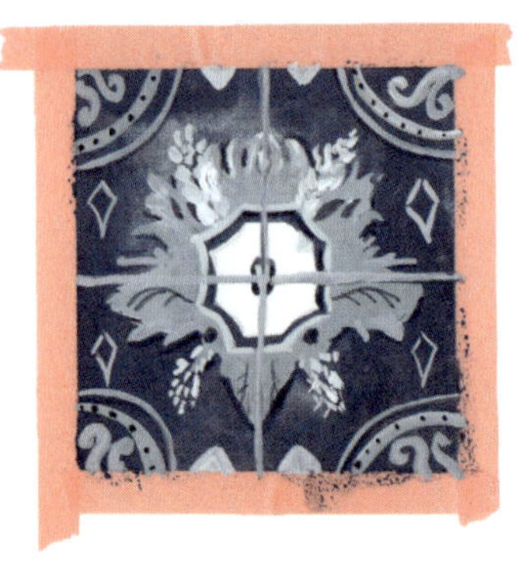

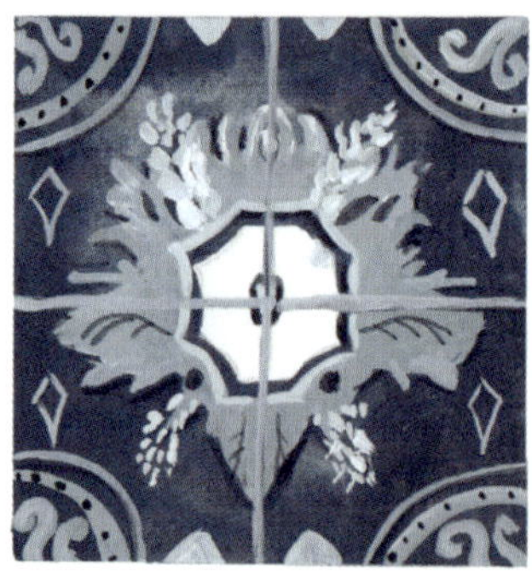

Background: yes or no?

Consider whether you want to add a colourful background. Paint the background using a large brush. Add more depth to your painting by mixing the paint with lots of water. Do this by adding a few more drops of water with a brush and gently spreading it into the box. This way you will notice that the paint appears lighter in some areas than in others.

Paint shapes

Add a general shape in the middle. Think of a square, circle, or an oval. Use a thin brush that allows you to work accurately. Experiment by adding a number of smaller shapes. Keep in mind that elements should mirror each other (think of circles on the side, and organic shapes like lines, crowns, and quadrangles).

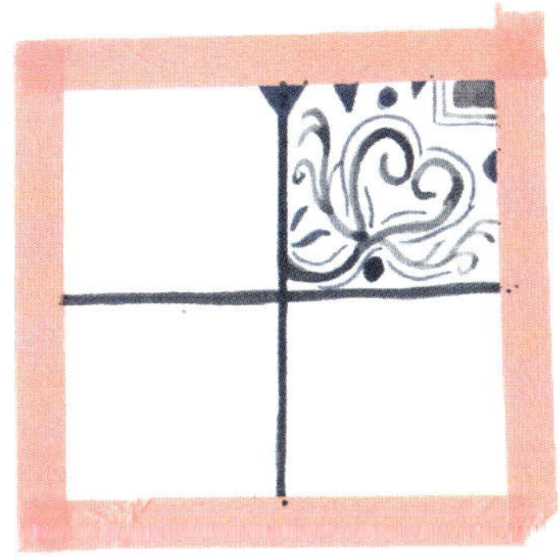
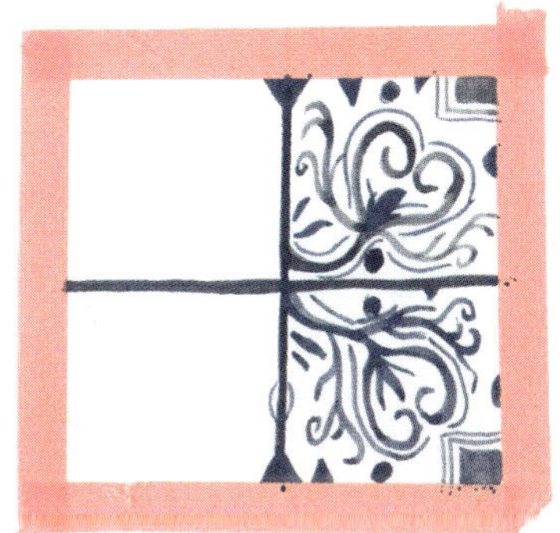

Add small drawings and accents

Place even more emphasis on your shapes by using white paint and the same precise brush or a fineliner. Add small drawings, such as a circle in the centre of your design. Paint new vertical and horizontal lines in the centre of your tile. Use a light colour on a colourful background, or a dark colour on a light background. Look closely at the example.

Remove the tape

Carefully remove the masking tape once your paint has dried. Don't wait too long, or the tape might stick and tear the paper when removed.

Start with a white tile first, and use only a dark blue to practice lines and shapes.

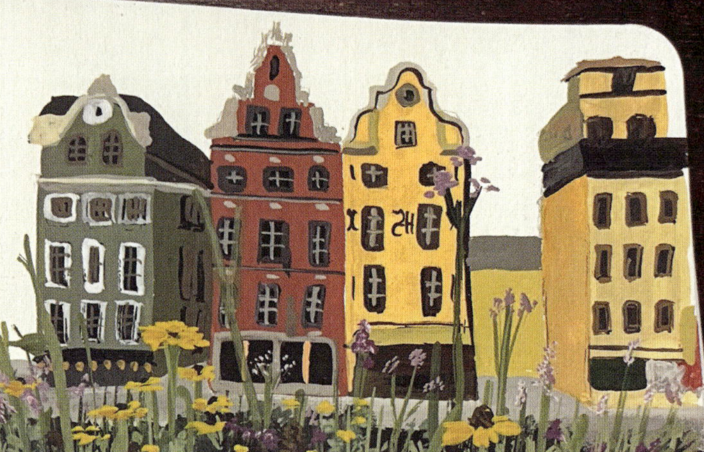

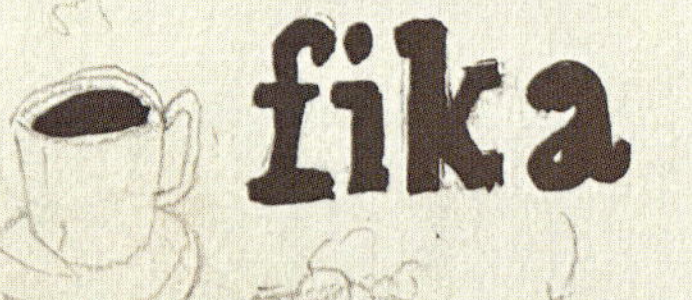

THE ART OF
THE SWEDISH
coffee break

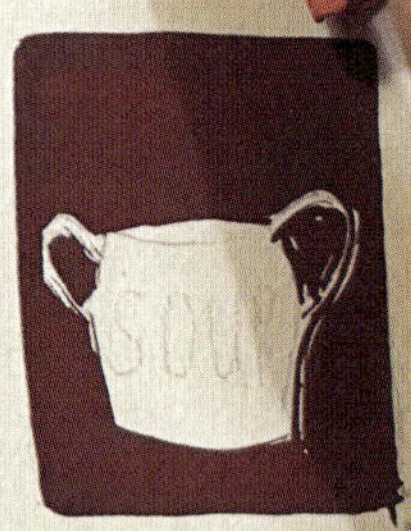

A SIGN I SAW
IN THE STREET

Capturing a city's essence

Bring only the essentials
Bring only two coloured pencils or just a fineliner and a sketchbook. That saves you from having to make choices about your materials on location, and you also challenge yourself by having to capture the environment with just a few tools.

Quick studies in public places
Practice by drawing many different people and their poses at a busy place, such as a café or train station. Challenge yourself even more by giving yourself a time limit of 30 seconds to 2 minutes per figure.

Avoid getting overwhelmed
If you find a building's details overwhelming, break it down and decide which elements to include. Make a list of what to capture, like 1) windows, 2) window frames, 3) a flowerpot on the balcony, and 4) a door and house number. You don't need to include every detail to make a building recognisable. The same applies when painting monuments and landmarks.

Practice makes perfect

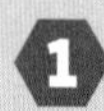

Fabulous façades

Draw canal houses, such as those found in Amsterdam or Bruges. These houses are typically tall, narrow, and deep, and there are beautiful details to be found in the windows and on the façade. First draw the skeleton of the buildings and then apply paint to bring them to life. Add more detail with a black fineliner to some of the houses to see what works better for you: with lines or without.

Change your background paper

Use different backgrounds for painting. Accents of white or light grey (for instance for the reflection in windows) are hardly noticeable on white or off-white paper, but on kraft paper they stand out very nicely.

Keep it simple

If you want to capture something unique about a place without using too much space, try focusing on a city icon. For example, in Granada (Spain), pomegranates are abundant as the city is named after them. You could illustrate a pomegranate or depict its various representations throughout the city, such as on pavers or in mosaics.

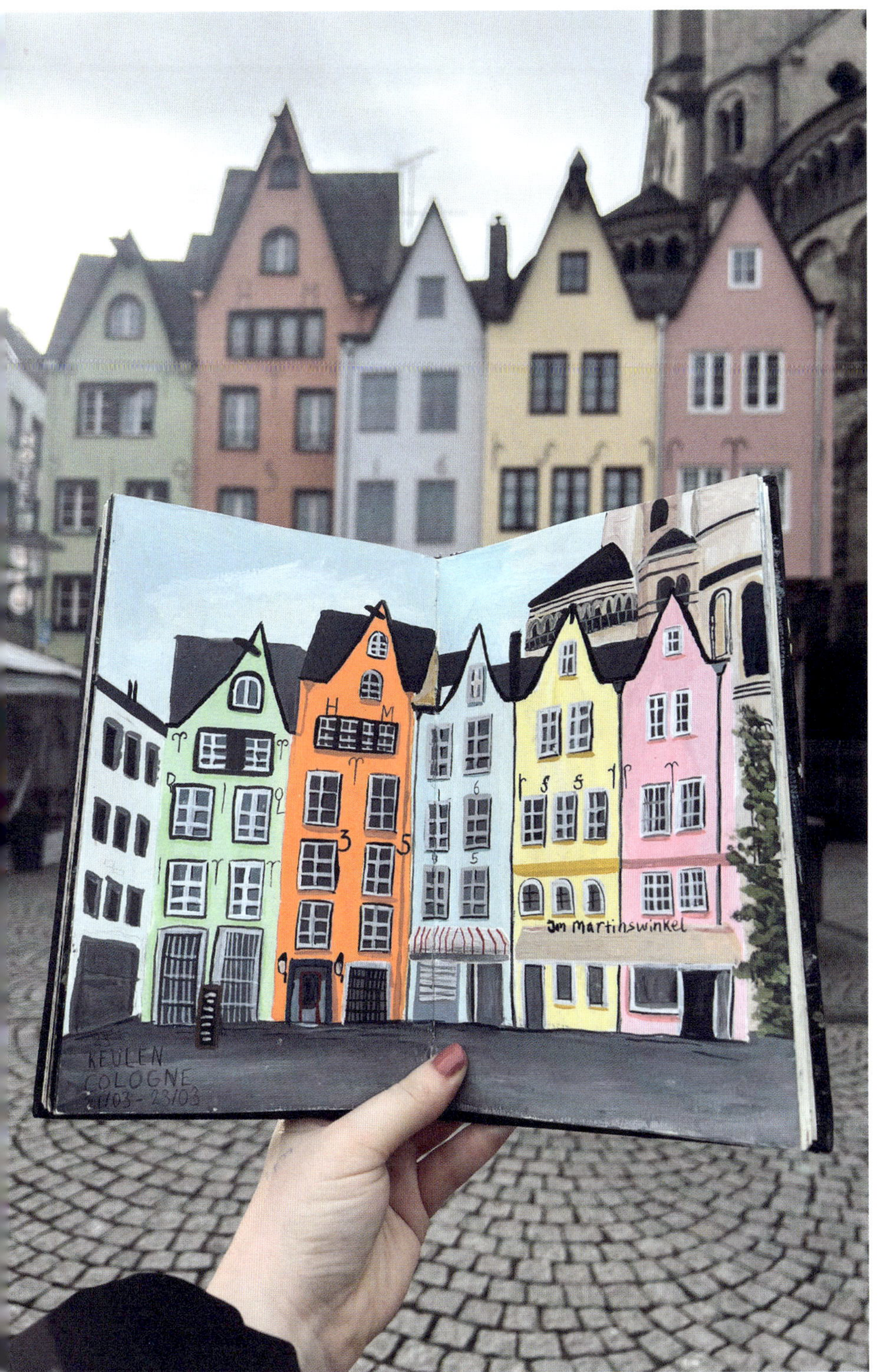

Im Martinswinkel
KEULEN
COLOGNE
21/03 - 23/03

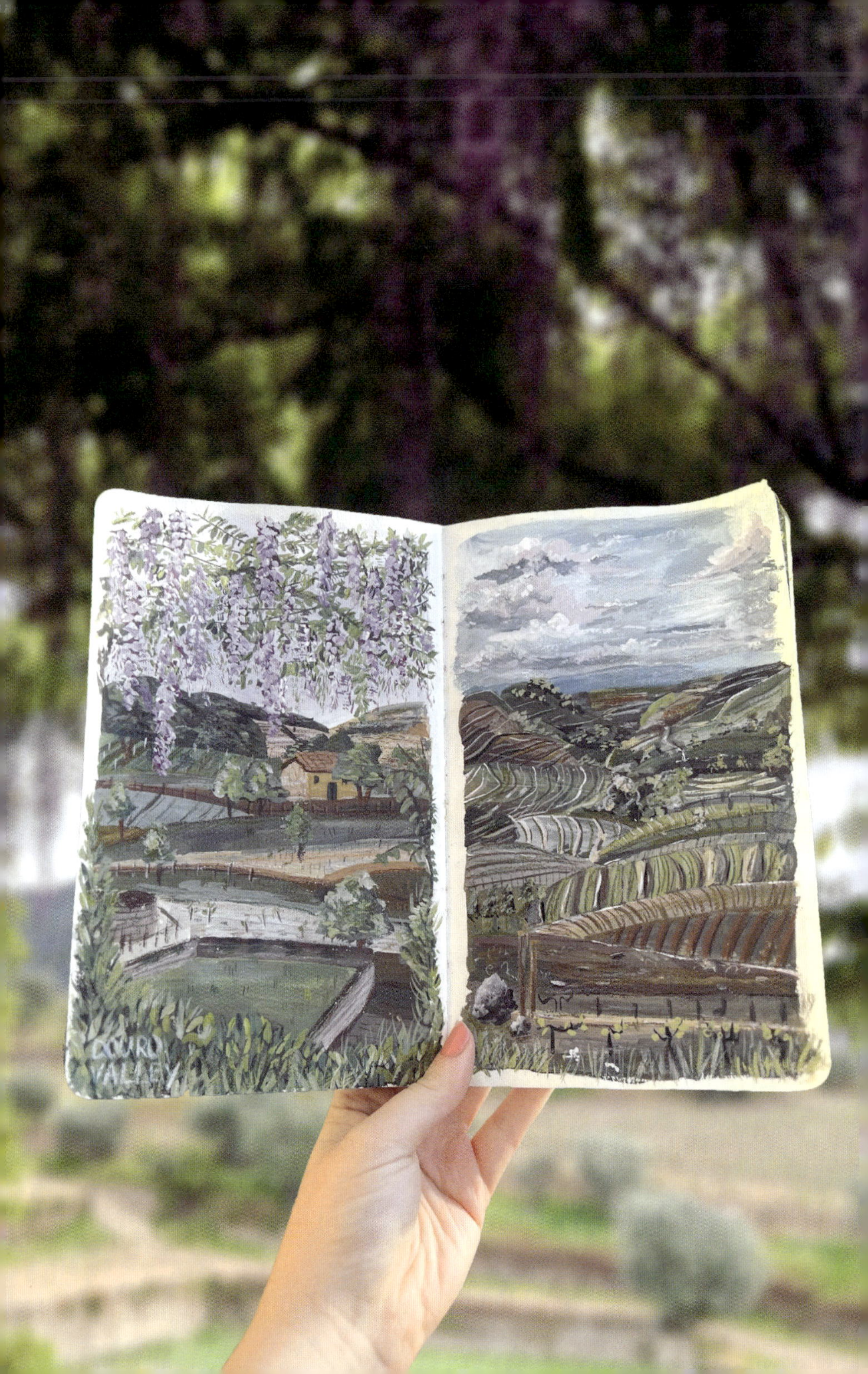

DOURO
VALLEY

CHAPTER 7

PAINTING NATURE

Have you ever gazed at a mountain peak from afar or hiked to a mesmerising lake, wishing you could capture the view in your memory? I certainly have. One way to bring that experience closer is by taking your art supplies with you and translating the colours and depth of nature onto paper.

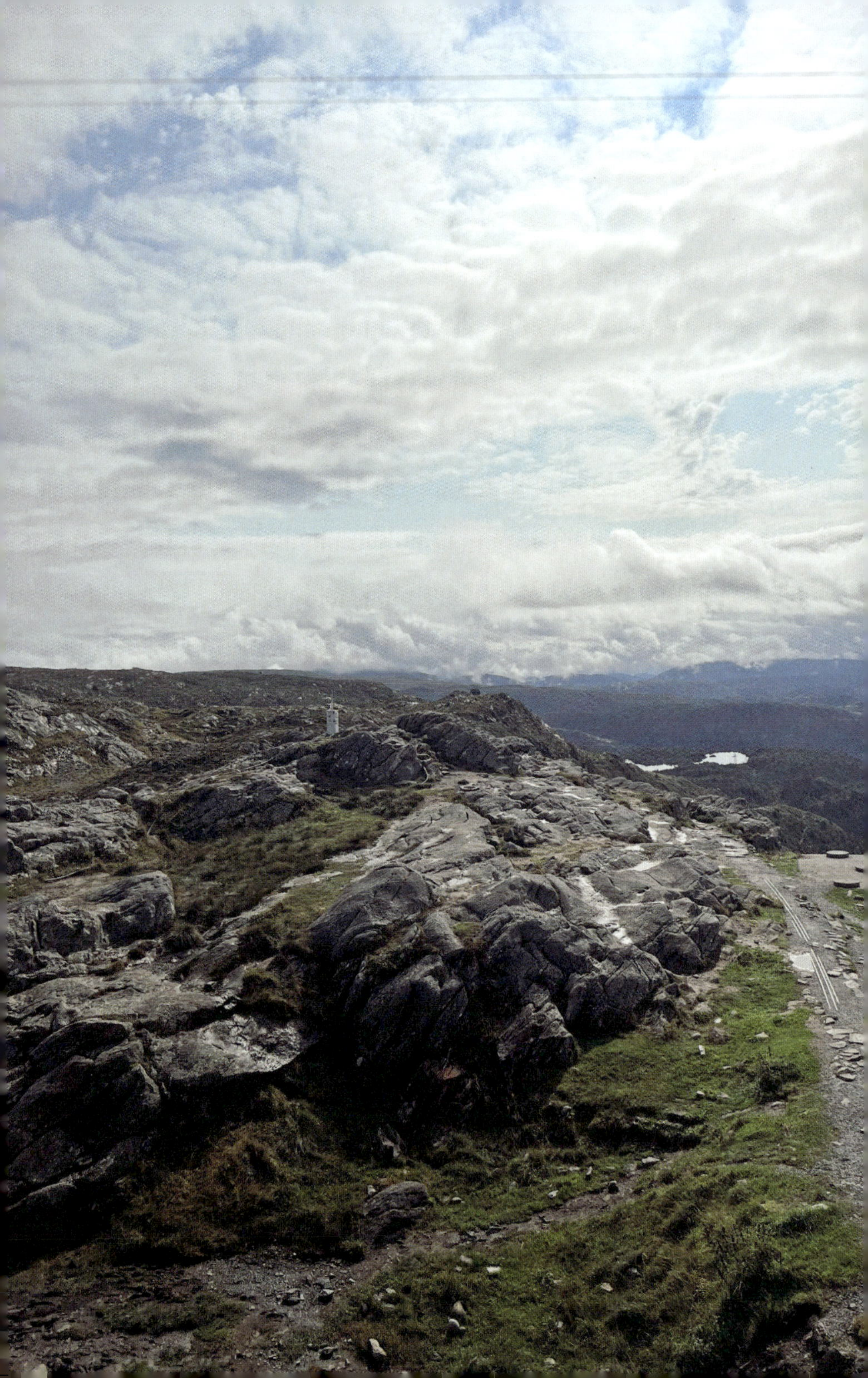

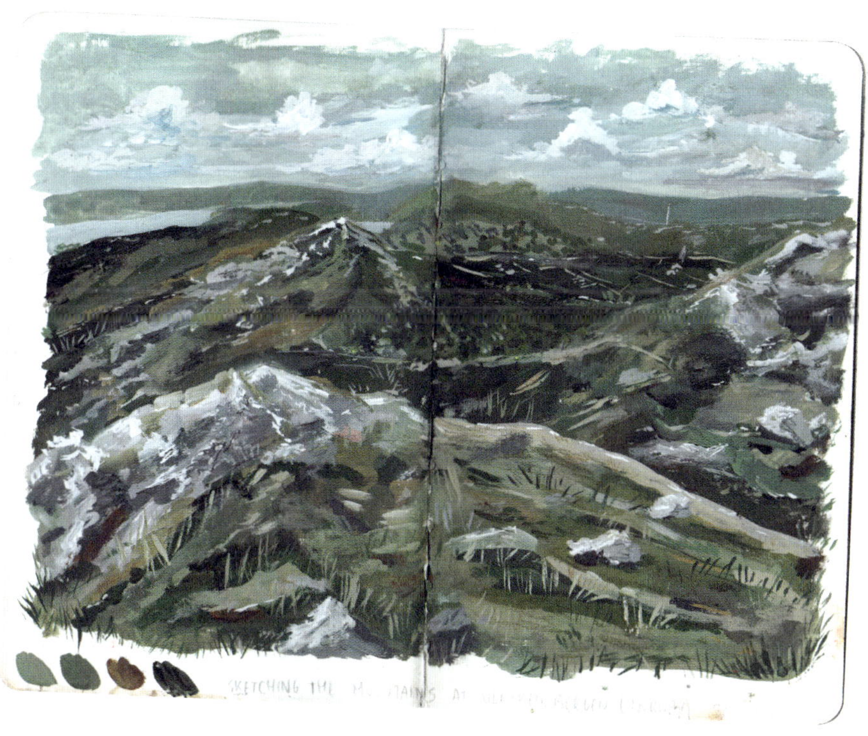

Peaks and panoramas

It was during one of my last days in Bergen (Norway) that I took the cable car up to mountain Ulriken. From the top, you have magnificent views of the city and the region, with the sea and rugged coastlines. The ground was rather muddy and not very suitable for further exploring. Fortunately, there were many spots on the terrace, on the rocks, and inside the nearby café where I could sit to capture my surroundings. I decided to paint what captured my attention most: the serene fjords with their deep blue waters and the mountains covered by lush greenery.

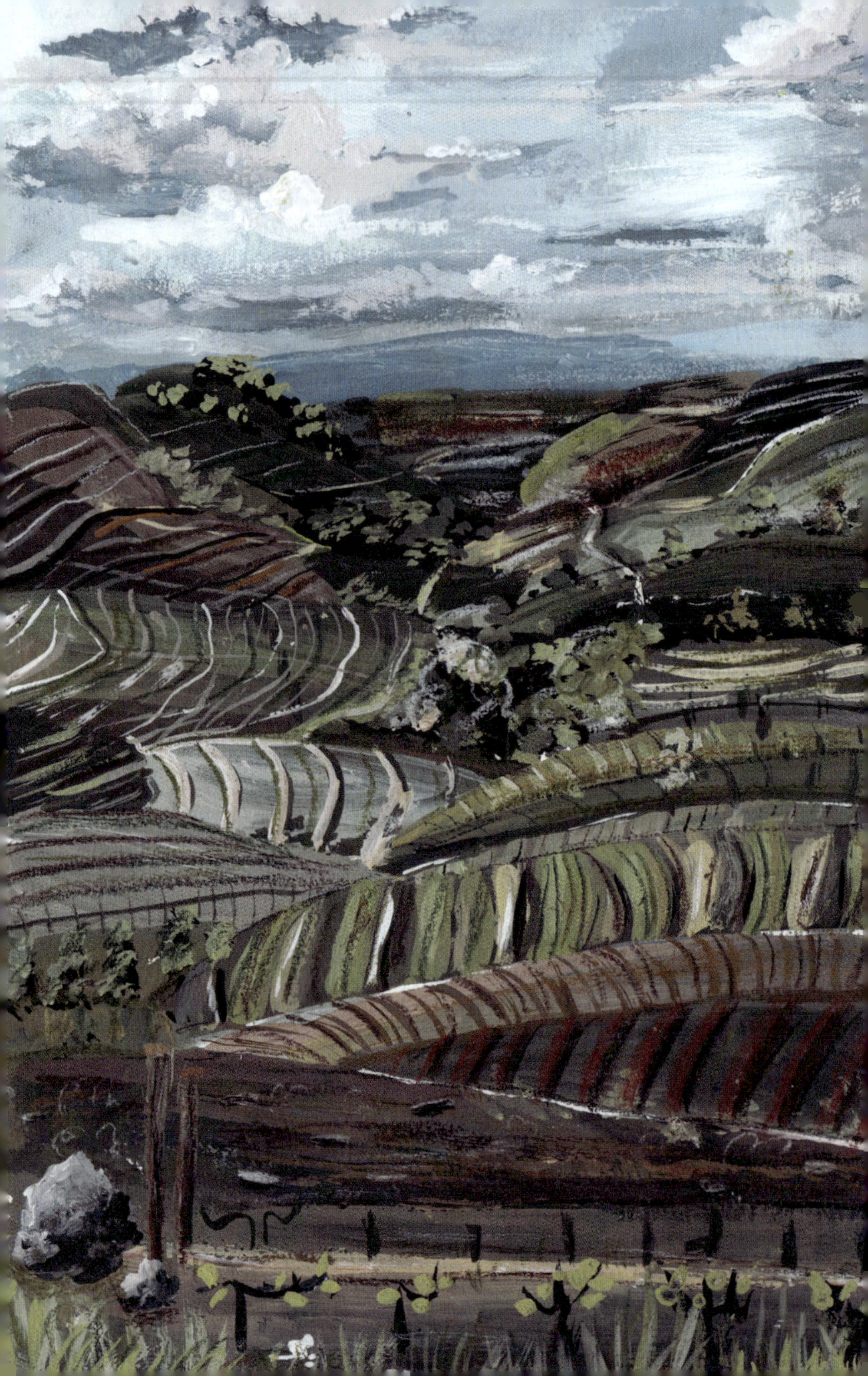

Painting rocks and mountains

Whether you're aiming to capture rocks or mountains, start by observing the contrasts between dark and light surfaces.

Sketch

Make a sketch of the outlines first.

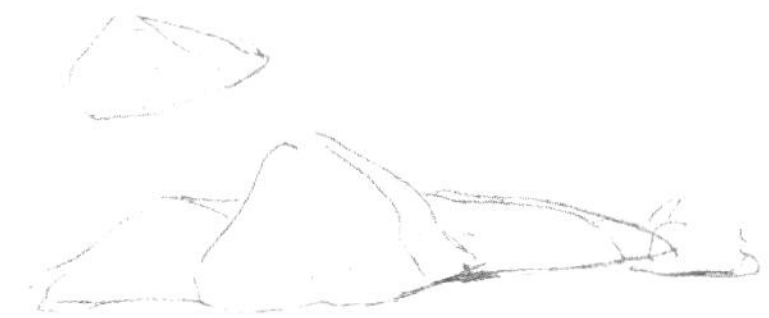

Paint

Use light and dark grey paints to match the values. Use earth tones like olive, ochre, umber, or burnt sienna for the surrounding nature. Grab a dark grey pencil to add textures by making irregular dashes and indentations.

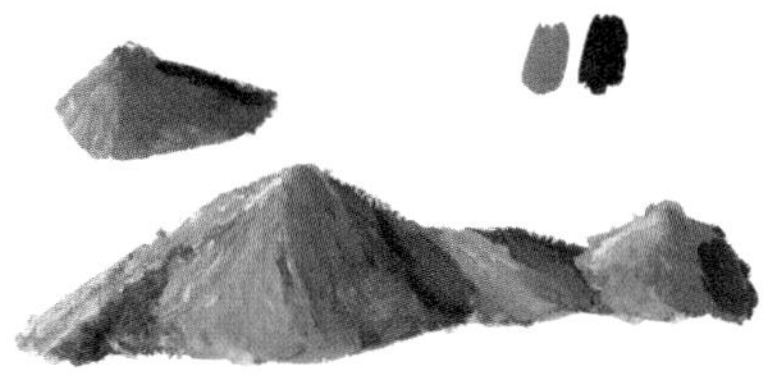

Adjust

It may take some time to achieve the right colours and gradients, so keep layering and adjusting until you're happy with the result.

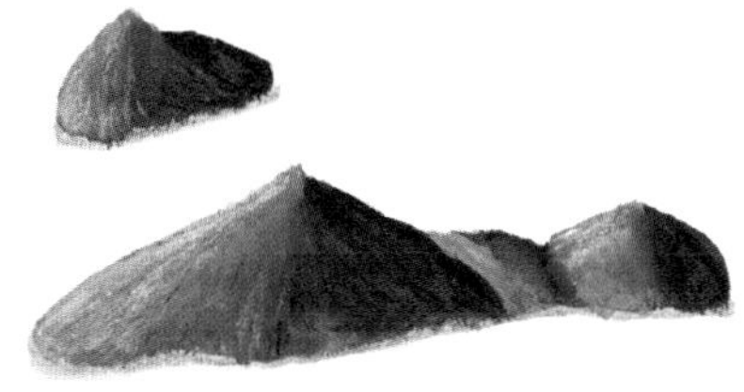

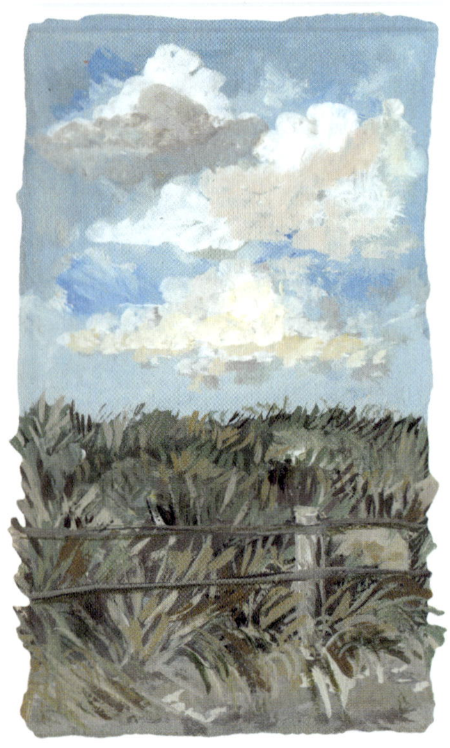 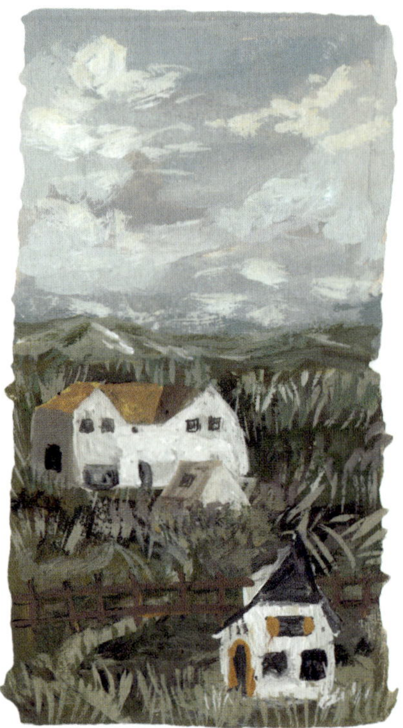

Adding shadows

Shadows are present in multiple places, such as on the opposite side of a light source, underneath objects (think of the edge of a roof or the brim of a hat), in crevices, cracks, folds, and wrinkles, and along edges where light falls off or meets another surface (such as the transition from river to bank).

Shadows in the foreground are usually darker and more defined, while those in the background are more diffused. In any case, shadows are rarely pure black; they are often hints of the surrounding colours and can vary depending on the light source. For example, outdoor shadows may have a bluish tone due to the sky's reflection.

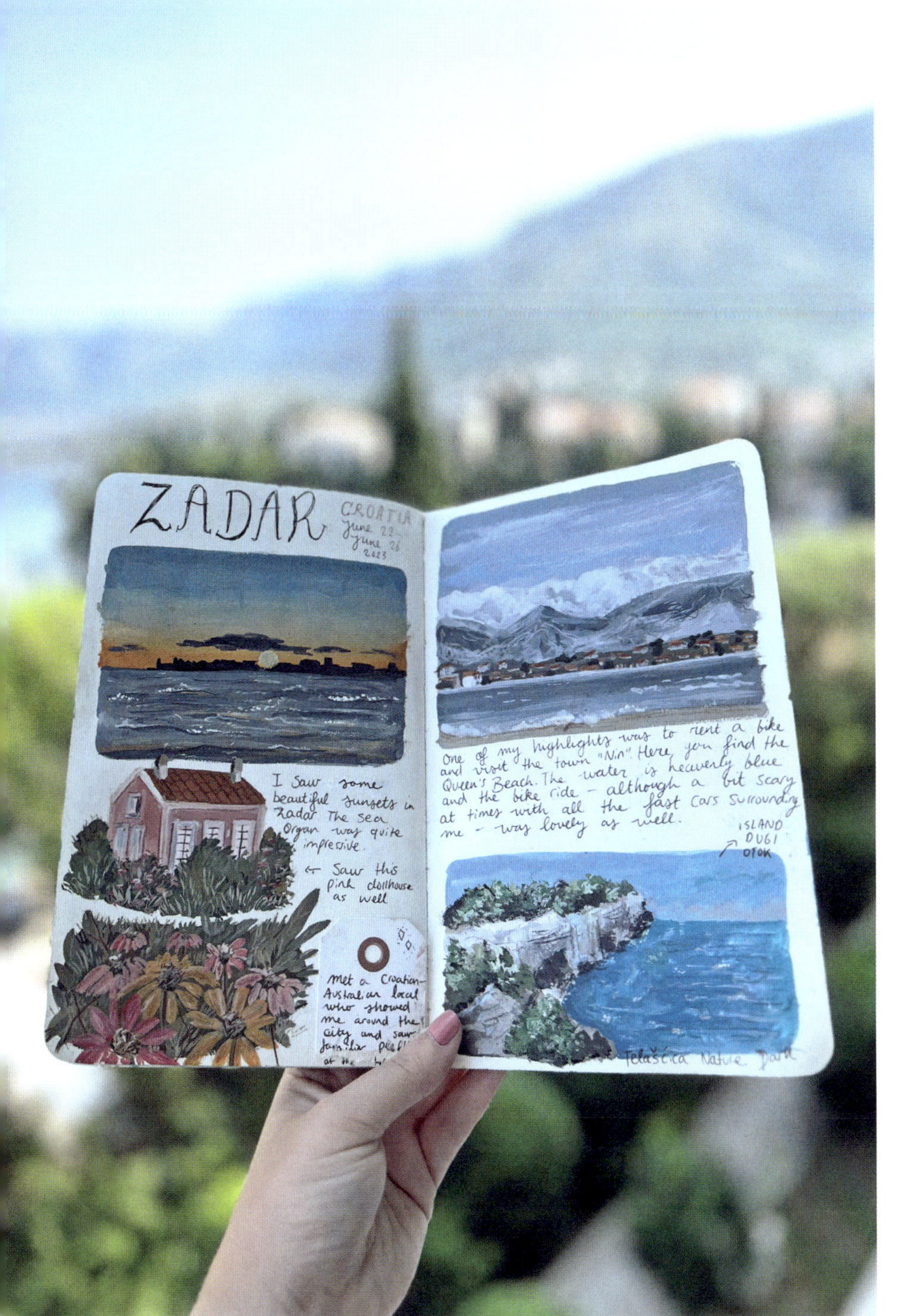

ZADAR
CROATIA
June 22 –
June 26
2023

I saw some
beautiful sunsets in
Zadar. The sea
Organ was quite
impressive.

← Saw this
pink dollhouse
as well

Met a Croatian-
Australian local
who showed
me around the
city and saw
familiar plants
at the

One of my highlights was to rent a bike
and visit the town "Nin". Here, you find the
Queen's Beach. The water is heavenly blue
and the bike ride – although a bit scary
at times with all the fast cars surrounding
me – way lovely as well.

ISLAND
DUGI
OTOK

Telašćica Nature Park

Painting trees

There are several ways to paint trees. If you're aiming for a more minimalistic tree, you can start by painting just its shape. Use a thinner brush to add the trunk and branches. If you wish to paint a more detailed tree, follow these steps.

Shape and size the tree

Carefully study the details of the tree trunk and sketch the shape with a pencil. This helps the tree's placement on your page. Pay attention to its size, especially the top, to ensure it fits well on your page.

Paint the trunk

Use various shades of brown. Start with a dark brown base and adjust the colour slightly each time: warm it up with red or ochre, or cool it down with blue or black. Consider adding darker colours on the left side and lighter colours on the right for depth and realism.

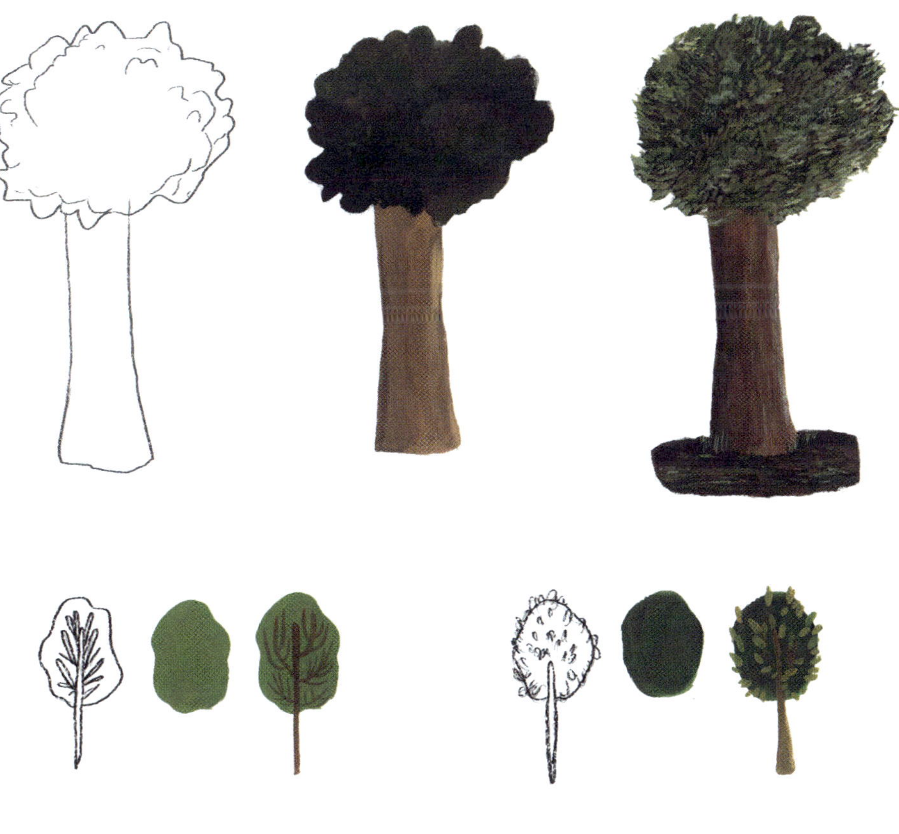

Paint the foliage

Use a round brush. Apply alternating shades of dark green in a circular motion, creating a cloud-like effect around the tree trunk. Paint various leaves and alternate colours and sizes by connecting arches above and below.

Add details

Apply greenery to the tree trunk and possibly on the ground, such as bits of moss and fallen leaves. Use a thin brush to add dashes and other details to the tree trunk. You may add branches to your tree, or blend them into the foliage to add a realistic touch.

Painting leaves

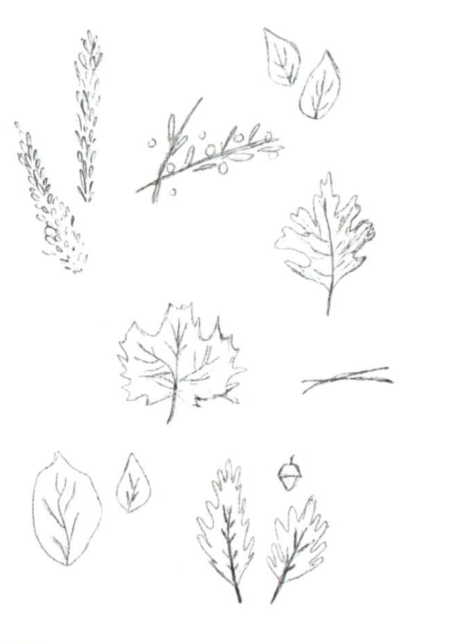

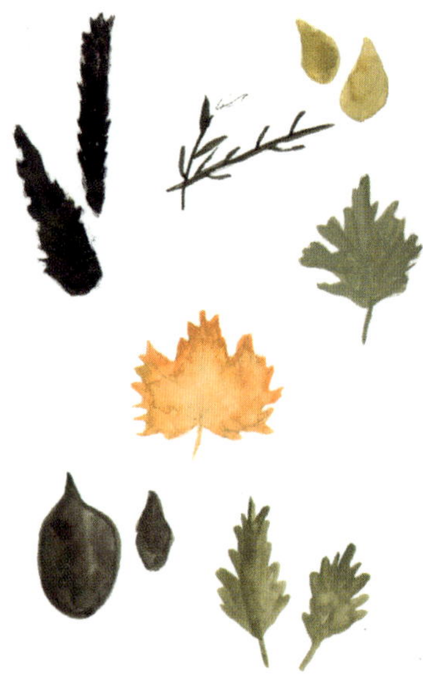

Study the leaf

Do this to understand its shape, veins, and texture. Explore a variety of leaves, either by researching different types or by gathering some from your garden, neighbourhood, or local woods for inspiration.

Begin with a light pencil sketch

Outline the shape and major veins.

Mix the appropriate colours

Typically, you'll need shades of green with variations for highlights and shadows. For autumn leaves, you can choose a warmer palette with browns and oranges. Blend the colours carefully, and avoid using too much water so you can still see the transitions between the colours and prevent them from blending into a muddy shade.

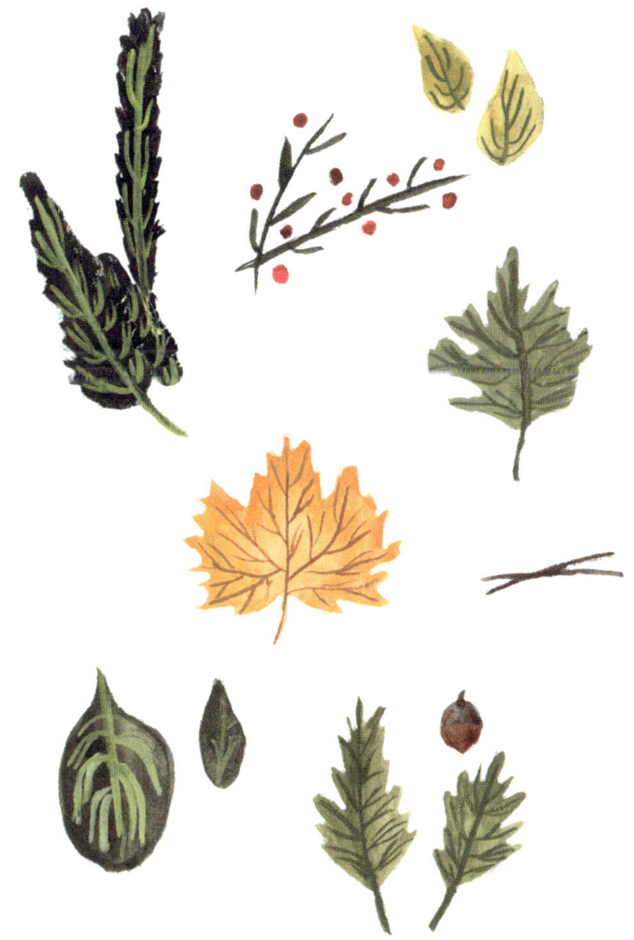

Start painting

Begin with a light wash of the base colour. Allow it to dry before adding more layers.

Add details

Paint or draw the veins using a finer brush or a coloured pencil. Pay attention to their direction and pattern. Apply darker shades of green for shadows and lighter shades for highlights. Together, they create depth and dimension.

Woodlands and forests

When painting woods or a forest, keep the background light to create a mysterious, misty look. Use a light green to paint trees in the background. Once the paint is dry, lightly moisten your work to make the trees appear slightly blurry. This creates distance and depth, making it look as if these trees are far away. Paint a second layer with slightly larger trees.

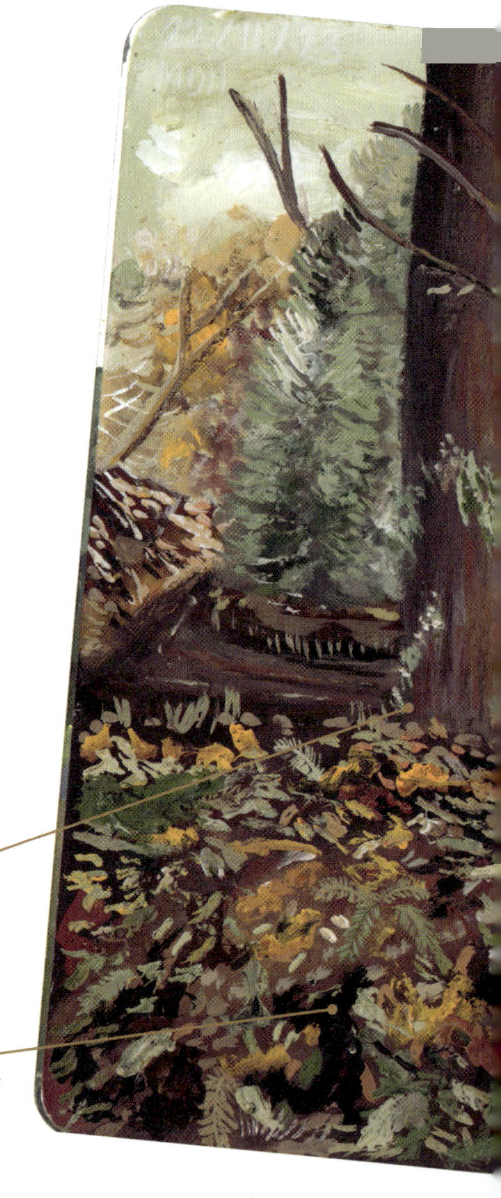

Finish your forest by adding shadows and highlights.

Adjust your palette to the season. Use warmer colours in autumn, and consider bare branches or snow in winter.

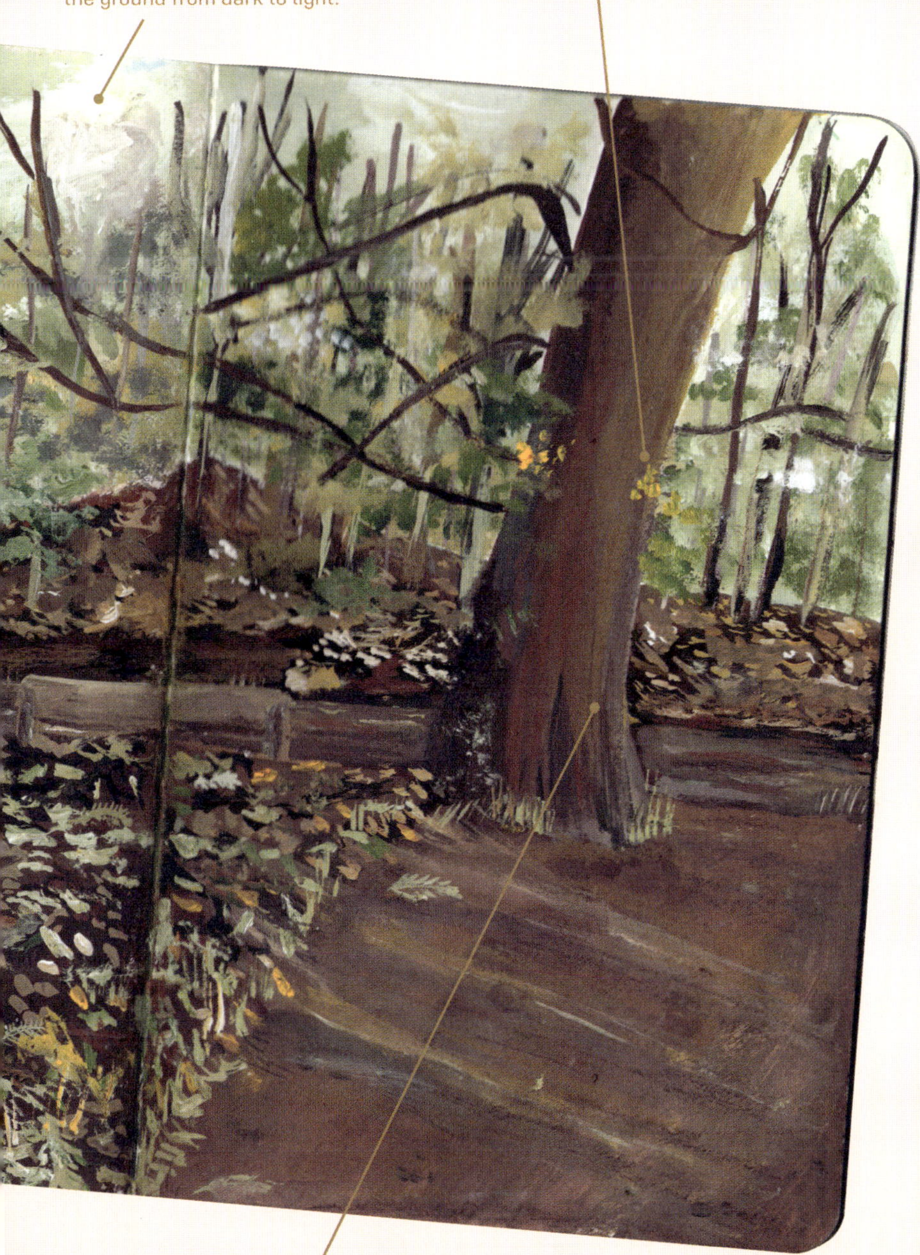

Remember to build up your sky and the distant trees from light to dark and the ground from dark to light.
Use a thin brush to add leaves, focusing mainly on the nearest trees.
The closer the trees are, the taller, larger, and more detailed they should appear in your artwork.

Dip your finger in white paint and dab this in circular motions on the paper to create the shape of a cloud. Add a bit of colour and blend it softly to integrate the cloud into the sky.

When painting clouds, use a round brush and make circular strokes to create the shapes. Layer clouds to add depth, and vary their shades to create contrast – darker at the bottom and lighter towards the top.

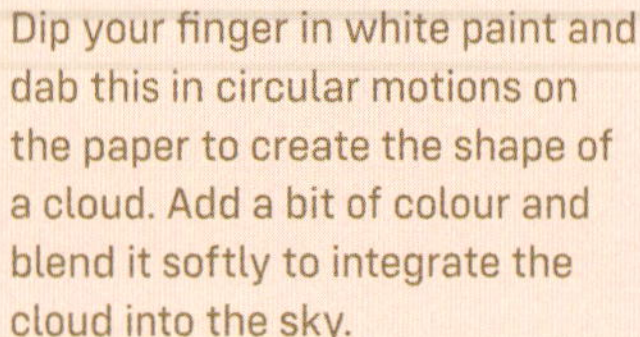

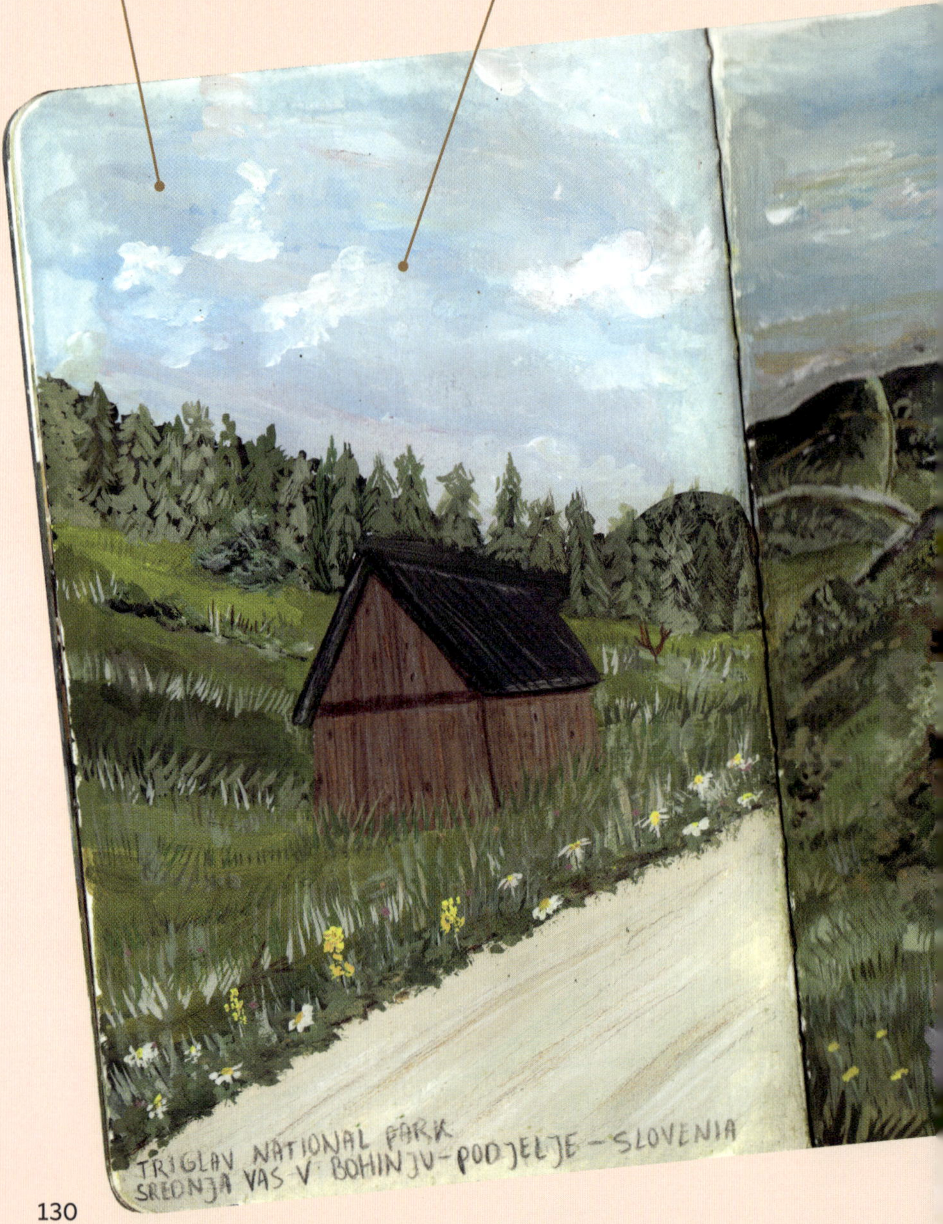

Cloudscapes

When I paint the sky, I work from top to bottom. I start with darker colours and blend gently to lighter shades. A large, flat brush works best as this covers wide strokes and large areas efficiently. To know which colours to use, it's useful to make swatches in advance as colours usually appear a bit different on paper than in tubes. When it comes to gouache paint, light colours dry slightly darker while dark colours dry lighter.

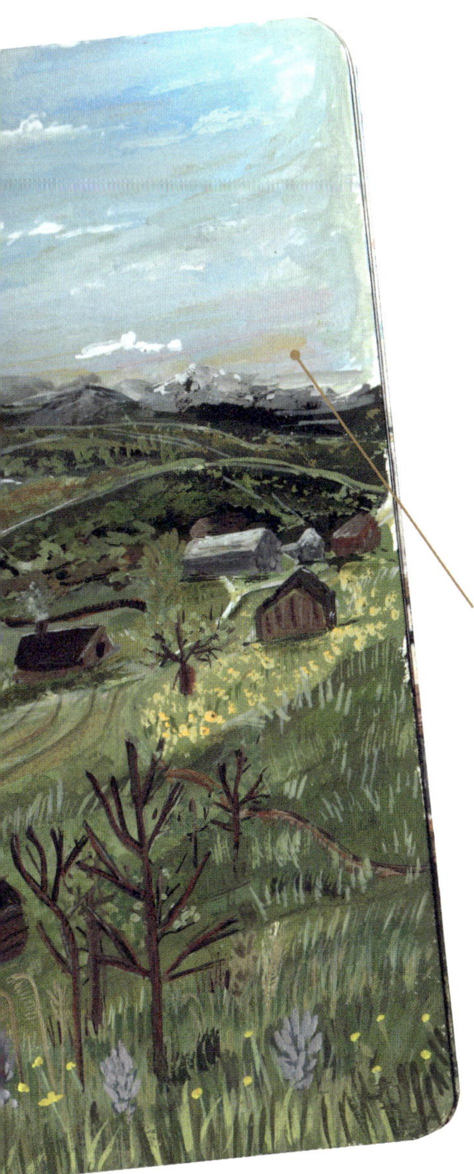

Add an unexpected colour to your sky, like neon pink. Blending it carefully can create an interesting effect. Pastel colours like lilac or Naples yellow also work well. Bonus points if you reflect these colours in a river.

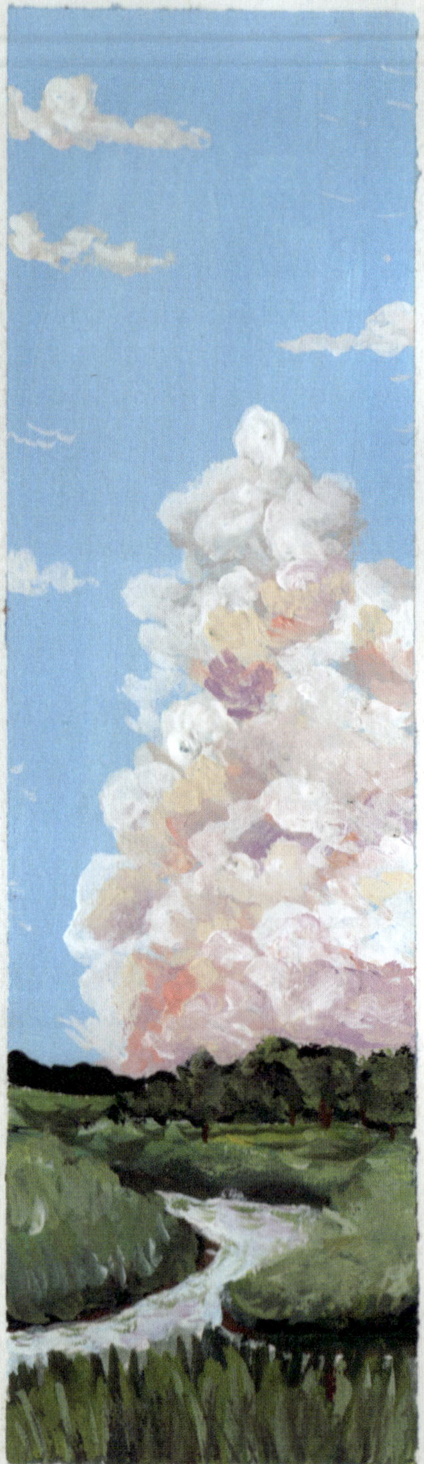

lost
in

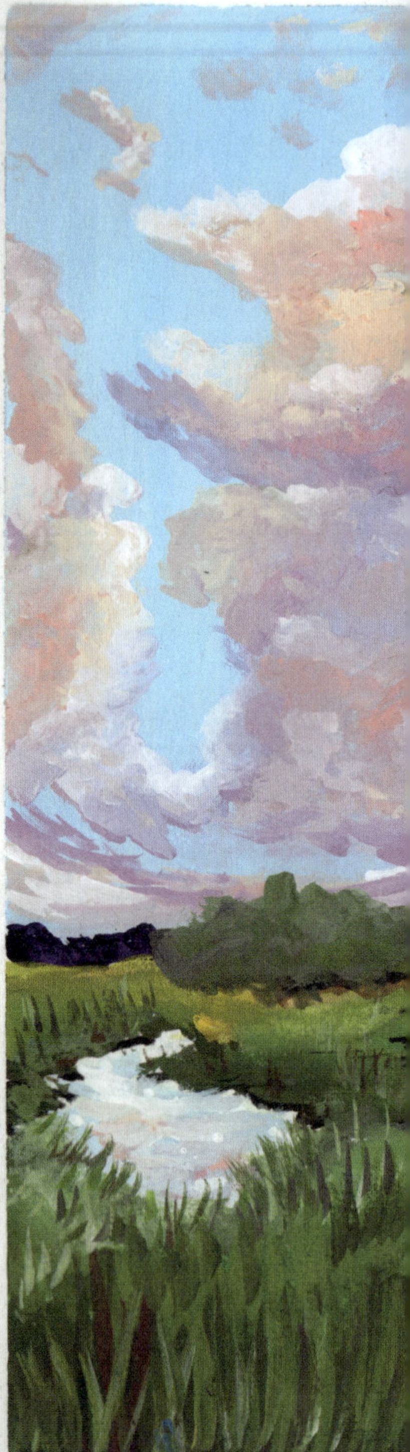

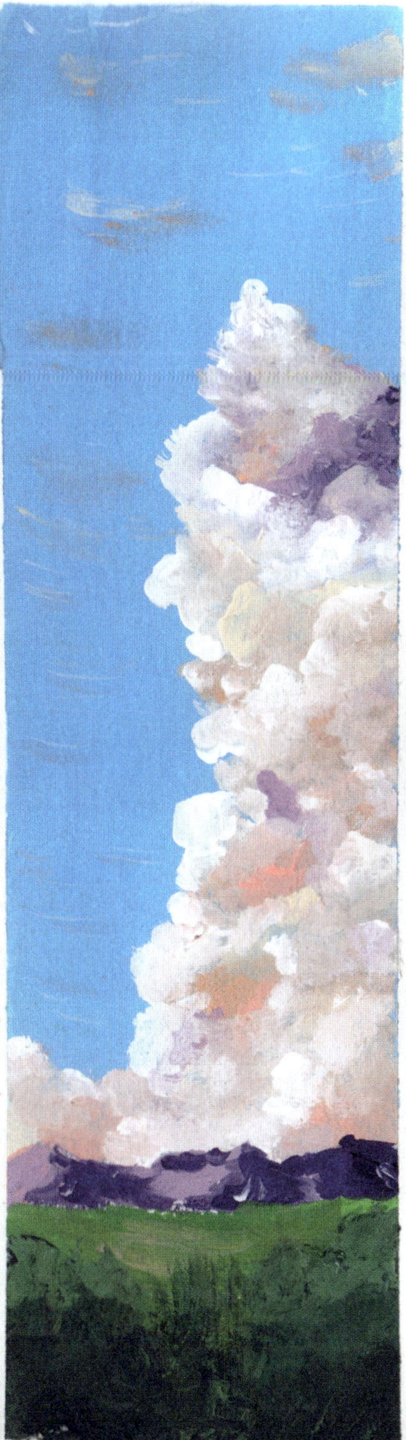

dreamy scenes

Painting landscapes

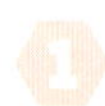

Map out what you want to paint
Use a reference photo or capture
the scene on location. Begin with
a loose pencil sketch to outline the
placement of different elements and
where the sky meets the landscape.
Choose your colours before you start
and mix your paints.

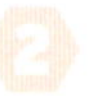

Work from top to bottom
Start with the sky. Whether it's
summer blue or stormy grey, use
a large brush and blend different
colours with water. Make sure the
sky is dry before moving on to paint
the landscape below.

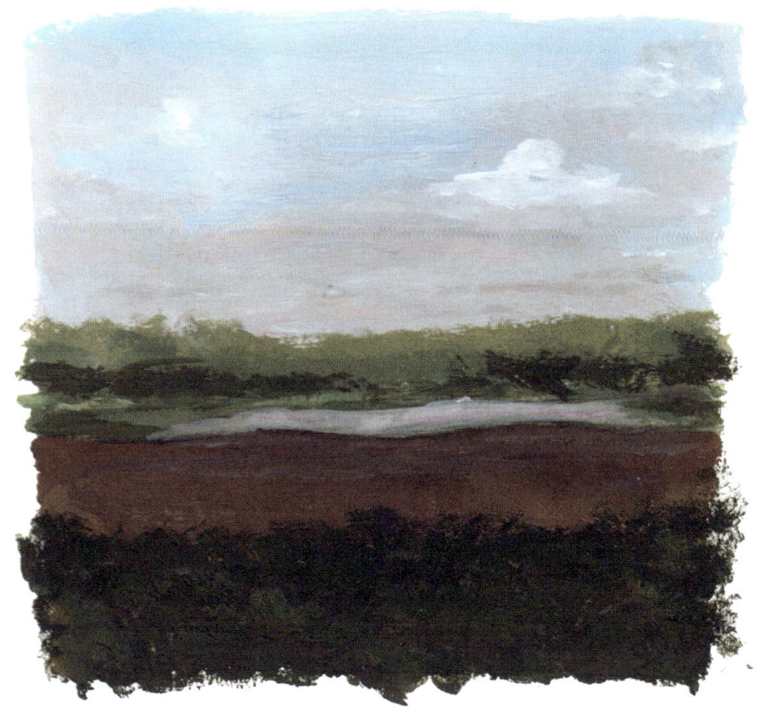

Paint the clouds and the ground
Do this after your sky has dried.
Build your landscape in layers. Start
by painting the ground for hills or
grassy areas. Add more layers if
needed to adjust colours or make
the area more opaque.

Add texture
Gently dip a dry brush into paint and
dab it onto the surface. Alternate
between colours such as olive green,
ochre, and dark brown or umber.

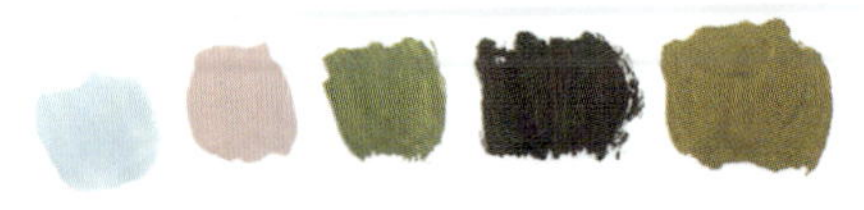

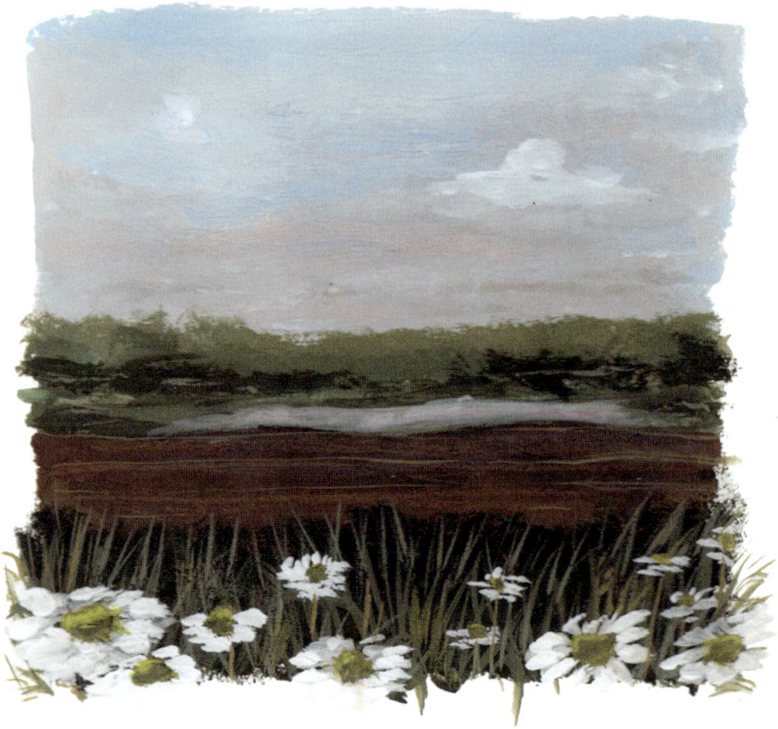

Add details

Use a fine brush to paint thin lines resembling (light and dark) blades of grass. Vary their sizes, and experiment with the paint-to-water ratio for precise strokes. Optionally, add flowers in the foreground and/or background. Paint highlights by mixing white with ochre to create a warm, light colour and add a few dots or dashes. Optionally, use earth-toned pencils like olive green, umber, yellow, burnt sienna, and light brown. Polychromos pencils are great because they apply smoothly, don't smudge, and can be layered. Wax pencils are also a good option for adding soft highlights or subtle shadows. Use them lightly to avoid smudging.

Remember while painting that objects in the foreground are much larger and more detailed than those in the background. Don't focus too much on details in the background, instead give attention to the elements that you place in the very front.

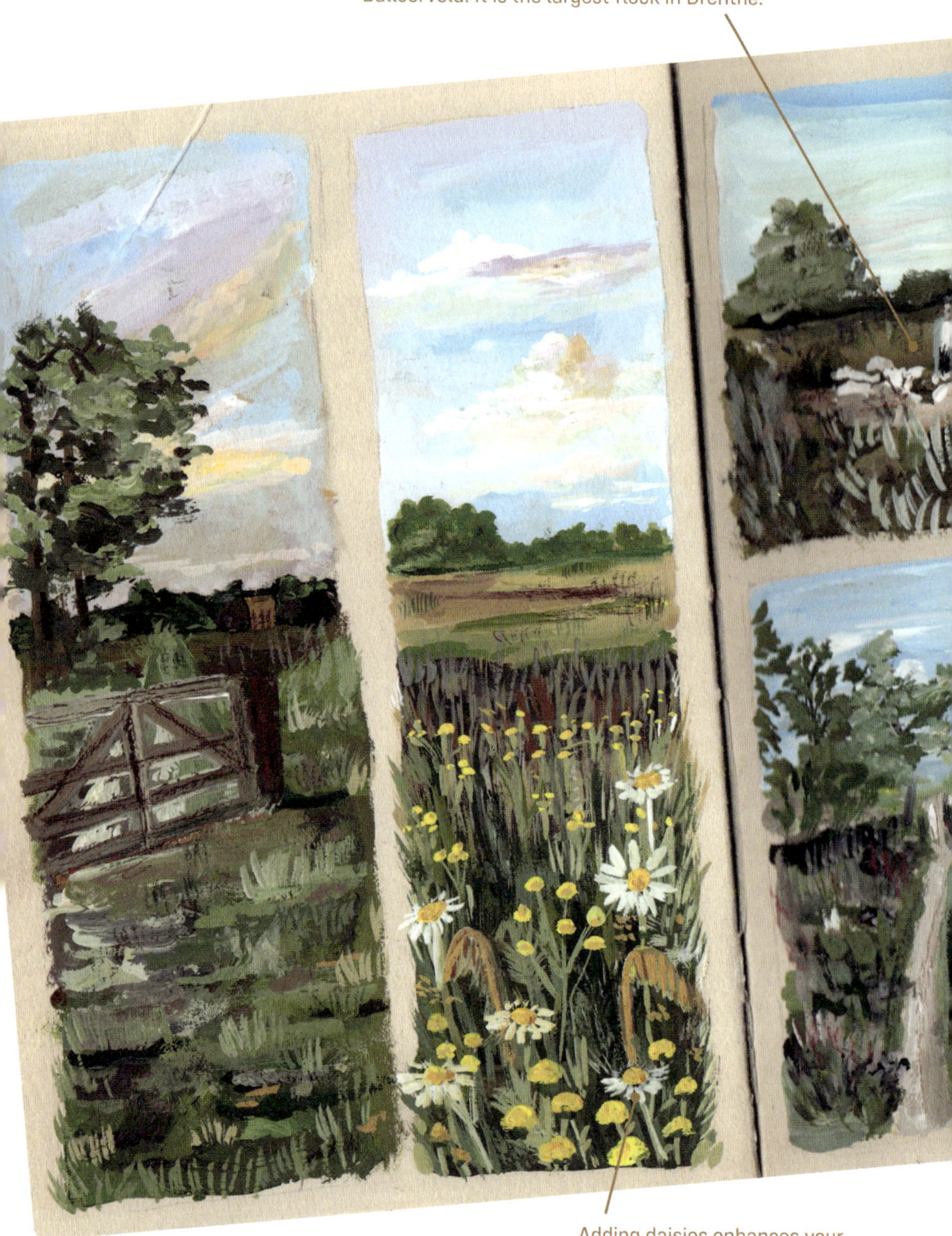

I captured the flock of Drenthe Heath Sheep on Balloërveld. It is the largest flock in Drenthe.

Adding daisies enhances your page. I enjoy including them to add interest to landscapes.

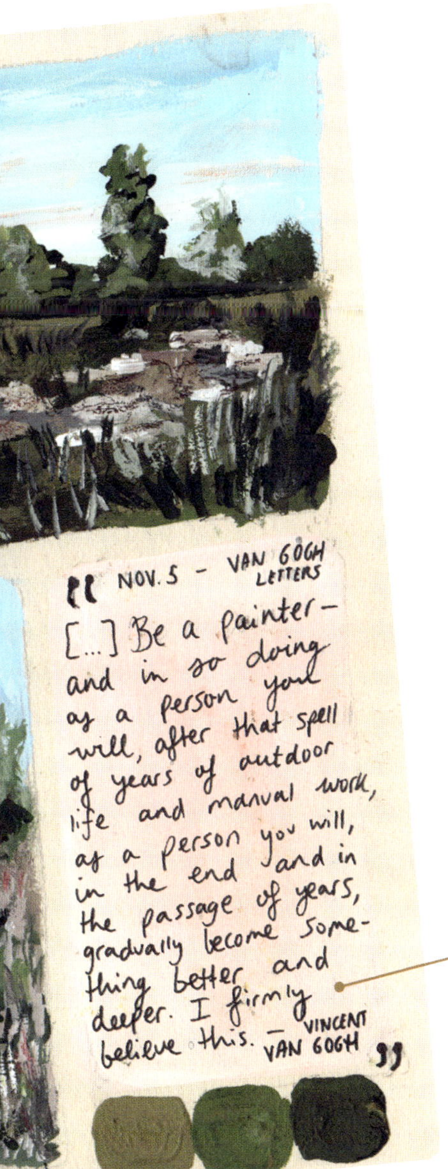

A painter's journey

For these pages, I followed in Van Gogh's footsteps. About a century before me, he arrived by train in Hoogeveen. He spent three months in the southeastern part of the Drenthe province of the Netherlands, producing a lot of works depicting farms with stacks of peat, workers, women on the peat moor, and landscapes. On these pages I captured Drenthe as it appears today: surrounded by beautiful moors and woodlands. Worth a visit!

Usually, I don't write much when I capture landscapes during my travels, but here I included a quote from one of the letters Van Gogh sent to his brother while living in Drenthe.

Capturing Ameland

Ameland, one of the Dutch Wadden Islands, is an ideal destination to recover from the hustle and bustle of everyday life. Looking at these painted scenes brings back memories of beach walks, sunset views, exploring quaint villages, and cycling along the coast. I used masking tape to turn these scenes into framed mini paintings.

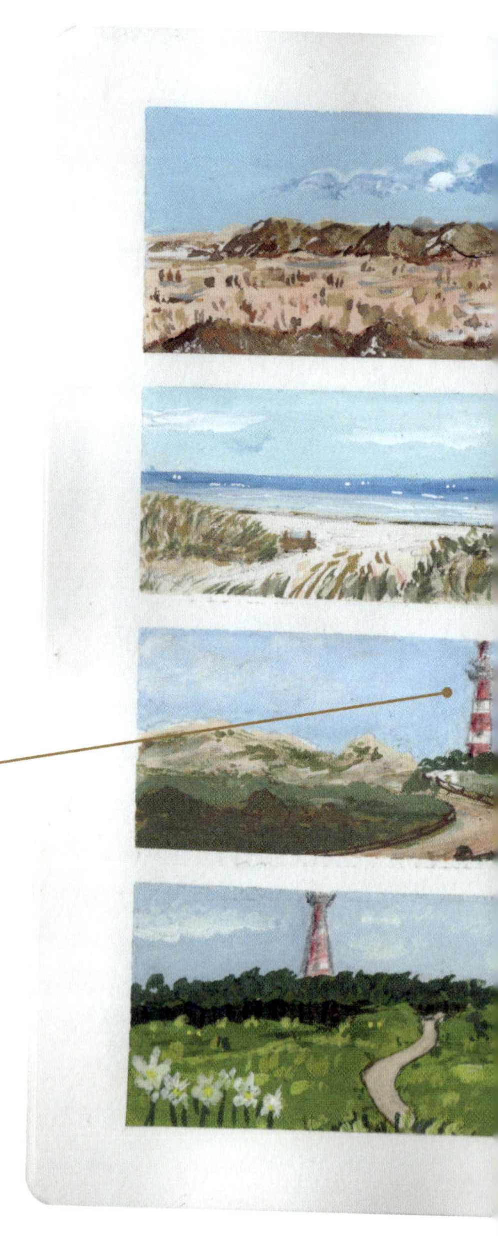

I painted the lighthouse by first outlining its shape with pencil. Afterwards, I filled it in with red and white paint. I added pencil, as the fine tips enable you to work more precisely, and it adds structure to the page. I used a dark red to add shadows, adding depth to the painting.

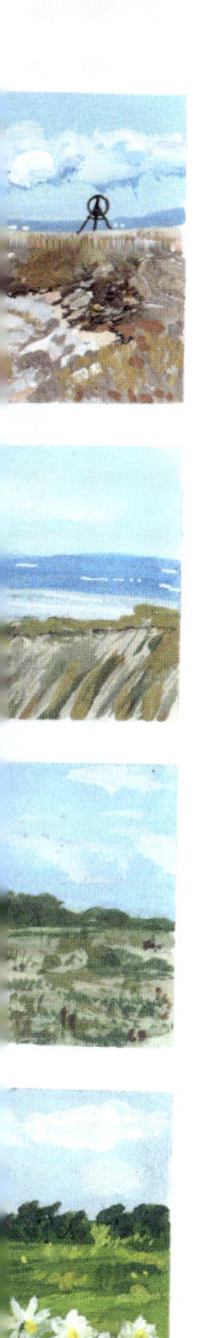

I used a cream colour for the dunes
and alternated it with dark green,
brown, and grey.

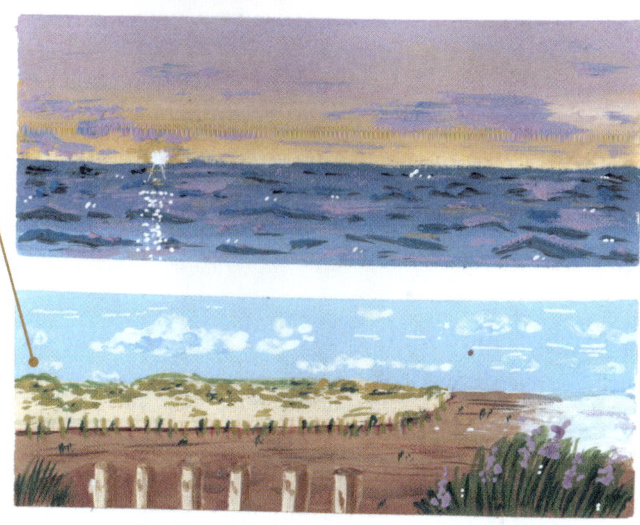

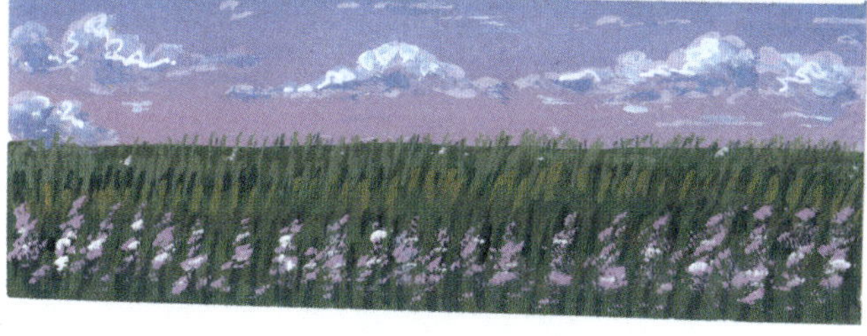

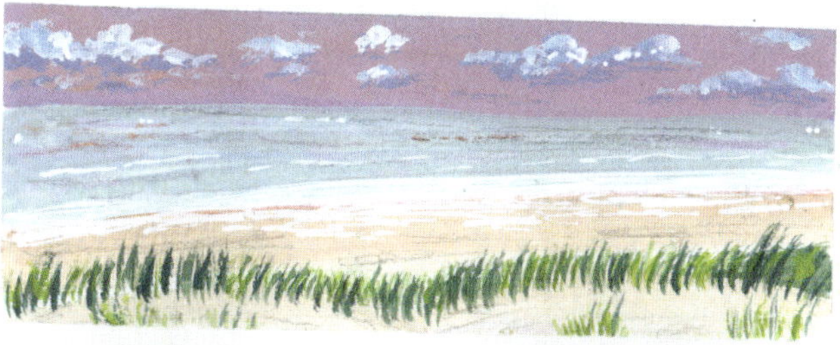

Painting water

When painting water, choose your colours carefully. Water often appears darker in the distance than up close. Use three colours that you can gradually blend into each other (think of navy blue to azure), and paint from top to bottom for a smooth transition. Make sure to reflect the sky's colours in it, this works especially well for a sunrise or sunset. Vary short and long strokes to depict flowing water. If you're painting calm water (such as a river or a lake), don't forget to include colours of objects, such as trees or bushes, near the water's edge.

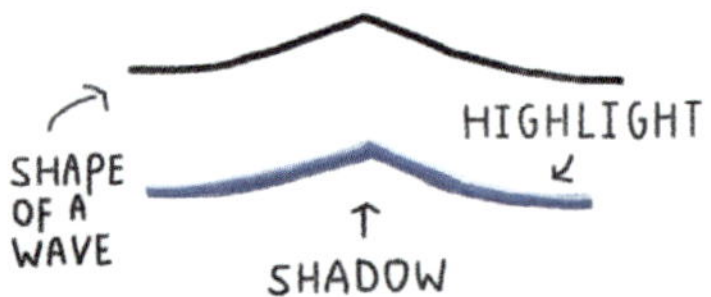

To create waves, use a thin brush and dark blue paint to create short, playful lines. Think of them as small peaks of miniature mountains.

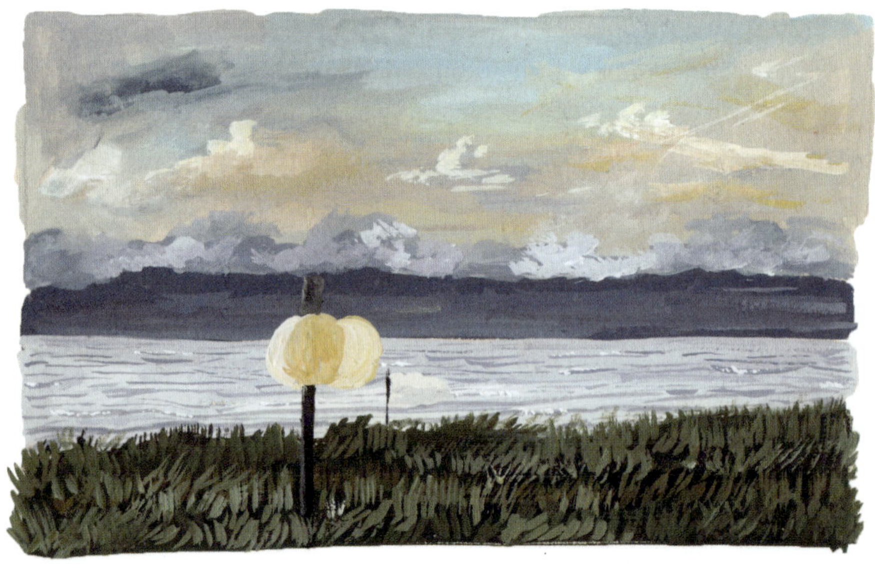

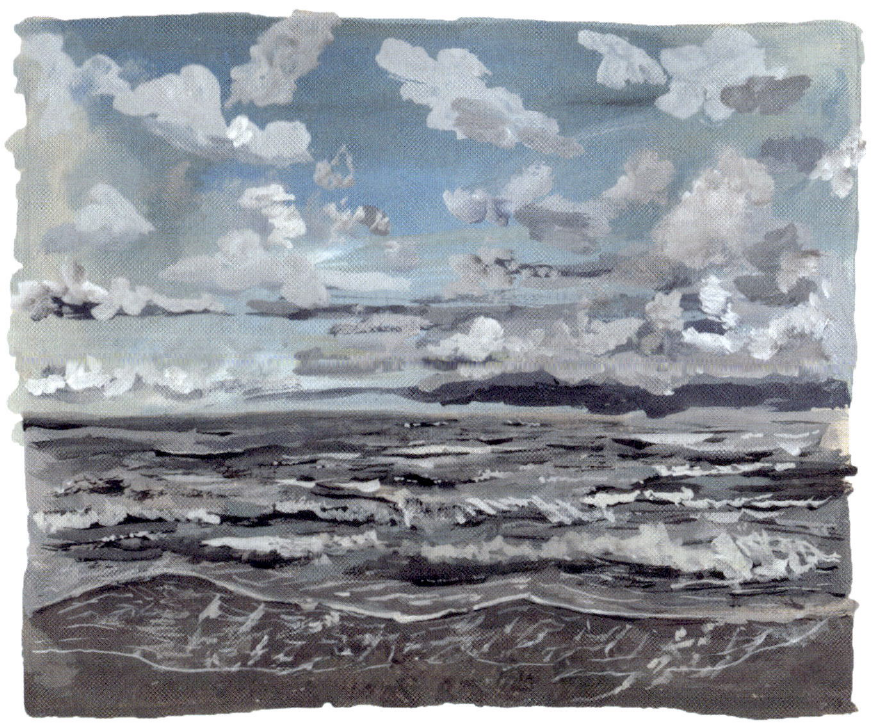

Start with smaller waves further away and gradually increase their size closer to the viewer. Use a darker colour beneath each wave and a lighter colour above to emphasise them. Add small dashes or dots at the tops of the waves to resemble foam or glimmers of sunlight. To make the foam stand out, use a dry brush dipped in white paint to gently stipple where you want it to appear. Use a white fineliner for highlights and coloured pencils for contrast, such as extra dashes in the water and a dark line to define the separation between the quay and the water.

Optional: add a boat, such as a canoe, motorboat, or yacht, to your painting. Start by sketching its shape to ensure accuracy. To add more life to your painting, you can also include people or birds, such as seagulls.

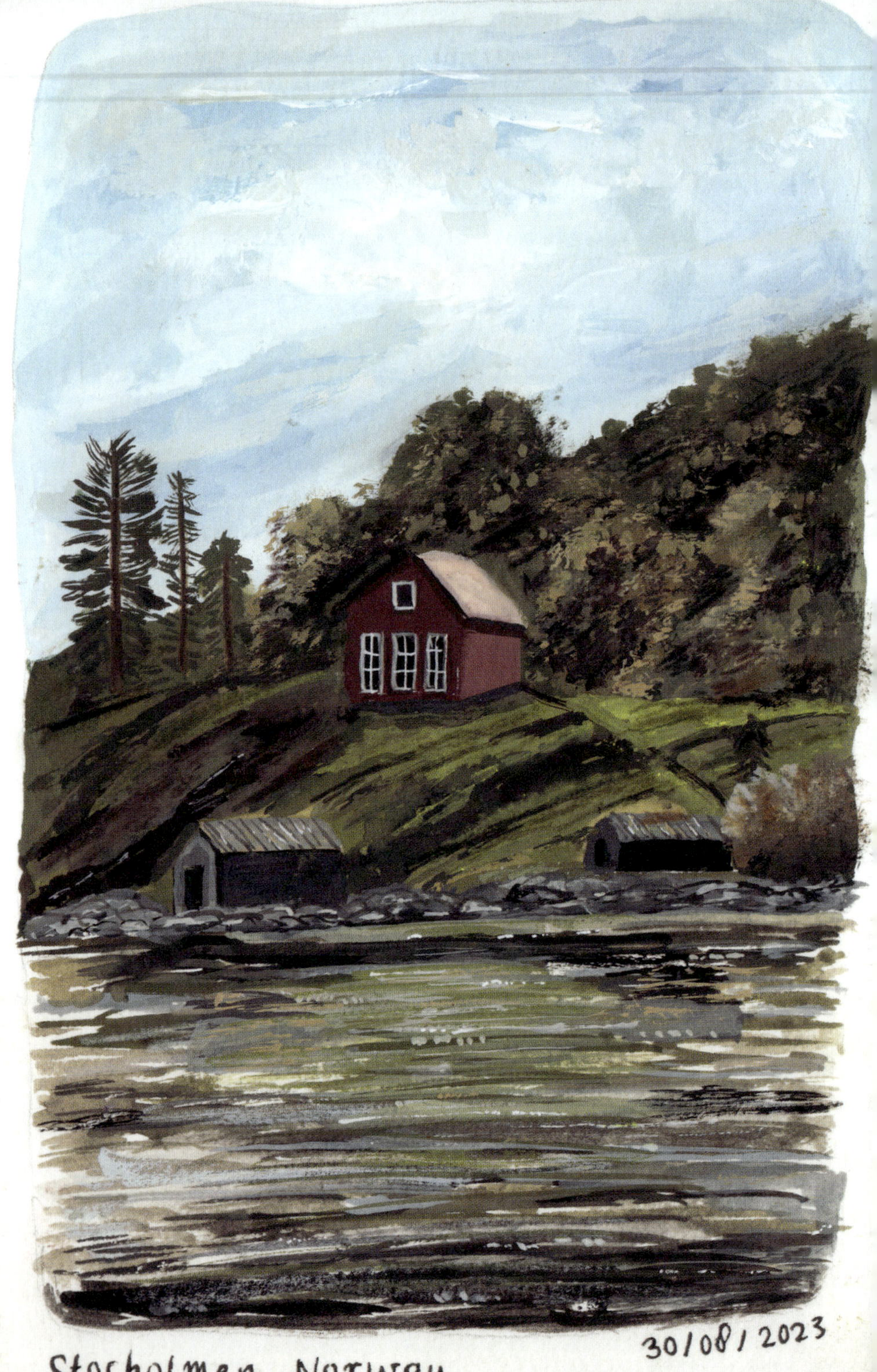

Storholmen, Norway
30/08/2023

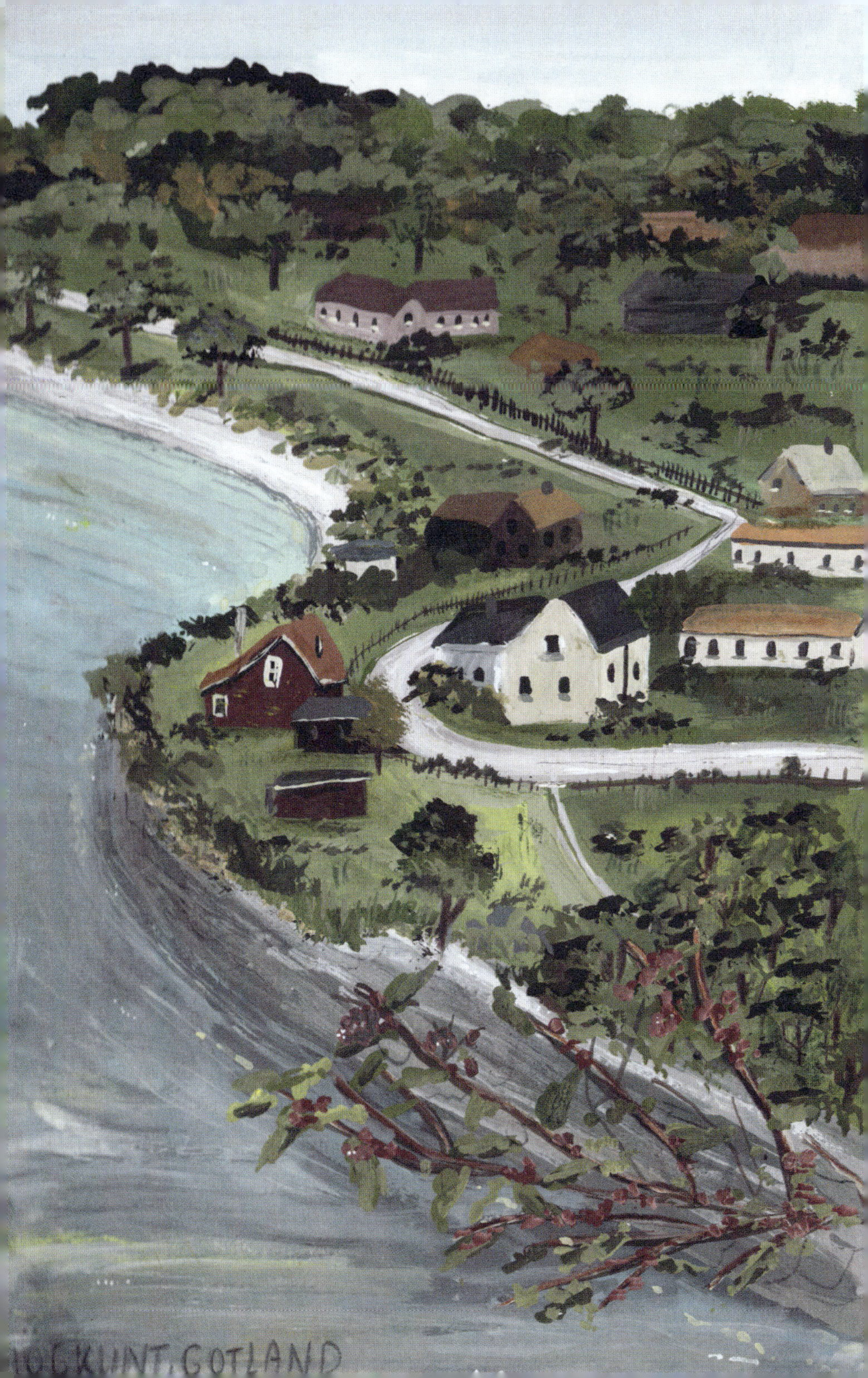

HOGKLINT, GOTLAND

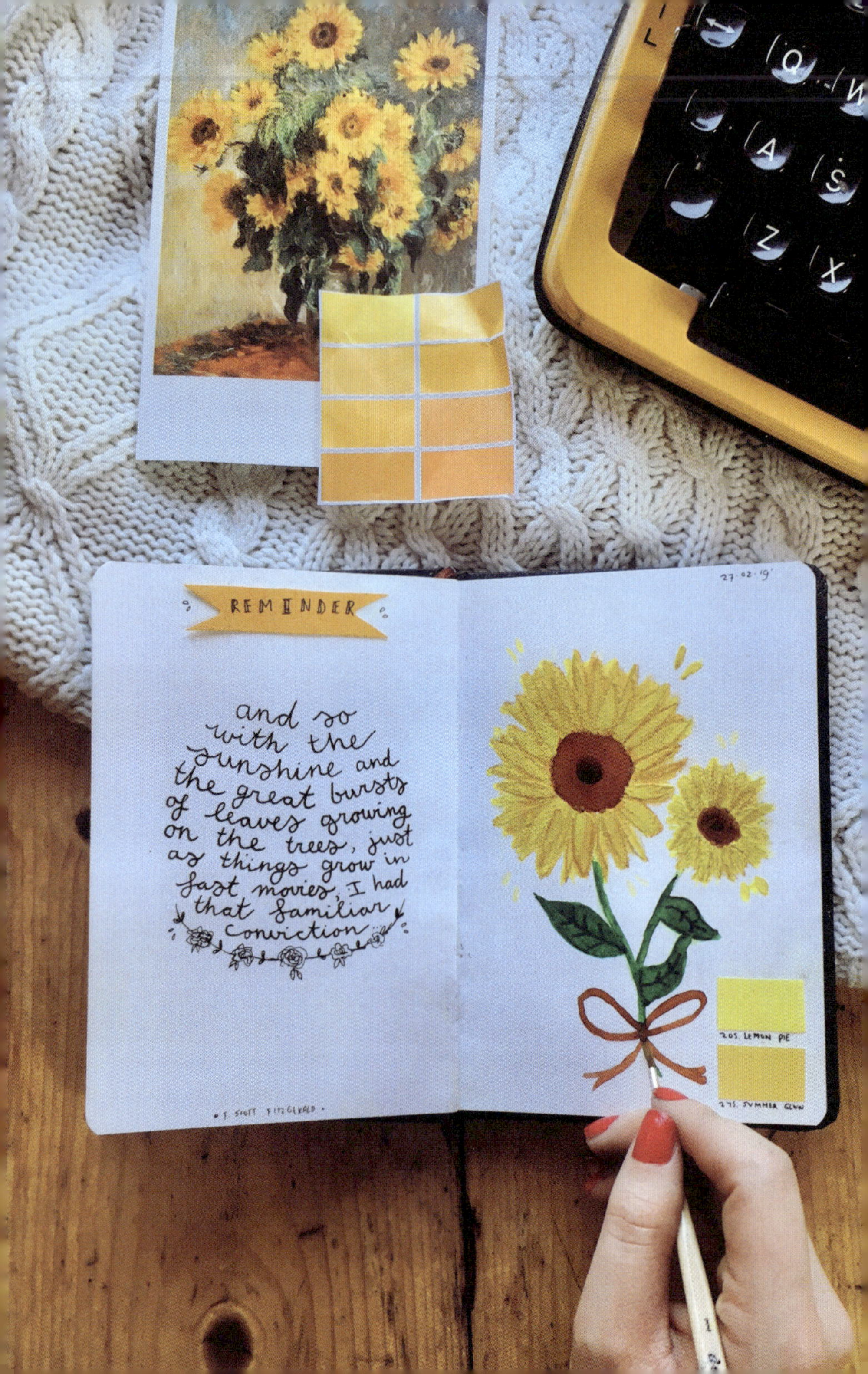

27.02.19
REMINDER
and so
with the
sunshine and
the great bursts
of leaves growing
on the trees, just
as things grow in
fast movies, I had
that familiar
conviction
F. SCOTT FITZGERALD
205. LEMON PIE
275. SUMMER GLOW

Painting flowers

When sketching flowers, I focus on the size and shape of the centres and petals rather than the small details. I draw the flowers in various shapes and sizes, including the stems and leaves. After that, I gather my colours and mix several variations (for example; I use cadmium red as well as maroon for roses) to paint the base layer, including the flower stem and leaves. If needed, I make adjustments along the way like adding petals, leaves, or enlarging the centre. I use a dark green to shade the stem and I extend it under the leaves.

I use a coloured pencil to bring more texture and focus to my painting. I use one that is similar to the colour of my flower petals and start outlining them. Sometimes I also use a contrasting green to emphasise the veins of the leaves.

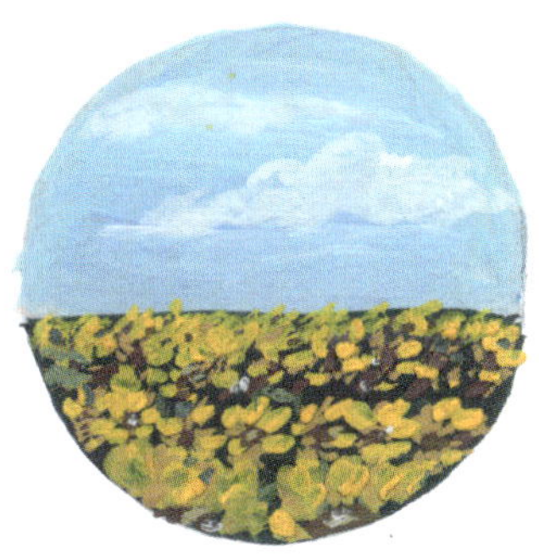
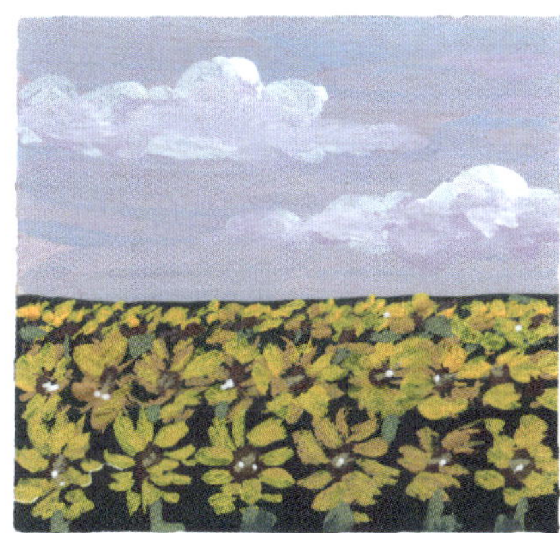

Painting a field of daisies

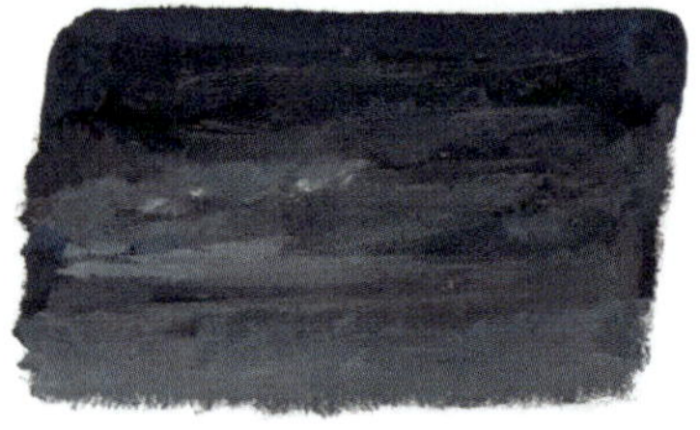

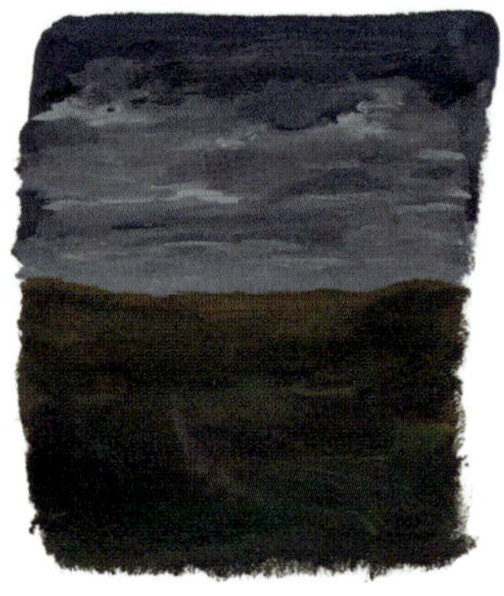

Paint the sky

Use a reference photo or observe the live sky before you start painting. Decide whether you want to use contrasting colours, or ones that are close on the colour wheel for a harmonious effect. A dark blue sky, either a sign of nightfall or just the calm before the storm, contrasts beautifully with the yellow of the daisies. They reinforce each other as blue and yellow are opposites on the colour wheel. A colour like ochre green is more harmonising and therefore it subtly enhances the warmth of the ochre yellow.

Add the base of the landscape

Use dark green paint with a touch of ochre. Alternate the colours until the page is filled. If needed, add a second coat for better coverage. Add many small yellow dots to the background using a primary yellow. The closer the daisies are, the larger they should be: increase their size every four or five rows. Place the flowers closely together, but leave space to add their stems and petals. Vary the height of the daisies to depict a realistic field of flowers.

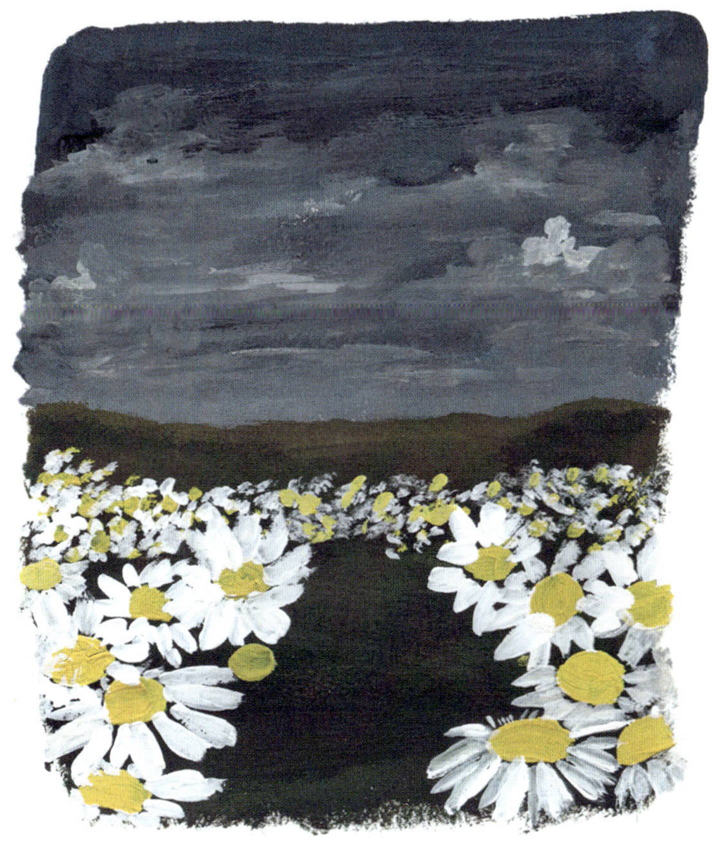

Paint the petals

Use a thin round brush to define their shapes. Let the paint dry before adding a second coat. As details are not visible at a distance, I paint small petals or numerous dots around the flower centres in the background to save time. Use ochre paint or a pencil to colour the edge of the flower centres. Apply the pencil lightly to avoid pressing too hard on your painting. Smooth out any streaks with a blending stump or gently blend them with your index finger.

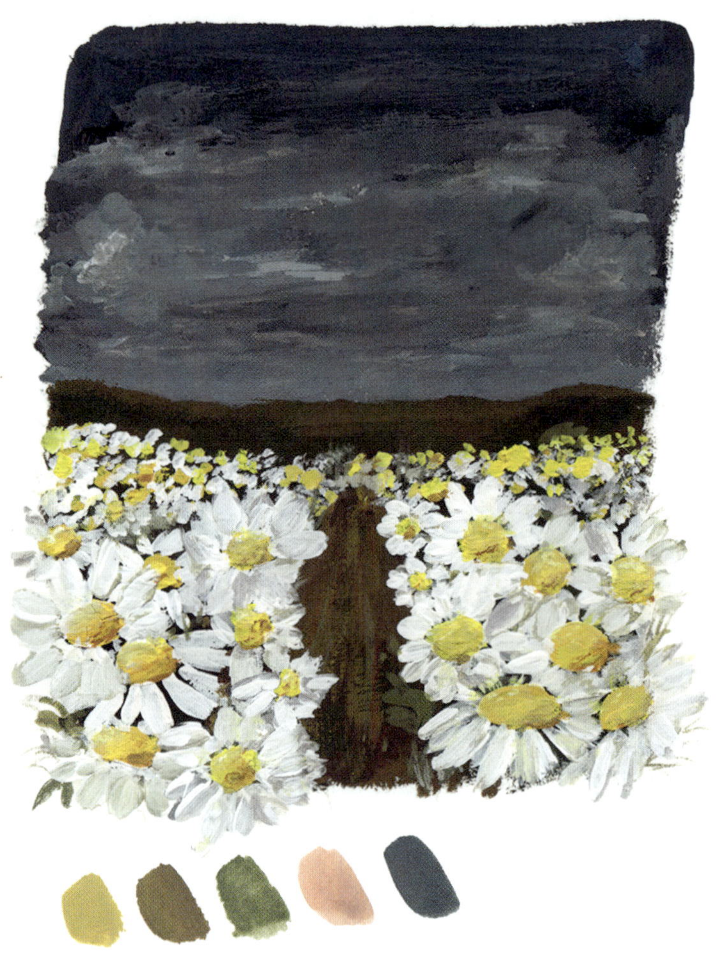

Add details

Highlight the top of the centres by gently applying a mixture of white with a bit of yellow paint and water. Alternatively, use a white pencil or fineliner. Finally, don't forget to draw fine lines to the petals with paint, marker, or coloured pencil.

From meadows to mountains

Avoiding stains

Work from top to bottom to avoid smudging. If you start at the bottom, your hand might touch wet paint and cause stains. If a stain does occur, gently dab with tissue paper or a sponge to remove some paint, or add more water to soften and blend the colours.

Adjusting your colour

You can easily lighten or darken paint by adding a drop of black or white. A dark brown such as umber works even better than black because it gives a more natural, earthy tone. To add warmth to a colour, add some red or yellow; to cool it down, add blue.

Don't wait, alternate

You can move to different sections of your painting if another part is still wet.

Recognising shadows

Do you want to capture subtle shadows that are difficult to discern? If you work with a reference photo, try to temporarily apply a black-and-white filter. This will make it easier to distinguish between highlights and shadows, helping you capture them more accurately.

Trying new things

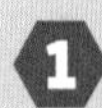

3D flowers

Use a small palette knife (triangular or rectangular; avoid large, spatula-shaped ones) to paint sunflowers. Load it with paint (go for a mix of primary yellow and ochre) and spread it on the paper with quick, firm motions. Apply enough pressure to create a thick layer, which will take longer to dry but will add a 3D effect.

Observation is key

The best way to learn to paint nature scenes is through practice and observation. For example, take a few minutes during your break to look at the clouds. Notice their shapes and see if you recognise anything in them. Take a photo of the sky, then look again fifteen minutes later from the same spot. You'll see how much the clouds changed, showing that there's no wrong way to paint them. Or take a picture every week of the same tree you see on your way home to see the seasons gradually change.

Make your own paint using natural elements

For green shades, use grass or leaves. Stones or clay can give you colours like red, yellow, brown, and grey. Finely ground sand adds texture and light, neutral tones. Flowers, berries, or bark offer different hues based on the plant. Prepare the pigments by grinding them into a fine powder or pulp. Sieve the mixture to remove impurities. To turn the powder into paint, mix it with a binder. You can use traditional binders like egg yolk, linseed oil, or gum arabic, or modern options like acrylic medium, gesso, or Mod Podge.

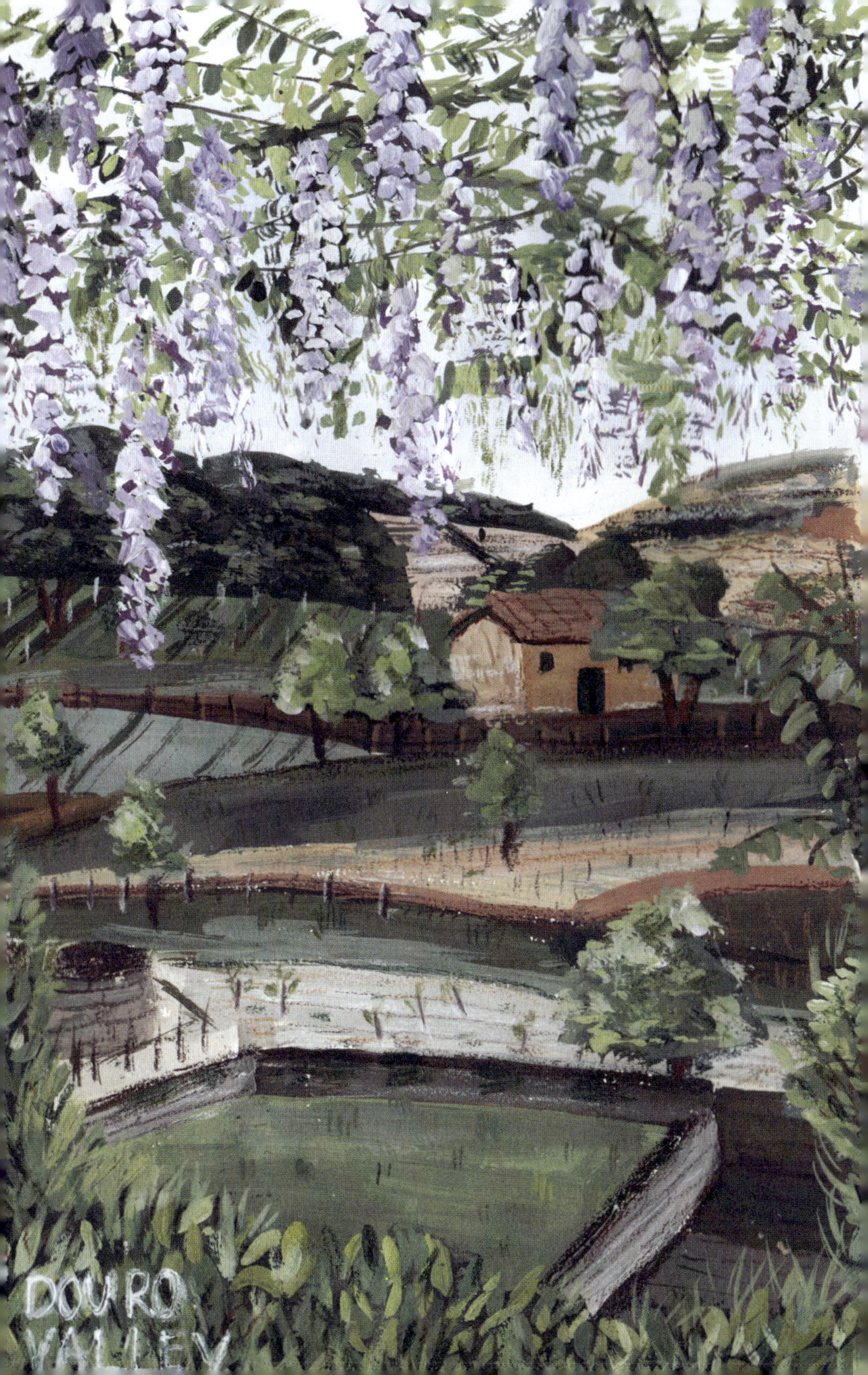

DOURO
VALLEY

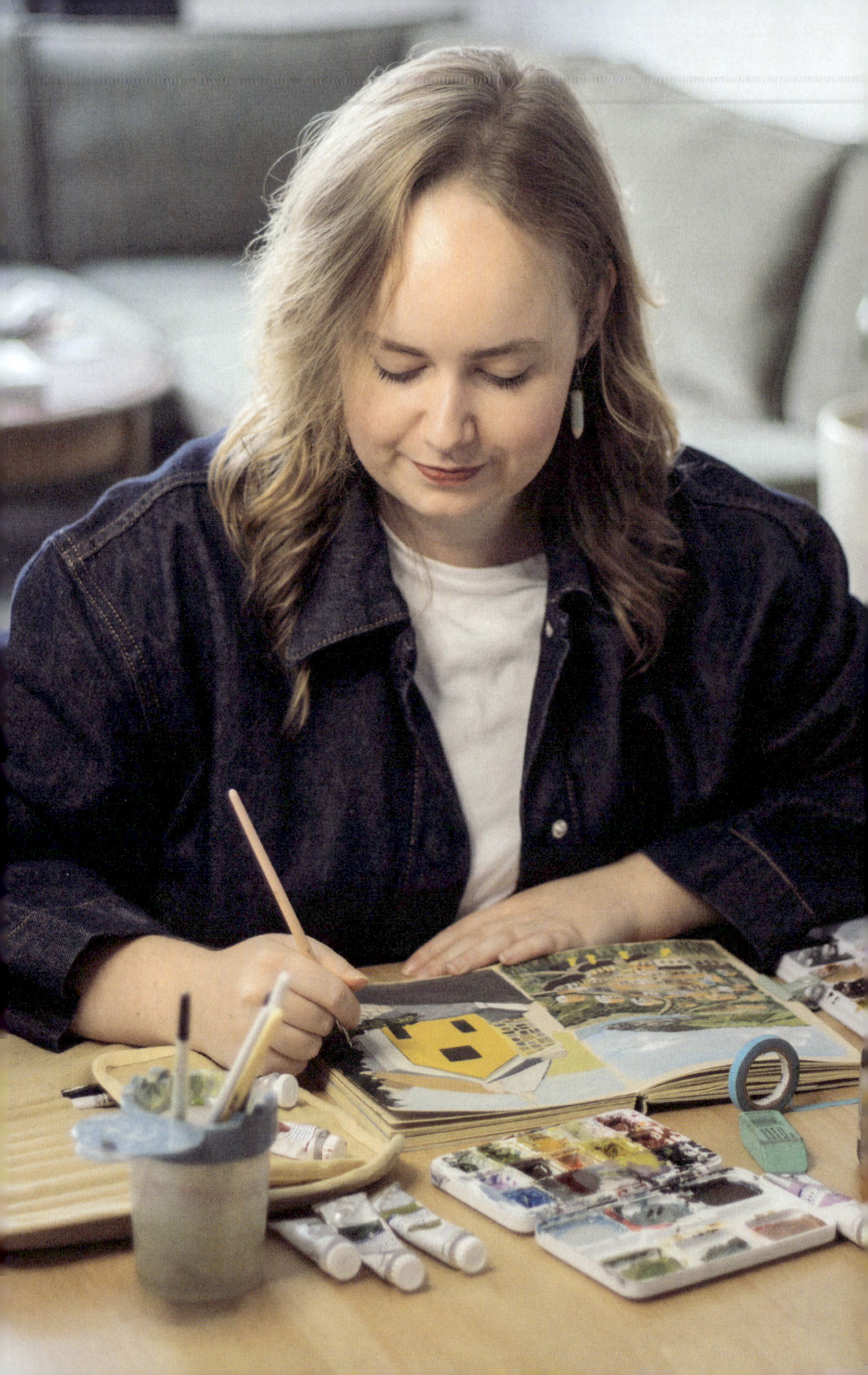

THE CROWNING BRUSHSTROKES

Would you like to fill the last empty spaces in your travel journal and try something new? In this chapter, I'll guide you through hand lettering and painting on different surfaces, and I will give you more tips and tricks to add extra flair to your travel journal.

When painting on unconventional surfaces, using gesso is key. This inexpensive chalk-based primer prevents paint from being absorbed or repelled. Apply about three coats to create a smooth, even base for your artwork.

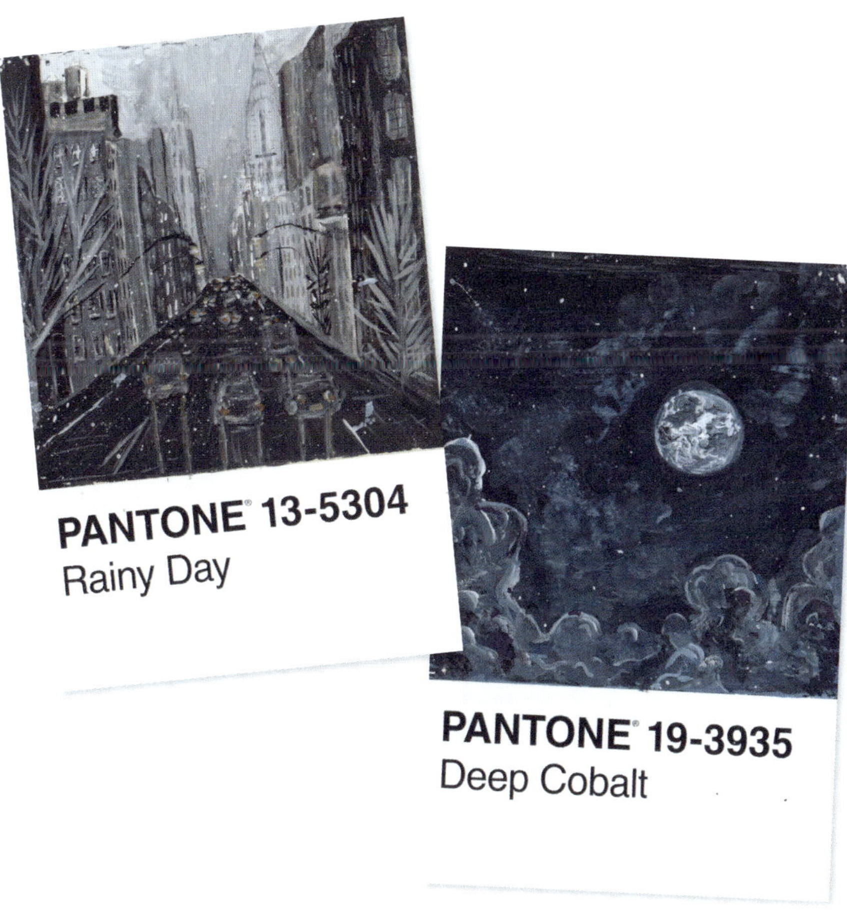

Unusual canvases

My passion for scrapbooking ignited when I stumbled upon colour cards at a DIY store. I took home dozens, not as inspiration for my walls, but to use as canvases for poems and drawings. It turned out the smooth paper wasn't the easiest surface to work on. Luckily, this beginner mistake can be avoided by using gesso.

Finish with varnish

Although I usually don't varnish my sketchbook illustrations, you might want to protect your works if they will be exposed to sunlight. Varnishing protects your paintings, enhances their colours, and gives a smooth finish. It also shields against dust and mould, and keeps the paint from fading, cracking, or flaking.

Allow for drying time
Ensure the painting is fully dry.

Choose the appropriate varnish
You can use either varnish from a tin or a spray-on lacquer. If you want a vibrant, shiny finish, go for glossy varnish. For a softer and more subtle look, choose satin varnish. Want to enhance your painting without adding shine? Pick matte varnish.

Test your varnish
Test a small area first to make sure the result is as desired.

Apply
Apply the varnish in a dust-free environment.

Add one to three layers
The number of layers depends on the surface and desired finish. Add extra layers for gloss or textured surfaces. Smooth surfaces usually need fewer layers. Brush-on varnish often needs less than spray-on varnish due to its thickness.

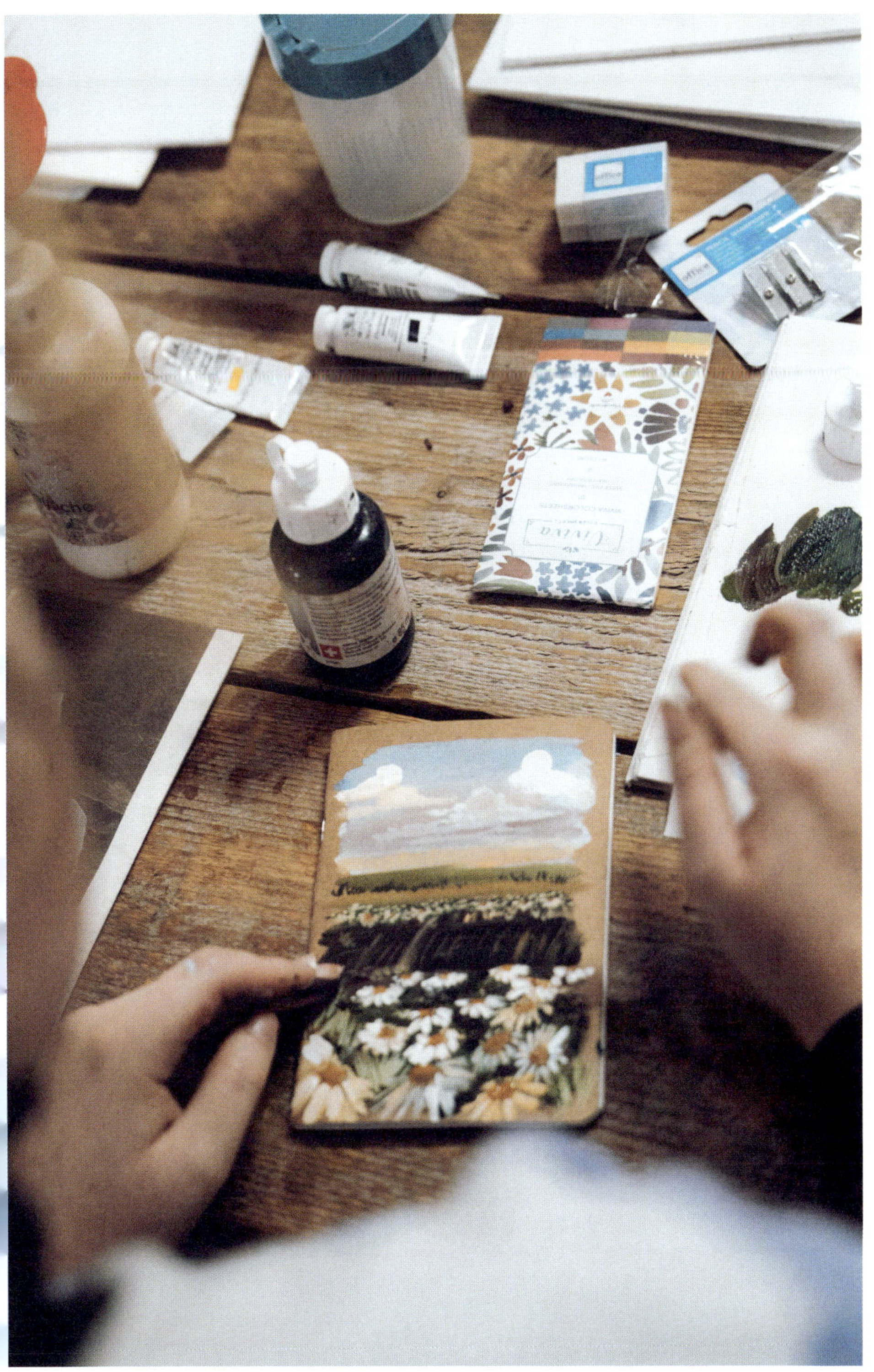

Coasters

During my first restaurant job, we received thousands of coasters weekly from a hospitality chain. One day, curiosity got the better of me, and I asked the warehouse manager of the restaurant if I could take some for a creative project. That day, I went home with more than two hundred coasters.

When travelling, collect coasters from bars or restaurants and add them to your journal. The blank side can be used for your own creations. Coasters absorb moisture, making them ideal for painting. If you plan to use them for drinks at home rather than sticking them in your journal, apply a coat of varnish to maintain their appearance, especially if you use them often.

I painted the left coaster with oil paint and the right with gouache. While oil paint isn't practical for journals due to its texture and drying time, it works well on coasters. Gouache and acrylic (when not heavily diluted) work as well, but watercolours get absorbed too quickly, and are therefore not recommended for this surface.

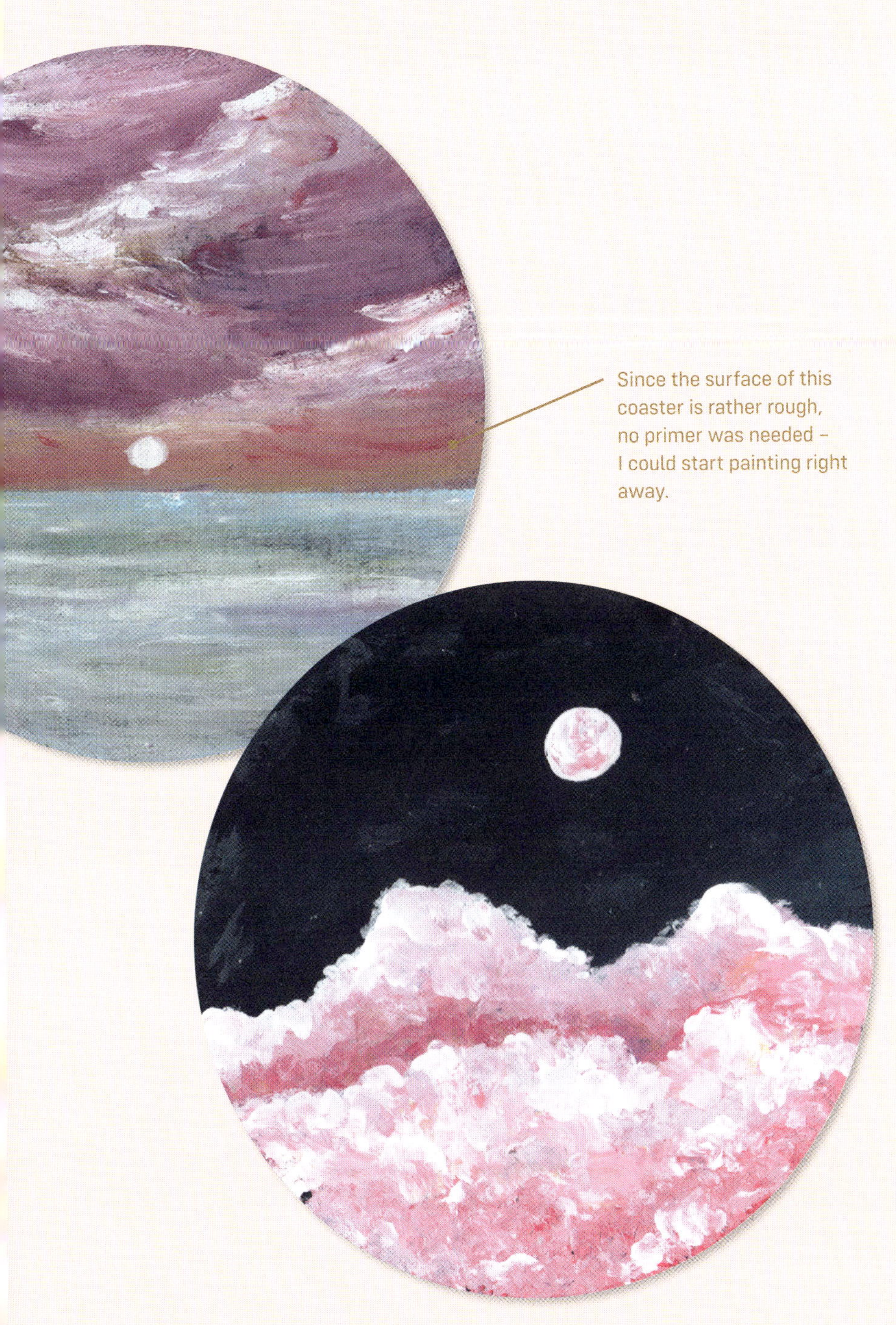

Since the surface of this coaster is rather rough, no primer was needed – I could start painting right away.

For lowercase letters, I prefer
decorative styles that feature
added strokes at the ends.

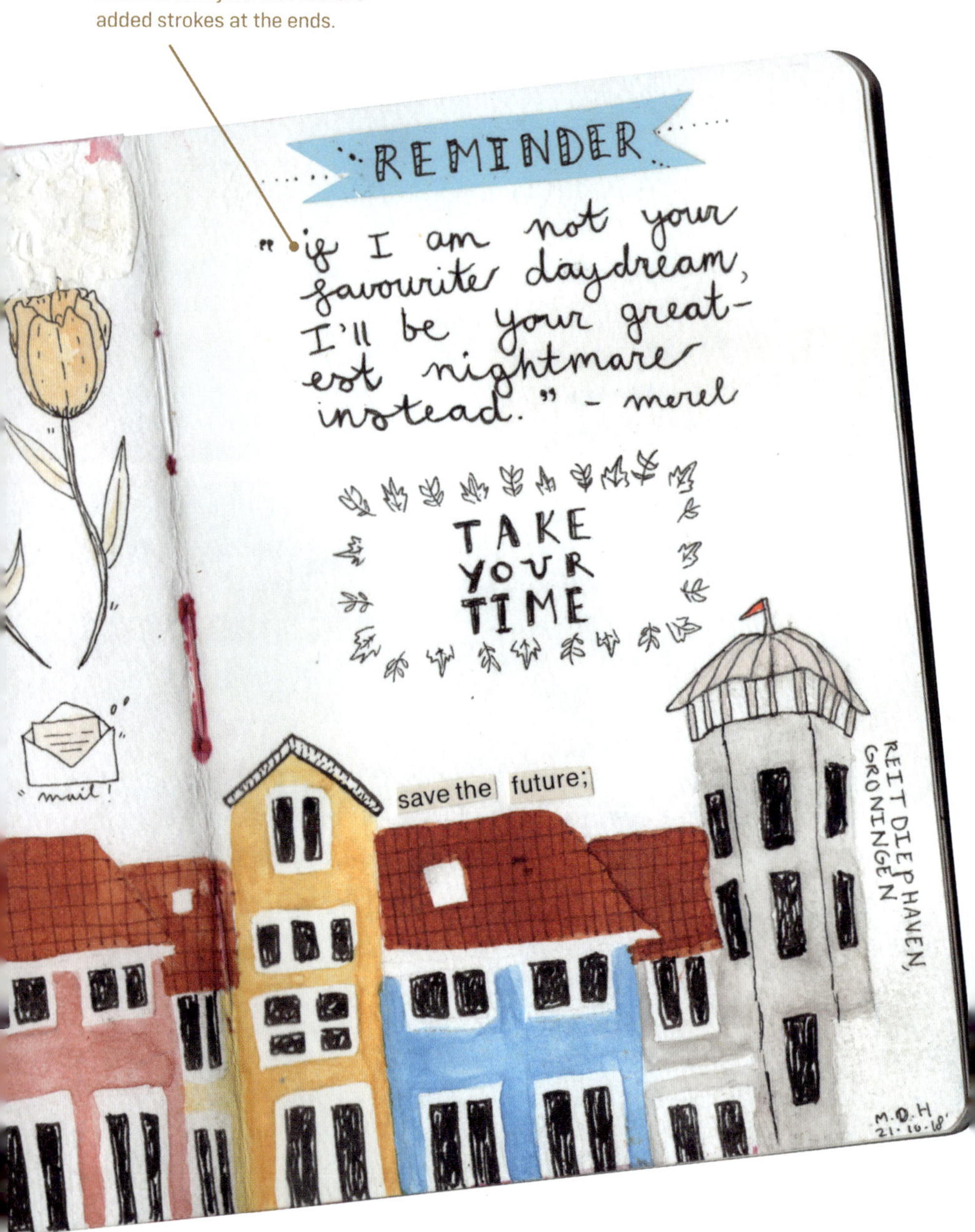
REMINDER

"if I am not your
favourite daydream,
I'll be your great-
est nightmare
instead." - merel

TAKE
YOUR
TIME

save the future;

mail!

REITDIEPHAVEN,
GRONINGEN

M.D.H
21·10·18

162

Hand lettering

Whether you wish to write a lot or only a little, hand lettering adds a
beautiful touch. It may take a while, so you might want to focus on just the
titles to make it manageable.

I prefer a thin, round brush with black paint and little bit of water. Be careful
not to use too much water, as it can make your letters too thick. Dab your
brush on a tissue to control moisture. Ecoline Liquid Watercolour inks are
great for hand lettering because of their intense colours and liquid consist-
ency. However, since Ecoline contains no pigments but dyes dissolved in
water, the paint may fade over the years.

Fineliners are perfect for beginners, offering precision and a consistent ink
flow, unlike paints, that require frequent adjustment. Small nibs (0.1–0.3 mm)
are ideal for delicate lines, while larger nibs (0.5–0.8 mm) are better for bold
strokes. For thicker letters and vibrant colours, try brush pens, such as the
Royal Talens Ecoline Brush Pens or Ohuhu markers.

How to improve your hand lettering

Keep it simple
Use a lined notebook to keep your letters uniform. Sketch in pencil first for easy corrections.

Add decorative elements
Include brackets or curls to achieve a different look.

Vary between strokes
Apply consistent pressure to create even lines. Go over one side of the letters multiple times to make it fuller or vary the pressure to achieve contrast between thick and thin strokes.

Experiment with different angles
Use either your brush or fineliner for varied effects.

Letter by letter

Hidden typography

As you walk around town, take note of different fonts you encounter. Cafés, hotels, libraries, museums, and universities often have special messages hidden in their logos that you might initially overlook. Take a photo of a beautiful font and recreate it in your own hand-writing.

Stacked and styled

For a playful effect, alternate lower-case and uppercase letters in a sentence, stacking words vertically.

Diagonal lines

Outline letters and add shading with diagonal lines as shown in *Granada* below. It is okay to leave some white space.

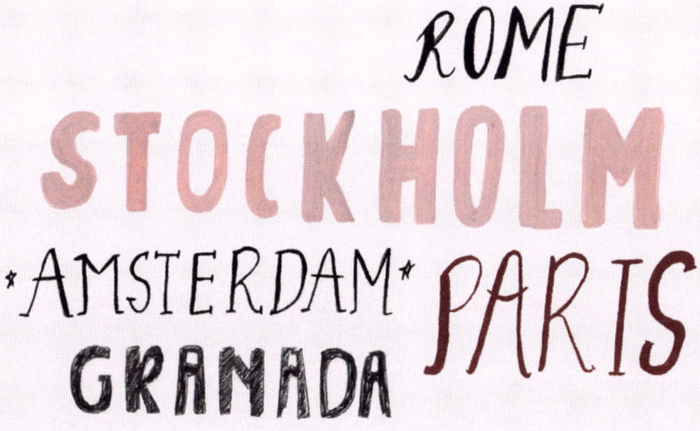

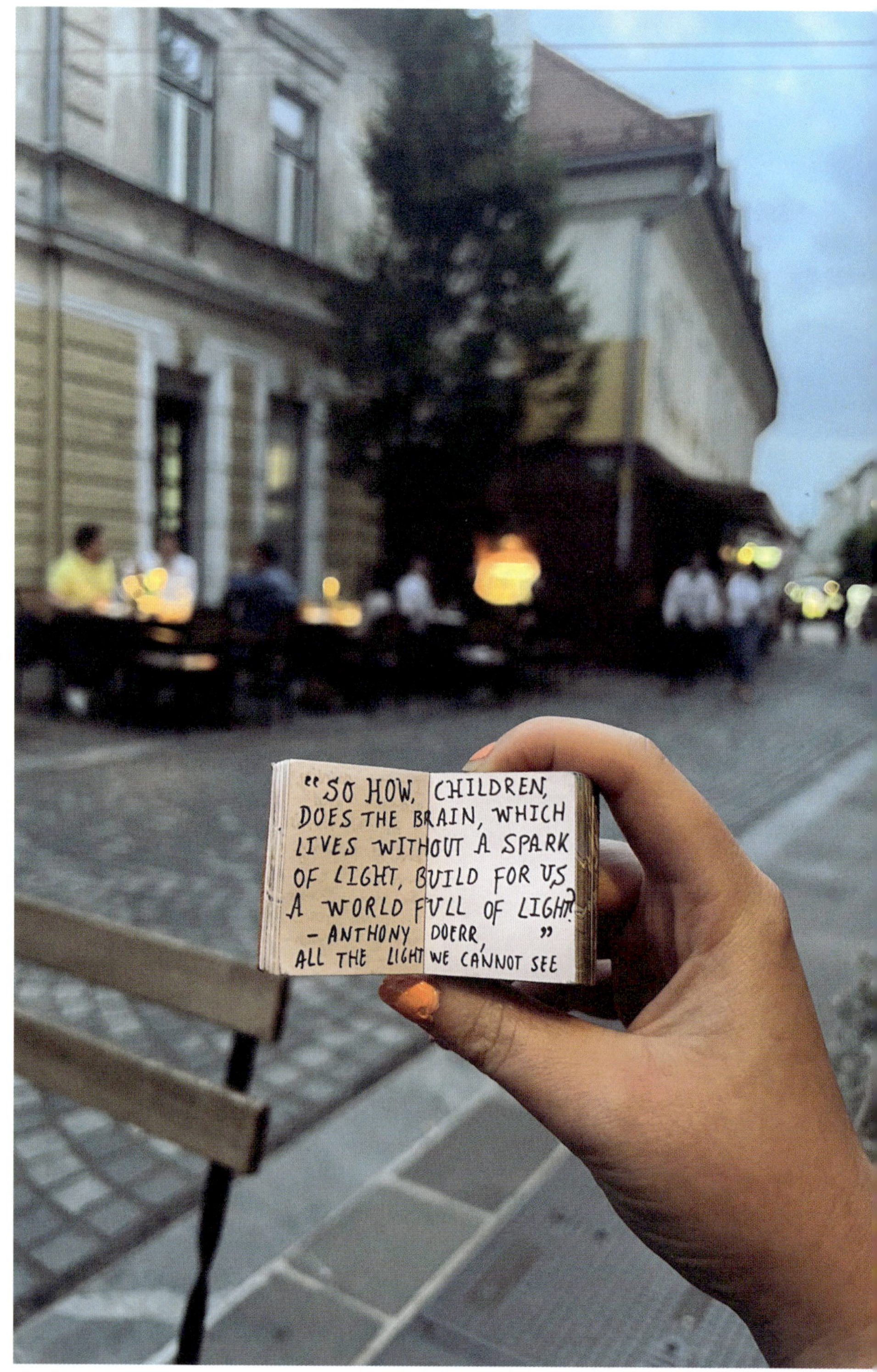

" SO HOW, CHILDREN,
DOES THE BRAIN, WHICH
LIVES WITHOUT A SPARK
OF LIGHT, BUILD FOR US
A WORLD FULL OF LIGHT?
- ANTHONY DOERR, "
ALL THE LIGHT WE CANNOT SEE

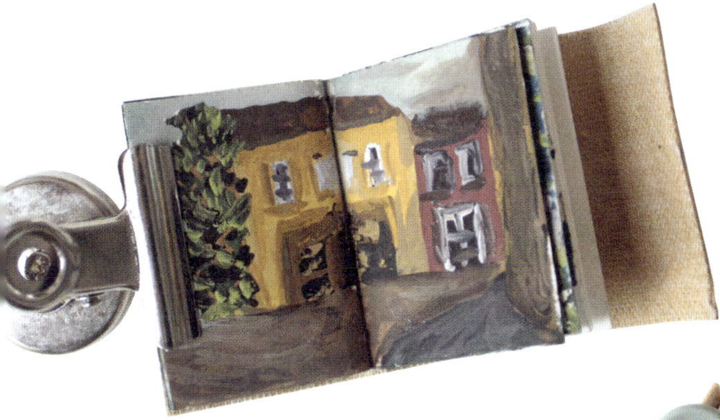

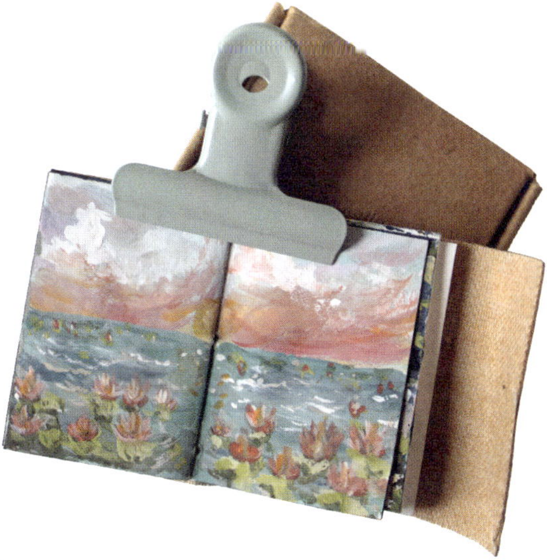

Tiny journals

A tiny journal is easy to carry and quick to fill. While you will need to work precisely with a tiny brush and the journal may not accommodate everything, it makes a great keepsake of your trip and a thoughtful gift for a travel companion. You can find small journals on Etsy or at hobby shops. Keep in mind that the paper is often thin and not of great quality. You can use acrylic paints or gouache in them, provided you don't use too much water.

For inspiration, watch my YouTube video
Fill a tiny journal with me.

Creating your own (tiny) journal

Limit your choices

Focus on one element: stamps from abroad, place names, sweet wrappers, painted sunsets, a special flower, or a snippet from a photo, such as a cat sleeping on a windowsill.

Make your own zine

A zine (pronounced [zeen], like the end of 'magazine') is a self-published booklet made from one or more sheets of A4 paper. It usually consists of about eight pages, including the front and back cover. Watch my YouTube video *Creating my first zine* to learn more about zines and making them.

Bind your own sketchbook

In for a challenge? Bind your own sketchbook! This takes time and effort, but it allows you to choose your own paper and cover. You can find many tutorials online.

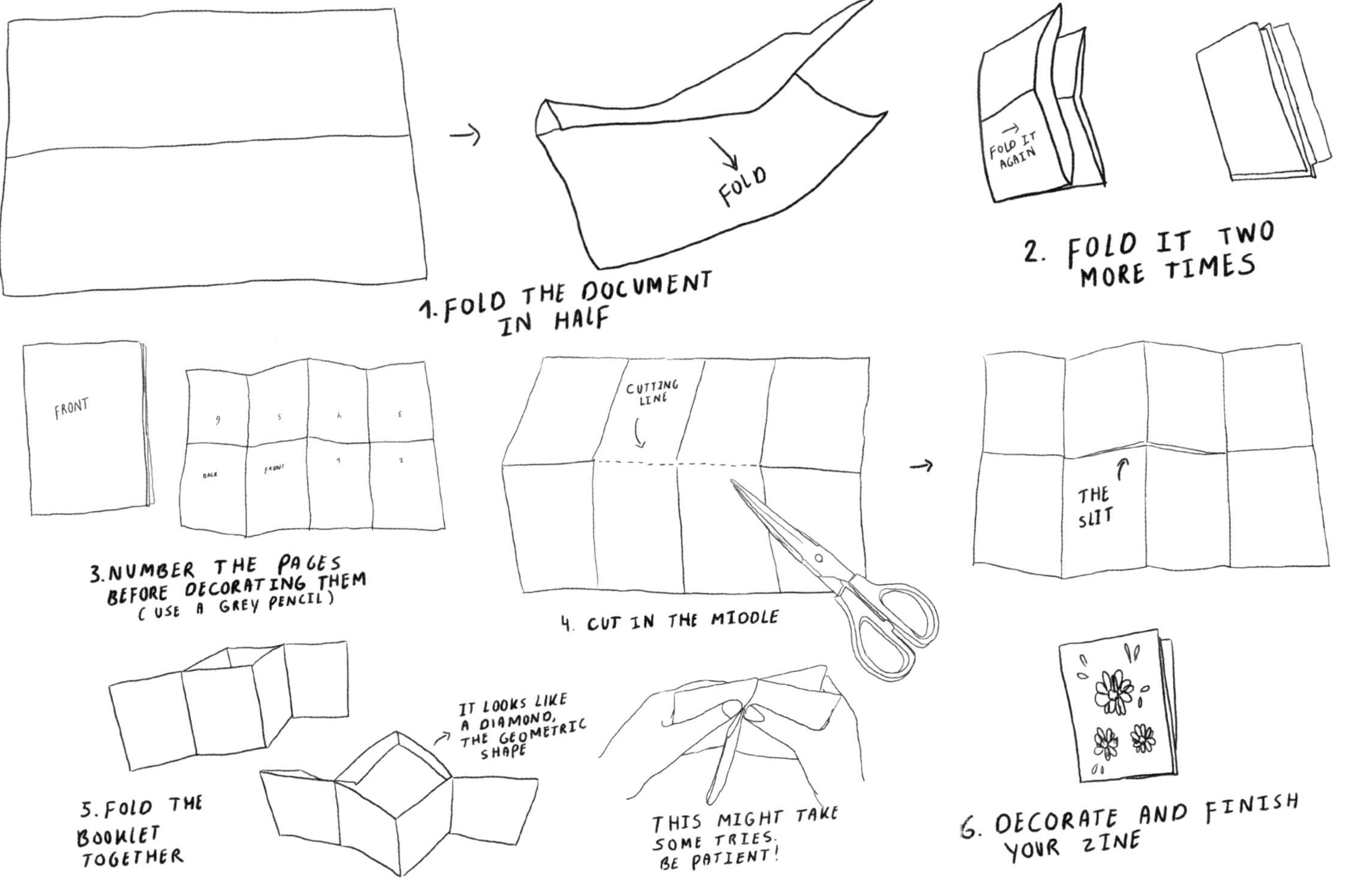
FOLD
1. FOLD THE DOCUMENT IN HALF
FOLD IT AGAIN
2. FOLD IT TWO MORE TIMES
FRONT
9
5
4
3
BACK
FRONT
1
2
3. NUMBER THE PAGES BEFORE DECORATING THEM (USE A GREY PENCIL)
CUTTING LINE
4. CUT IN THE MIDDLE
THE SLIT
IT LOOKS LIKE A DIAMOND, THE GEOMETRIC SHAPE
5. FOLD THE BOOKLET TOGETHER
THIS MIGHT TAKE SOME TRIES. BE PATIENT!
6. DECORATE AND FINISH YOUR ZINE

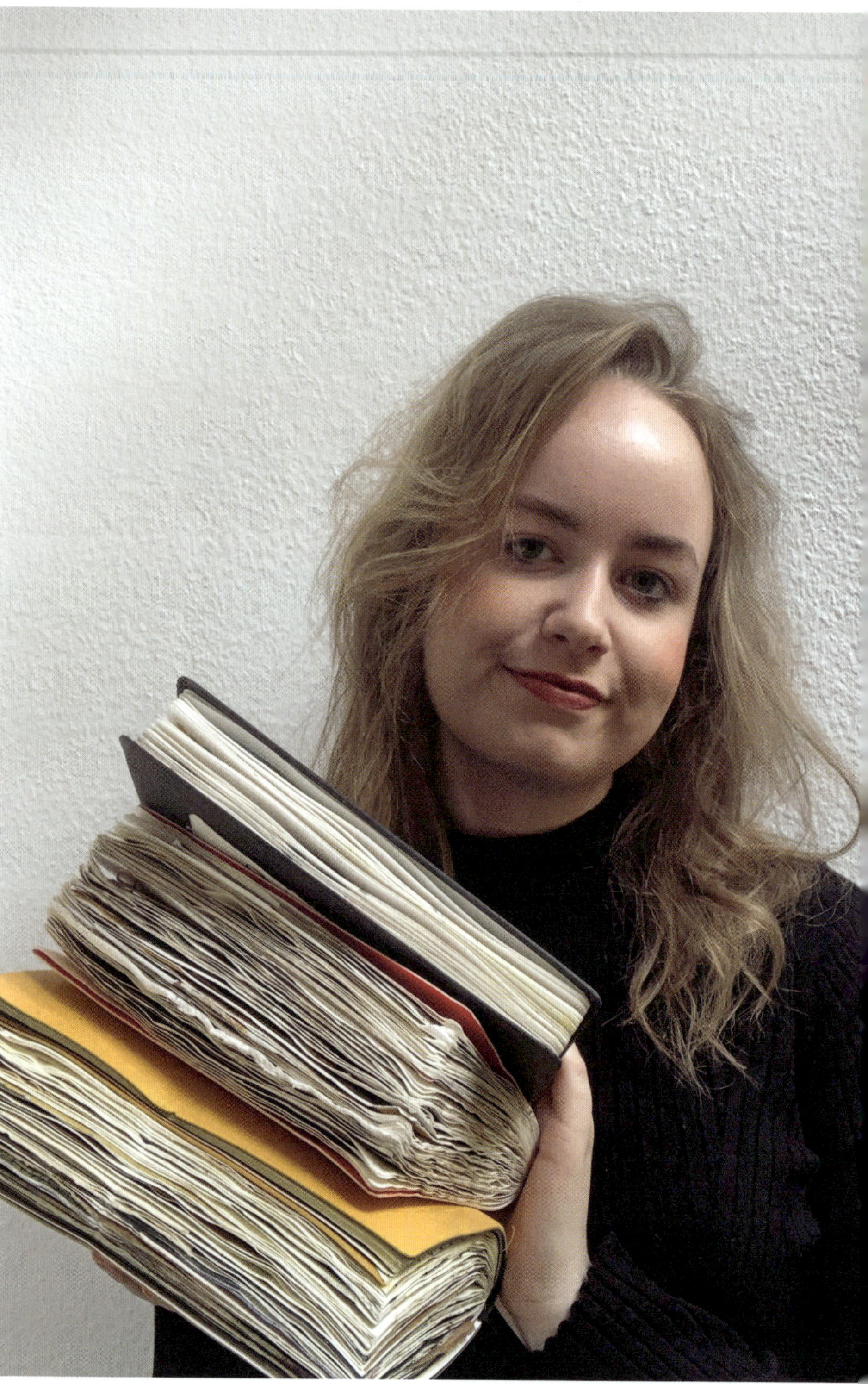

ACKNOWLEDGEMENTS

This book is dedicated to my fellow travel journallers eager to observe the world and capture it on paper. My hope is that you'll explore the world, even if it is just a small part, and document it in your own unique way. Remember that creating travel journal entries is not about the amount of time spent or the quality of the materials you use; it's about engaging with your memories, and preserving them for years to come.

When I began sharing my creative diary online in 2017, I never imagined I would inspire so many people to start journaling. The overwhelming response – the likes, comments, and people approaching me in public – has been incredibly rewarding. This support has allowed me to work with amazing clients who trust my creative instincts, and meet wonderful people online, during my travels, and at workshops.

I want to thank my family, friends, and colleagues for their unwavering support and for listening to my endless ramblings about this project. A special thanks to the wonderful team at mo'media for guiding me, and especially to Lotte for being a fantastic editor and assisting me throughout the creation of this book.

Love,
Merel

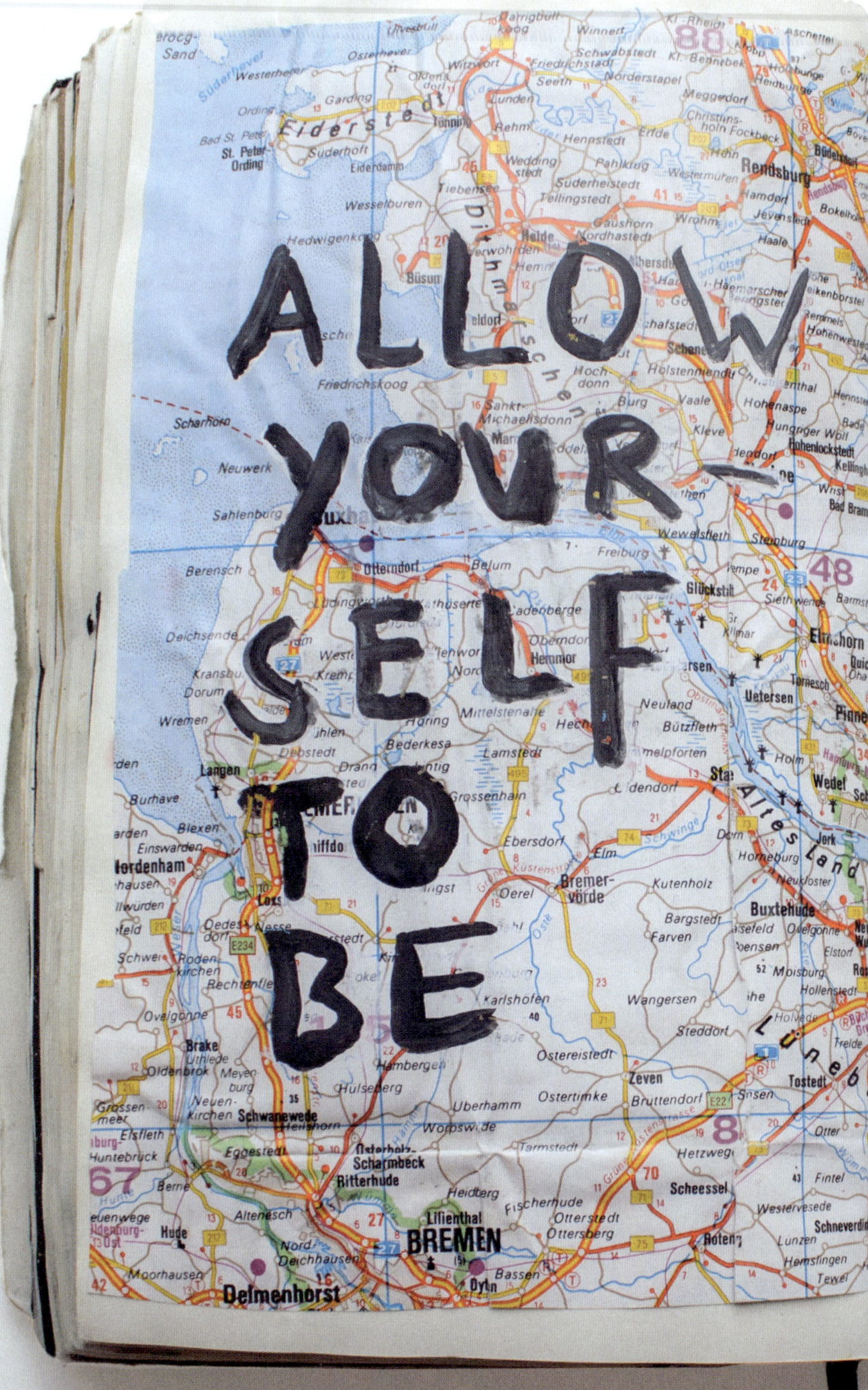

ALLOW YOUR-
SELF
TO
BE

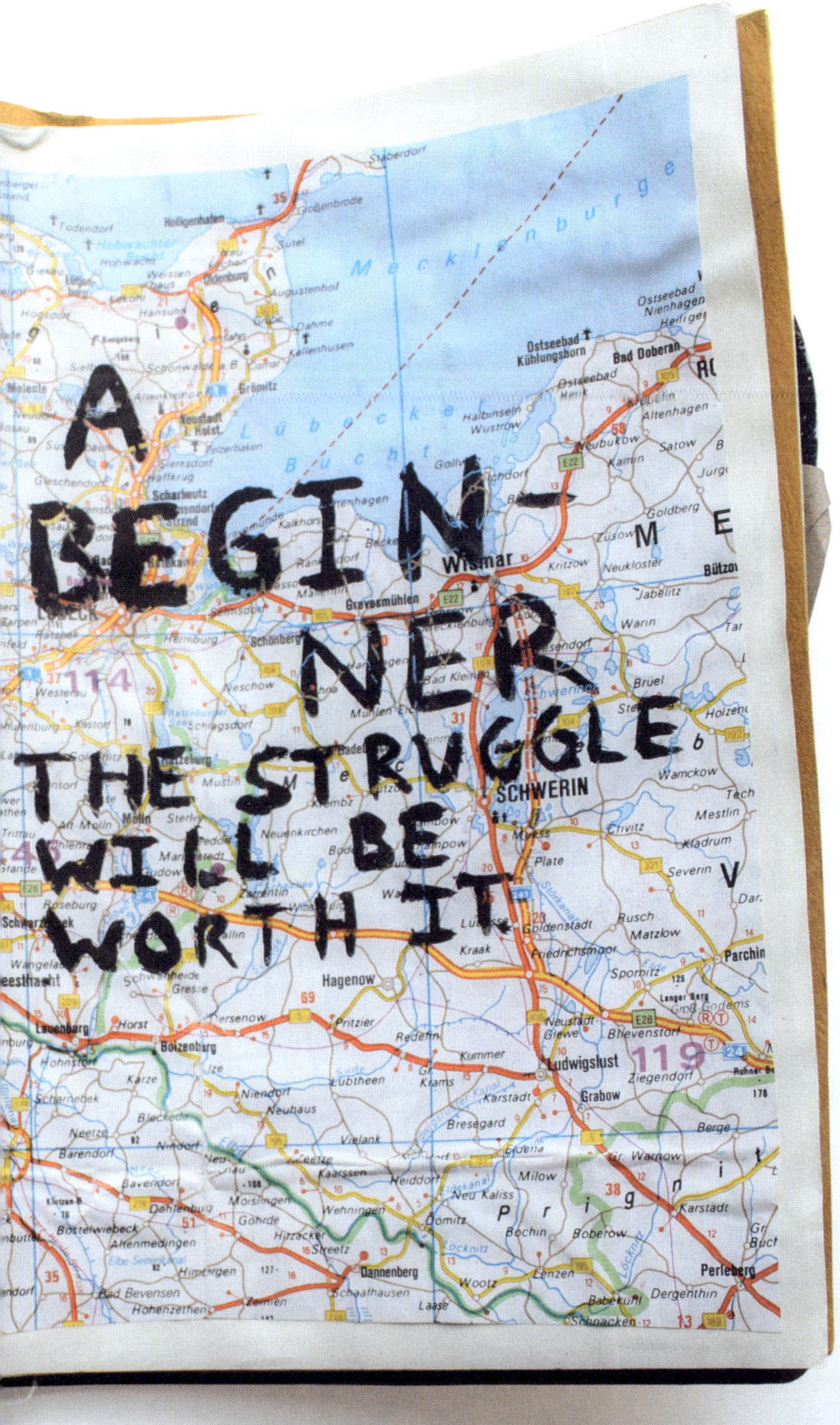
A BEGIN-
NER
THE STRUGGLE
WILL BE
WORTH IT

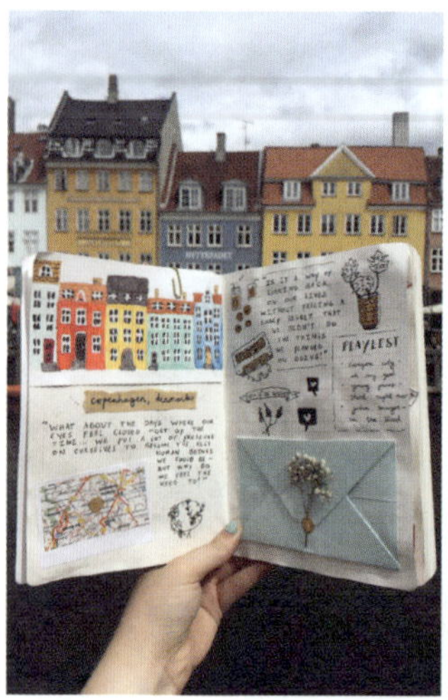

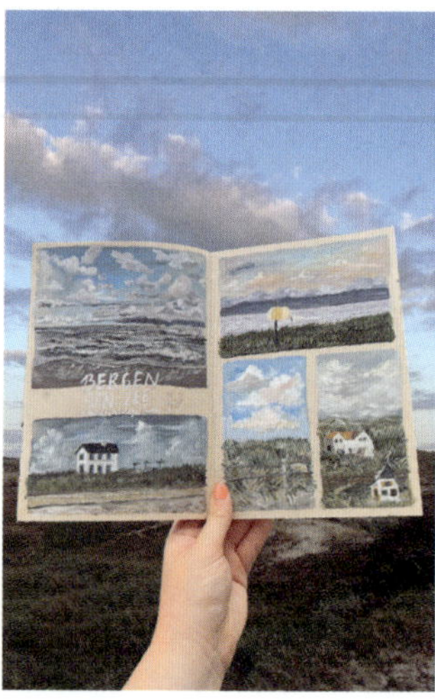

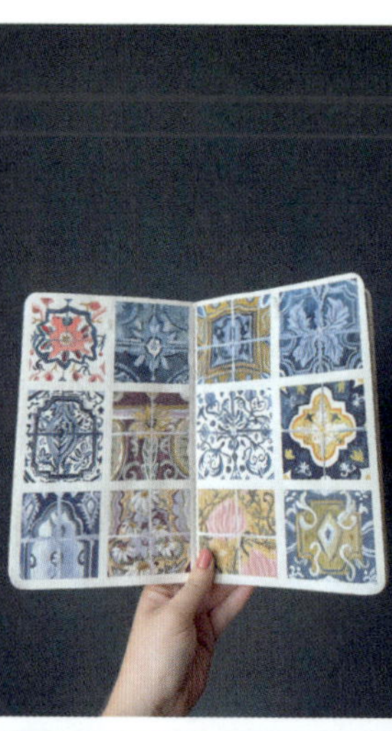

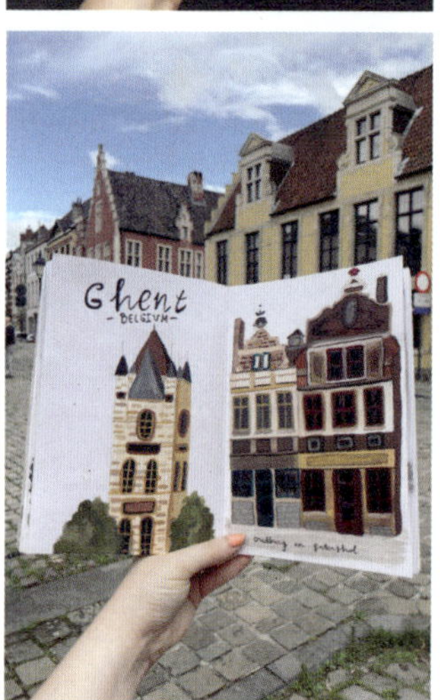

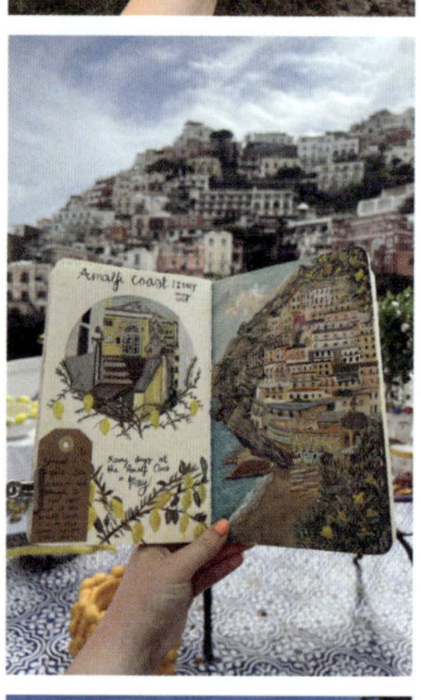

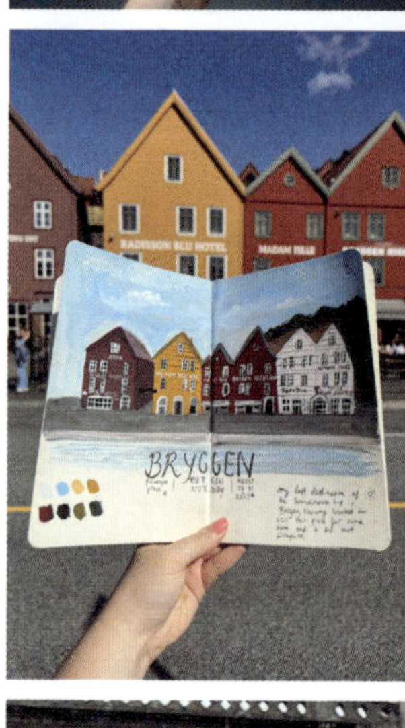

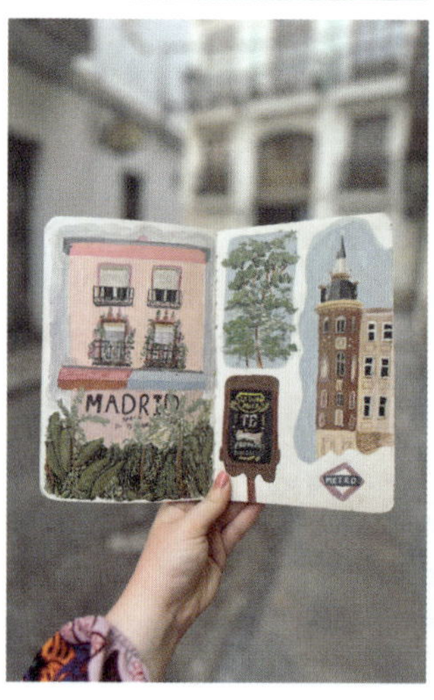

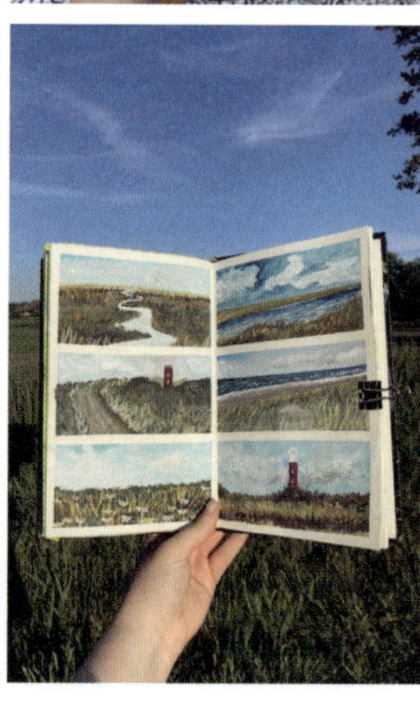

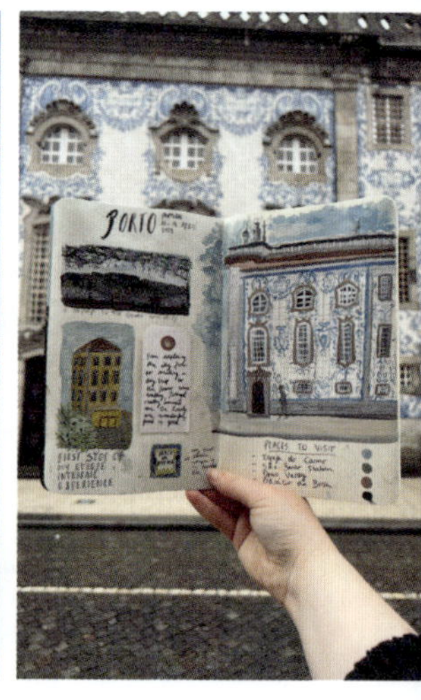

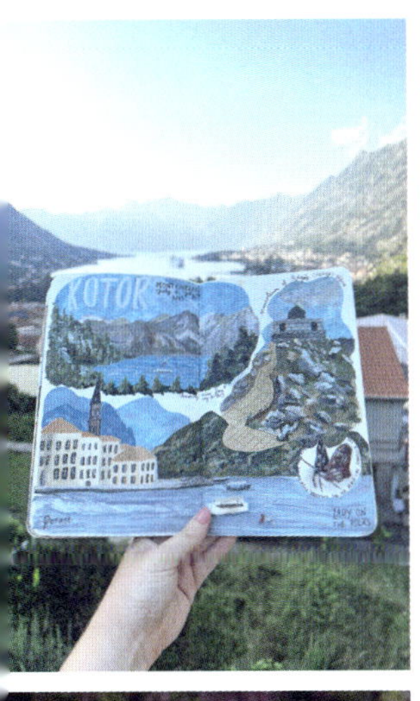

KOTOR

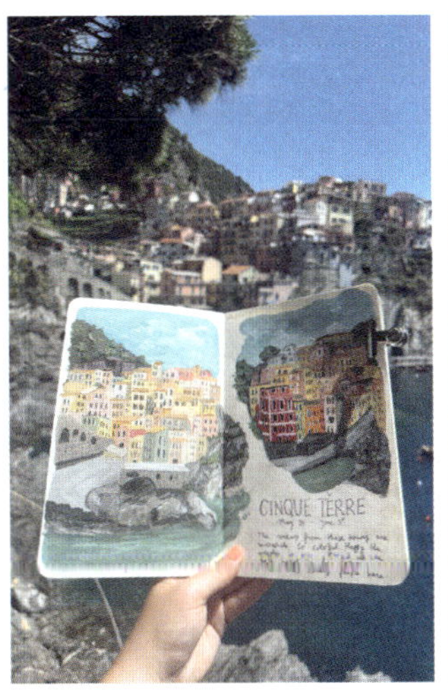

CINQUE TERRE

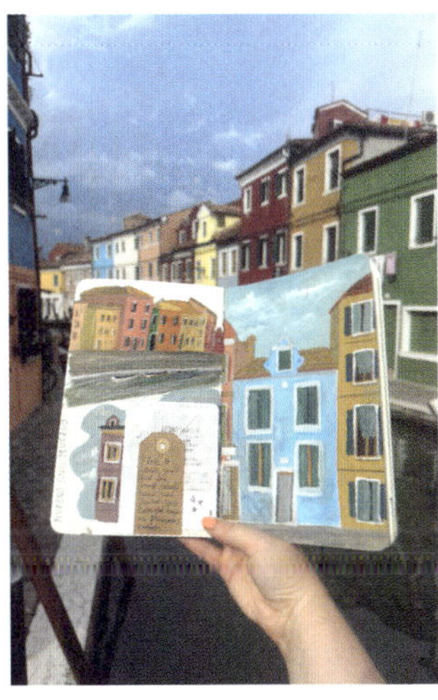

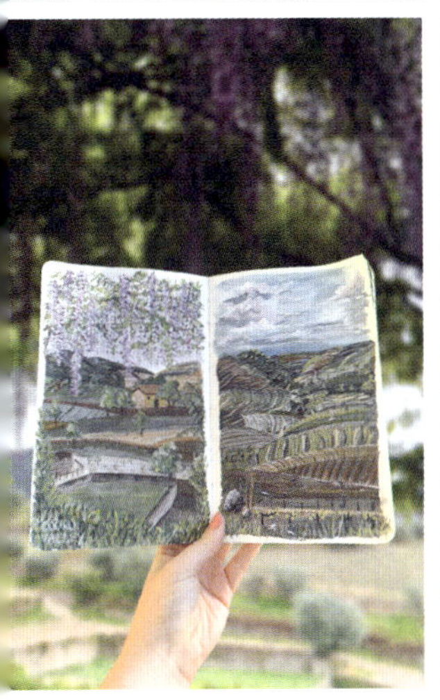

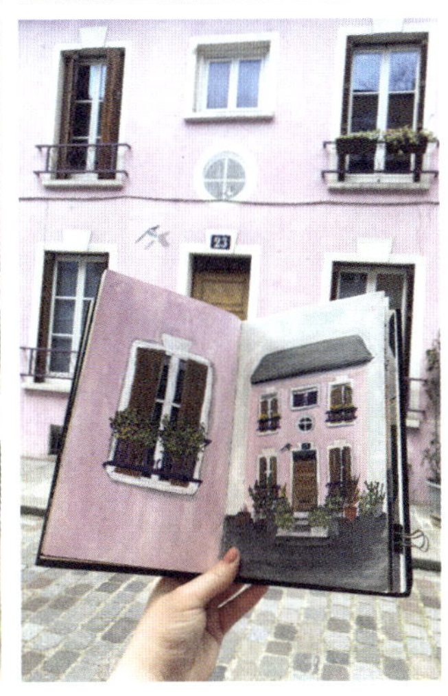

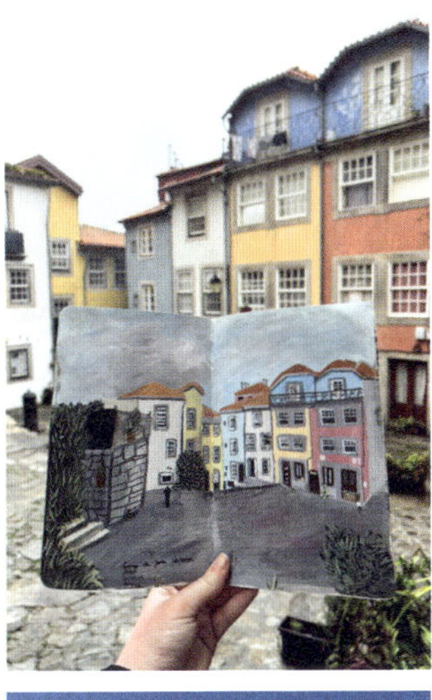

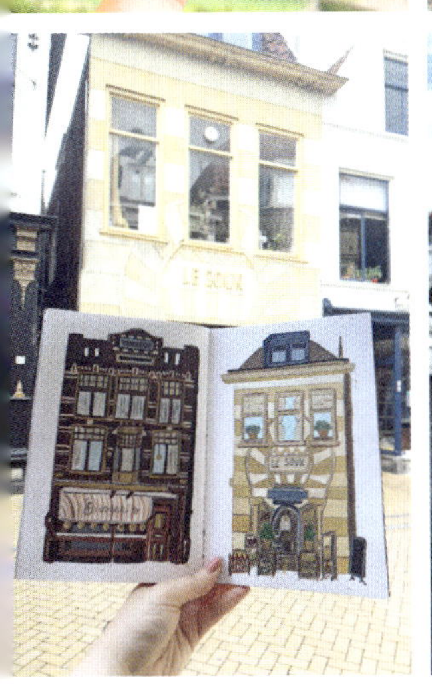

LE SOUK
LE SOUK

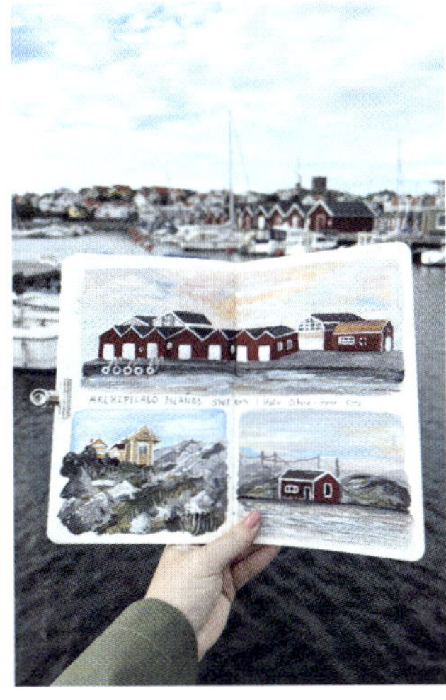

ARCHIPELAGO ISLANDS

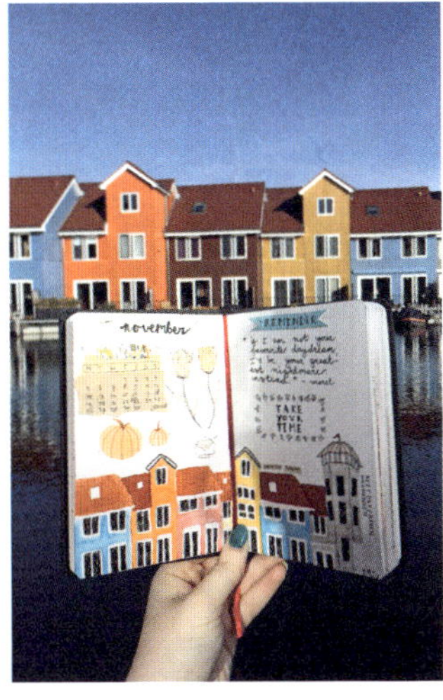

november
TAKE
YOUR
TIME

PAINT, PAPER & GOING PLACES
A Guide to Creative Travel Journaling

Author and illustrations
Merel Djamila Hoekstra

Editing
Ezra van Wilgenburg

Graphic design
Bianca Enthoven

Author's portrait
Myrthe Hoekstra

Photography
Merel Djamila Hoekstra, Myrthe Hoekstra (p. 2, p. 8, p. 28, p. 40, p. 62, p. 63, p. 154), Emgarro Photography (p. 6, p. 71), Nino Knezevic (p. 74), Ashwien Jurawan (p. 159), Eric Laudonien (p. 88), Victor Martín (p. 101)

Special thanks to
Lotte Leeuwis, Maaike van Steekelenburg, Myrthe Hoekstra, Christa Hoekstra, Rens Hoekstra, Ids Nicolai

Source definition p. 22:
Oxford Pocket Dictionary of Current English

Published in 2025 by mo'media
P.O. Box 359, 3000 AJ Rotterdam, The Netherlands, mo'media.nl

Paint, Paper & Going Places
ISBN 978 94 93 338 234
NUR 510, 476, 450

Publisher's note
Every effort has been made to ensure that the information in this book is accurate at the time of going to press. The publisher welcomes any information or suggestions for correction or improvement. Please send us an e-mail at *redactie@momedia.nl*.

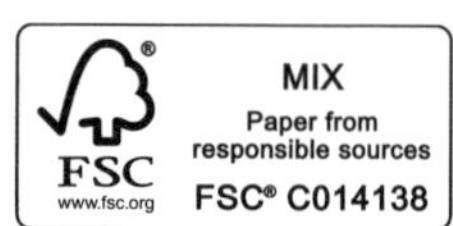